Contemporary Problems of Pakistan

Published in cooperation with
the American Institute of Pakistan Studies

Contemporary Problems of Pakistan

EDITED BY
J. Henry Korson

Westview Press
BOULDER • SAN FRANCISCO • OXFORD

Pak Book Corporation
LAHORE • ISLAMABAD • KARACHI

Published in 1993 in the United States of America by Westview Press, Inc., 5500 Central Avenue, Boulder, Colorado 80301-2877, and in the United Kingdom by Westview Press, 36 Lonsdale Road, Summertown, Oxford OX2 7EW

Distributed in Pakistan by Pak Book Corporation, 21 Queen's Road, Lahore

Library of Congress Cataloging-in-Publication Data
Contemporary problems of Pakistan / edited by J. Henry Korson.
p. cm.
ISBN 0-8133-8768-X
1. Pakistan—Politics and government—1988- . 2. Pakistan—Economic conditions. 3. Pakistan—Social conditions. I. Korson, J. Henry.
DS389.C66 1993
954.9105—dc20 93-29531
CIP

Printed and bound in the United States of America

The paper used in this publication meets the requirements of the American National Standard for Permanence of Paper for Printed Library Materials Z39.48-1984.

10 9 8 7 6 5 4 3 2 1

For Tom, Mary and Andrew

and for

my wife, Sabra Rogers MacCleod, without whom. . .

Contents

Preface

Shortly after the turn of the century, the eminent sociologist William Graham Sumner claimed that the "maintenance [economic] mores are basic to the well being of every society." Regardless of whatever economic philosophy a nation has pursued, this truism has stood the test of time. At its founding, Pakistan was primarily an agricultural society with a minimal industrial base. Today the industrial/commercial part of the economy is closely approaching that of agriculture in importance.

This volume offers a discussion of some of the most important problems that continue to confront the government of Pakistan, many of which will challenge the nation's leadership for years to come.

Aside from the brief effort of Zulfikar Ali Bhutto, Pakistan's leaders have avoided any attempts to institute Draconian measures to establish a Marxist economy, and Zia ul-Haq's efforts to impose his Islamization program have been diverted from full fruition. Nawaz Sharif, on the other hand, has set the nation in the direction of a market economy by denationalizing some basic industries that Bhutto nationalized.

Shahid Javed Burki points up some of the major failings as well as strengths of previous administrations and indicates the positive aspects of the nation's early leaders, who eschewed the adoption of ideologically based measures in an effort to seek a Utopian paradise. Nevertheless, a measure of success was achieved over the years when one considers the monumental problems that confronted the fledgling state at its birth. Much of the success, however, was due to generous aid from abroad, particularly the United States. In the last two decades remittances from Pakistanis employed in the oil-producing states have played an important role in contributing to a rising standard of living. With the impending end of aid from the United States and with the decline of employment opportunities for Pakistani workers in the Middle East, the nation's leaders will have to revise their development programs to include these changes.

Burki also points out the potentially devastating effect the continued high fertility rate will have on the future development prospects of the nation. In spite of current difficulties, Burki presents a ten-point agenda that could contribute to the continuing economic development of the nation by the year 2000.

Closely related to the economic development of the nation is the continuing problem of a rapidly expanding population. At partition, Pakistan had an annual growth rate of 1.8 percent per annum in its population, but it has since increased to 3.1 percent per annum. Lee Bean points out that Pakistan has had and continues to have one of the highest fertility rates of all the developing nations in the world. In spite of millions of dollars/rupees the several administrations have spent on fertility control programs, hardly more than 9 percent of married women avail themselves of contraceptive measures, and only 12 percent have ever used such measures. The result: the population has doubled approximately every twenty-three years, or each generation.

A World Bank Development Study of 1991 predicted that if the current rate of increase continued, by the year 2050 Pakistan will have a population of 557 million, third only to India and China, in that order. Contributing to the problems of the rapidly expanding population is the failure over a period of years of the government to establish a mandatory system of registering births and deaths, so that such problems as the "missing eight million females" in various demographic studies continue to haunt the efforts of demographers.

Gender and urban-rural inequities continue, especially in terms of the areas of social development. Nonetheless, public health measures have increased life expectancy for both males and females by about twenty years since Pakistan came into being. Smallpox has been eliminated, although malaria, history's greatest killer, continues to take its toll.

Closely allied with the economy and increasing population pressure is the problem of the status of women in Pakistani society, more specifically, the medical care available to women. In spite of statistical data that show the expansion of the medical establishment in the last two decades, medical care available to women, and inevitably to children, has lagged. Anne Sweetser's chapter raises some critical questions concerning the problem. Although life expectancy has risen dramatically in the past decades, infant mortality continues at an annual rate of 10.4 percent, and as recently as 1984-1986, maternal mortality was estimated to be between four and eight per 1,000 live births.

As a traditional Muslim society, purdah is a dominating factor in the relations between the genders. In the population at large, not many women will seek medical care from male physicians, and female physicians are a distinct minority and are found largely in urban areas. The concept of *izzat* -- family honor -- is the burden women carry as reflected in their behavior. It is safe to say that with the exception of educated urban women, in terms of medical care, they are treated as second-class citizens.

Nasir Jalil has reported on one of Pakistan's long-standing and basic problems -- the educational institution. Every administration since Pakistan gained independence has proclaimed the solution of the high level of illiteracy in the nation as one of its top priorities. In large measure each administration has failed because of two major factors: inadequate funding and the continued high fertility rate, which has resulted in an increase of almost a million illiterates added to the population each year.

Actual expenditures have usually not approached the amounts appropriated by the government. The amounts spent on the three levels of education (primary, secondary and tertiary) have been disproportionate to the basic needs of the population. Probably because of their political power the middle and upper classes have supported the expansion of the college and university systems, with the secondary system receiving the next proportional amount of support and the elementary system receiving the least amount. There is further evidence of the disproportionate amounts spent on urban versus rural schooling and boys' versus girls' education. Since all schooling below the university level is segregated on the basis of gender, education for girls has lagged behind that of boys. Successive administrations have put forward Five Year Education Plans, but each has met with only limited success.

The status of women in Pakistan has been the subject of much discussion and controversy ever since the nation's founding. Anita Weiss presents the matter of gender inequities in compelling fashion. Women's status varies from one Muslim society to another, from the very conservative to the liberal. Pakistan might be considered as "traditional" in the judgment of some. Nationally, at the primary level 51 percent of the boys are enrolled in school compared to 28 percent of the girls. At the secondary level the disparity is even greater with 26 percent of the boys enrolled against 11 percent of the girls. At the tertiary level the ratio returns to a 2 to 1 basis in favor of males. (Curiously, at the University of Karachi, women have outnumbered men for the last three decades.) Discrimination against women in professional schools is very evident. At the professional level, women have been traditionally limited to teaching in women's institutions and working in the field of medicine, but with increased access to higher education over the last three decades, more women are entering traditionally male preserves in government and commerce. There has also been an increase in female employment in industry.

In the field of social service, the All Pakistan Women's Association was founded soon after partition to help feed and care for the millions of refugees from India. It was founded by the late Begum Ra'ana Liaqat Ali Khan. APWA concentrated its efforts in the field of social service, establishing schools for girls and homes for needy widows, and tried to improve conditions for working women. Political action was not their forte.

In the early 1980s the Women's Action Forum (WAF) was organized by members of the Pakistan Women Lawyers Association in opposition to what they considered was legislation inimical to women's welfare. Although there is universal suffrage and a few women have served in the national assembly in "reserved seats" for women, only one woman, the current ambassador to the

United States, Begum Syeda Abida Hussain, was ever directly elected to the National Assembly. The WAF has consistently fought against legislation considered inimical to women's rights and welfare.

Ethnic dissension and even violence appear to have become pandemic, and Pakistan has not been spared. Islam expects Muslims to offer hospitality to those in need. Partition of the subcontinent in 1947 created a monumental flood of refugees -- moving in both directions: Hindus leaving newly established Pakistan for India, and Muslims leaving India for Pakistan. Only rough estimates of this population exchange have ever been established. Muslim refugees were welcomed in both East and West Pakistan.

As Afak Haydar has pointed out, Muslims from West Bengal moved to East Pakistan and Punjabi Muslims from East Punjab migrated to West Pakistan. Urdu-speaking migrants from various parts of India migrated to Sindh, where Sindhi was the native language and where the migrants could easily be identified. The Bengalis and the Punjabis had little difficulty in adapting to their new homelands, but the new arrivals in Sindh were confronted with difficult problems of adjustment. Many of the new arrivals were professionals who were able to fill posts in colleges and government positions left vacant by the departed Hindus. Over the years native Sindhis gained sufficient education to qualify for professional and government positions but found the situations filled by the mohajirs. What had been a language problem became an economic (employment) problem.

When a superpower invades a small neighboring state, it is cause for concern among other nearby nations. But when the invasion results in as many as a third of the population fleeing to neighboring countries, the host countries are certainly confronted with monumental problems. Such has been the experience of Pakistan and Iran when the Soviet Union invaded Afghanistan in 1979 following the takeover of the Kabul government in a local communist coup.

In the 1980s an estimated three million Afghanis sought refuge in Pakistan and another two million in Iran. The United Nations High Commission for Refugees (UNHCR), the Government of Pakistan, and many private voluntary organizations (PVOs) as well as foreign governments supported the refugees in their camps, which were established in the North West Frontier Province and in Boluchistan, close to the Afghan border. The Government of Pakistan is said to have spent many millions of dollars/rupees in the relief effort, about 45 percent of the total cost.

Marvin Weinbaum reviews in considerable detail the myriad problems that confronted the Government of Pakistan, as well as the other aid givers. Although the Soviets withdrew in defeat at the hands of the mujahidin, fighting has continued among various factions and the final outcome is far from clear.

Lawrence Ziring analyzes Pakistan's larger role in the geopolitical environment of the subcontinent. From Pakistan's birth as a separate identity, the nation's leaders have had two concerns in its foreign affairs: first, its relations with India, from which it had an unhappy and strife-ridden divorce, and second, the development of a functional relationship with other neighbors as well as the major players on the international scene.

After independence and partition, it was not long before India forged a link with the Soviet Union, possibly because India's early leaders viewed a state-controlled economy with optimism while Pakistan's leaders opted for a market economy. Pakistan also developed a strong relationship with China to counterbalance India's ties with the Soviet Union. The arrangement might be considered a "double axis."

Although Pakistan became a member of the Central Treaty Organization in response to U.S. efforts to contain Soviet expansion, the United States was largely looked upon as a reliable and generous supplier of economic and military aid -- minus a commitment to send military personnel in case of a conflict.

Despite the bilateral arrangements described above, Pakistan maintained friendly relations with the Soviet Union and even received some aid, while India received considerable economic assistance from the United States. The Soviet Union's invasion of Afghanistan brought foreign troops to Pakistan's borders, and a few doomsayers predicted that the Soviets would march through Boluchistan to the Arabian Sea in order to gain a "warm water port."

Two facets of Pakistan's foreign affairs continue to be problematic. One is the continuing dispute with India over Kashmir. India continues to ignore the United Nations' mandate to hold a plebiscite to permit the right of self-determination for its inhabitants, claiming that Kashmir is an integral part of India. The other is the discontinuance of foreign aid from the United States because of American claims that Pakistan is developing a nuclear device and that under the terms of the Pressler Amendment, Pakistan no longer qualifies for American aid -- this in spite of the fact that India exploded such a device in 1974, almost twenty years ago, and has obviously expanded its nuclear capability. Pakistan believes it has not received equitable treatment, which appears to be the case.

In his chapter, "Another Try at Democracy," Robert LaPorte traces the development of Pakistan's leadership since partition with a review not only of the personalities involved but also of the economic, political and social forces that impinged on their efforts to achieve a polity that would respond to the problems and challenges of the fledgling nation.

Mohammed Ali Jinnah, a western-trained lawyer, was the architect of the successful effort of the Muslim League to establish a separate homeland for the Muslims of the subcontinent. From his years spent in England, he had learned the elements of a democratic polity and tried to implement such with the help of other leaders who had supported his efforts. Although Pakistan was envisioned as a homeland for the Muslims of the subcontinent, he was determined that his country would not be ruled by a theocracy and would allow freedom of religion.

However, what Jinnah had inherited from the British was not a democratic system but rather a viceregal system the principal functions of which were to "maintain law and order and revenue collection." Not until 1956 was a constitution adopted by the National Assembly, followed by new ones in 1962 and 1973. Even so, amendments have since been added, some more controversial than others. From time to time governments have failed and the army would take over and establish military rule, so that Pakistan has had military rulers for more than half its life. But with the death of President (General) Mohammed Zia ul-Haq in 1988, the electoral process brought Benazir Bhutto, the leader of the Pakistan People's Party (PPP) to power as the prime minister, the first woman to head a Muslim nation. Her tenure was brief, followed by the election of Nawaz Sharif as the new prime minister when the PPP lost the next election. In the summer of 1993, the attempted reconciliation of differences between Benazir Bhutto and Nawaz Sharif came to naught, and the political tug-of-war between the president and prime minister continues unabated.

Just as no writer writes alone, no editor works alone. I am grateful to the contributors of the several chapters of this volume, for their patience and forbearance in meeting the requirements of a camera-ready project. Their contributions are of a uniformly excellent quality, and if they suffer from anything, it has been the need to limit their enthusiasm for their topics. None of this volume would have seen the light of day without the wise and supportive counsel of senior editor Susan McEachern and her staff at Westview Press. This volume is published with the cooperation of the American Institute of Pakistan Studies, which supports scholarly efforts on Pakistan. I am also indebted to the Sociology Department of the University of Massachusetts at Amherst for its support and to Professor Gene Fisher, who solves all mysteries of the computer with a wave of his wand; and last, but not least, my thanks go to Catherine Lewis-Sanderson, who saw this volume to its completion with skill, patience and good humor.

J. Henry Korson
Amherst, Massachusetts

1

Pakistan's Economy in the Year 2000: Two Possible Scenarios

Shahid Javed Burki

Introduction

The subject of this chapter demands an unorthodox treatment. Instead of starting with a series of arguments or hypotheses and then using them to work toward a set of conclusions, I will follow a different approach. I will first state the conclusions I wish to arrive at and then suggest the reasons for reaching them.

I want to adopt this approach for a simple reason. In the few days I spent in Pakistan in the summer of 1992 -- days spent in reading the daily newspapers and current issues of weeklies and monthlies; in talking to relatives, friends and former colleagues in the civil service, and in travelling fairly extensively in the country -- I was struck by the extraordinary amount of pessimism with which people seem to view their country's future. Pessimism can be self-fulfilling. This is true for all situations and for all societies. To take one example: lack of consumer confidence in the United States has prolonged an economic recession well beyond its normal duration. Similarly, pessimism about the future of the Pakistani economy has begun to affect economic life in several different ways. The stock market, after reaching dizzying heights, has been in a long downward slide; large scale private investment remains well below its long-term potential; foreign investors, after having flocked to the country in impressive numbers, now seem to be waiting for the clouds of uncertainty to clear. There is a general malaise -- a sense of fatigue -- which I find hard to understand. To lift it Pakistanis should not be looking at the short term; they should, instead, think in long strategic terms. They should also take a good, sober look at the fundamentals of their economy. They should investigate the weaknesses in the economy as well as its many strengths in order to deal with the former by making use of the latter. It is this kind of analysis that has helped me to reach the following four conclusions:

First, if we choose to focus on the positive side of the economic ledger, there is no reason to believe that Pakistan should do less well in the next decade or two compared to its achievement in the past 46 years.

Second, it does not require a great deal of economic expertise to draw up a list of policy measures that need to be adopted in order to keep the country moving forward at a brisk pace.

Third, only politicians, and not bureaucrats, can lead the country forward. On many occasions in its history, Pakistan was tempted to place its life in the seemingly safe hands of the civil and military officials only to find that they were not capable of dealing with the deep structural problems the country faced.

Fourth, and finally, instead of depending on the largesse of its erstwhile friends in the West, Pakistan will have to rely on its own resources for building its economic base and for erecting a durable structure on top of it.

A Brief Retrospective

To reflect on Pakistan's future, we must understand its past. The past for Pakistan's economy began in 1947 when the country started rather hesitantly the difficult task of creating an economy independent from that of India. In retrospect it is surprising that the Indians should have helped Pakistan's fledgling government to cut itself loose from their much larger economy. This they did probably in the belief that some early shocks to the new country would keep it in line with their own economic destiny. The result, unexpectedly for both India and Pakistan, but to the understandable delight of the latter, turned out to be quite different from that apparently intended by the first generation of Indian leaders. Pakistan emerged economically stronger from the trade and water wars fought with India in the late forties. These wars and the dozens of disputes over the division of assets of British India between the two successor states and over the movement of millions of people across the boundary between the two states convinced the Pakistanis that their survival depended on their ability to develop a totally independent economic system.

While the purpose of this essay is not to offer a detailed account of Pakistan's economic history, it is nevertheless helpful to look back at the long distance the country has travelled since it gained independence 46 years ago, and the place from where the original journey began. There is a definite need for such a retrospective if only to underscore that Pakistan's economy has been through some very shaky periods before. One hears a great deal of pessimistic talk these days about Pakistan's economic future. There is a growing feeling that the country may not find the resources it needs to put its economic and political house in order. There is a widespread impression that for the first time in Pakistan's history the country is faced with economic problems it may not be able to surmount. Abandoned by the United States and largely ignored by the western world, Pakistanis seem to feel that they now have to live in a singularly hostile world. Ethnic tensions, particularly in the province of Sindh but not too far below the surface in other parts of the country, seem to suggest to some that the very existence of Pakistan as a state may be threatened once again; that what happened in 1971 when East Pakistan left to become the state of Bangladesh may be repeated for the second time.

While there is considerable substance in these fears, a look at Pakistan's brief history helps to put them in some perspective. It is useful to remember that Pakistan began its existence as an independent country in a situation considerably worse than the one in which it finds itself today. To start with, it is helpful to recall that Pakistan's birth as an independent state was not treated with wild enthusiasm by the world.

The British would have wanted to leave a united India as the most worthy legacy of their two century rule over the subcontinent. The United States administration, reminded perhaps by its own war of independence against the British crown, was impressed by the way Gandhi and the leaders of the Indian National Congress had waged their struggle against British rule. The Americans, given their own experience with secessionist movements, were also not well disposed toward the breakaway tendencies in the post-colonial states of Asia and Africa. They saw the effort to create a separate homeland for the Muslims of British India from the prism of their own Civil War experience. Accordingly, they were not particularly warm toward the idea of carving out Pakistan from the territory of British India. Totally unexpectedly for the leaders of Pakistan, their country's birth was not viewed as a development of great consequence by the world's Muslim states either. Afghanistan was the only country that voted against the entry of Pakistan into the United Nations. Other Muslim countries also showed little enthusiasm for the creation of a country whose very birth was motivated by the desire to create a separate political entity for a large segment of the world's Muslim population. In other words Pakistan's birth took place in an environment which if not totally hostile was at best indifferent toward the new state.

Pakistan's Economy in 1947 and 1993

Pakistan's economy in 1947 and for several years after its birth was in a very fragile state. At the time of independence, Pakistan was a predominantly agricultural country with the sector of agriculture responsible for nearly two-thirds of its gross domestic product. It did not have an industrial sector of any consequence and there were few signs of the presence of such modern sectors of the economy as banking, insurance, construction and air transport. Lahore was the only city that could be called truly urban; even Karachi and Rawalpindi were small garrison towns with defense as their only industry. The country traded a small part of its products with the outside world. Even internal commerce was quite underdeveloped.

Today, only four and a half decades after its birth, Pakistan has a much more robust economy. By far the most significant change that has occurred is with respect to the prevalence of poverty. Pakistan does not have the kind of poverty which was common at the time of its birth and which is still highly visible in other countries of South Asia. Much of this change occurred in the last two decades, particularly with the migration of millions of people to the Middle East in the seventies and eighties. These migrants sent billions of dollars worth of savings to their dependents who, in turn, used a large proportion of them to improve their living standards.[1] While firm estimates are not available on the incidence of poverty, my guess would be that no more than 15 percent of its current population -- or about 20 million people -- is absolutely poor. A very large number of the remaining poor are concentrated in less accessible regions of Boluchistan and the Frontier Province and in the rural areas of Sindh.

But Pakistan's economic achievements go beyond the elimination of the worst forms of poverty. It is a relatively modern economy with the share of manufacturing in gross domestic product approaching that of agriculture. Agriculture itself has modernized, no longer producing what is required only for subsistence. A number of Pakistan's agricultural products have entered world trade. The country now counts among the top half dozen exporters of rice and cotton and there is now a sizeable export of fruit and fruit products. Unlike a number of poor countries, the structure of Pakistan's industry is diversified and technologically sophisticated. The manufacturing sector has proceeded well beyond the simple task of processing agricultural commodities toward the production of sophisticated transport and electrical equipment and consumer electronics. Nearly a third of the country's population lives in urban areas spread all over the country. Pakistan has two mega cities, Karachi and Lahore, with populations close to ten million in each. Another dozen cities have populations of more than or approaching one million. The service sector is able to handle sophisticated transactions. In spite of a poorly developed educational sector, Pakistan can boast of a well educated work force that numbers several hundred thousand. It has developed skills of world standard in banking, hotel management, airline operations, shipping, and computer software development. It has a large pool of people working abroad, many of them in highly skilled occupations, and several thousand of them with access to capital that they would be willing to invest in the country.

In other words, it is safe to say that in many respects Pakistan is no longer a poor South Asian country; it has many features of a middle income nation. According to one way of estimating national income, Pakistan's per capita income is close to $2,000, twice that of India's.[2] Conventional ways of national income comparisons put per capita incomes of Pakistan and India very close to each other: according to the latest figures available from The World Bank, 1990 per capita incomes for Pakistan and India were estimated at $380 and $320, respectively.[3]

Insofar as Pakistan's external economic environment is concerned, it is much more supportive now than it was at the time of the country's birth. It is easy to exaggerate the consequences of Pakistan's current difficulties with the United States and the consequent suspension of aid by that country. There are a number of entries on the positive side of the ledger. Some unforeseen trading opportunities have opened up in Central Asia after the collapse of the Soviet Union; the economic revolution quickly unfolding in China could have a number of positive implications for Pakistan, particularly in terms of trade in the commodities that have yet to enter the world market; the maturing of the economies of East Asia present Pakistan with additional opportunities to obtain direct foreign investment; the presence of a large and growing expatriate Pakistani community in Europe and North America could become an important source of investment capital and managerial talent for the home country.

Finally, it is also possible to become despondent about Pakistan's ethnic problems and the seeming inability of many of its diverse people to live together in peace. Again, the situation now is not much worse than it was immediately after independence when the arrival of millions of refugees into the country was viewed with tremendous hostility by the natives of the areas that became Pakistan. The states of Boluchistan had to be won over to the Pakistani side by the show of considerable force by the central authority; the tribes of the North West Frontier Province remained restive; even Bahawalpur did not seem anxious to be fully absorbed into Pakistan. All this does not mean that there is no reason to be concerned with ethnic strife in many parts of the country and the damage it is doing to the economy. That notwithstanding, it is important to note that differences among Pakistan's many ethnic groups are not of recent origin and that on many previous occasions the authorities have had to resort to the use of great force in order to secure law and order in the troubled areas.

One useful message to come out of this brief review of history is to recognize that the reasons cited by those who chose to be pessimistic about the country's future are not the product of some recent developments. If anything Pakistan today is in a much better position to move along the path of rapid economic growth than it was at the time of its birth. If Pakistan could survive the trauma of its birth and continue to grow at a rate that would have been considered impossible even by those who were optimistic about the new country's economic and political future, then there is no particular reason, other than the common tendency to feel with greater intensity the pain and discomfort of the moment, to be particularly despondent about the future. Given the history of the country, there is not much justification to be totally pessimistic about the future at this time.

Four Happy Developments

I will now return to the reading of Pakistan's economic history for another type of reflection; to identify the reasons for the country's relative economic success in the four and a half decades since independence. From a reading of our history I reach the conclusion that Pakistan's economic leaders contributed to the country's enormous success in overcoming a number of difficulties faced early in the country's life by getting four things right.

First, they made a very effective use of the competent civil service they inherited from the British raj to handle the large number of economic crises that hit the country soon after it gained independence. These included the trade and water wars with India, the arrival of millions of Muslim refugees from India in the short space of a few months following independence, the situation created by a number of serious floods that visited the provinces of Punjab and Sindh in the first few years after independence, the equally serious situation that resulted from the massive crop failure in 1954 which turned Pakistan for the first time in its history into a food deficit area. The civil service managed these crises extremely well but, unfortunately, in the process also took over the responsibility for all economic decision-making. The civil servants were well trained to manage crises but were not well equipped to undertake strategic economic planning. To succeed, the latter required consensus among a number of powerful social groups, which could not be produced by the civil service. Accordingly, a number of difficult structural rigidities in the economy remained unattended to for a long time.

The second happy development for Pakistan's economy was the lack of interest by the first generation of leaders in getting the state involved in a highly intrusive way in the economic life of the country. While the government of Jawaharlal Nehru in India was putting the state on the commanding heights of the economy, the administrations of Mohammed Ali Jinnah and Liaqat Ali Khan were quite content to leave the economy in Pakistan basically in the hands of the private sector.[4] No serious effort was made to institute medium or long-term planning. The state was required to play a supportive role providing the private sector with the infrastructure it needed, the funds it required to augment its resources for investment, and protection the domestic industry felt it needed in the initial stages from the more mature industries in the industrial world. It is interesting to note that central planning came to Pakistan not as the result of an ideological belief in it on the part of the leadership of the day, but as a consequence of pressure from foreign donors, in particular the United States, that a planning framework was required to ensure the efficient utilization of the foreign resources that were being provided to the country.

The third fortunate development for Pakistan was the consequence, in turn, of the government's willingness to allow the private sector a major role in the economy. Accordingly, small entrepreneurs in the industrial sector and middle-sized farmers in the countryside invested heavily in the sectors of industry and agriculture, thereby broadening the bases of both sectors of the economy. This development, often unnoticed by the students of the Pakistani economy, has lent a degree of robustness to the economic structure which is not usually found in most developing countries. The small industrial entrepreneurs saved the sector from devastation when the government of Prime Minister Zulfikar Ali Bhutto nationalized large-scale industries. They were also responsible for Pakistan's second industrial revolution that started in the mid-eighties and is still unfolding. While the first industrial revolution in the fifties introduced industry into the Pakistani economy, the second revolution is changing its structure by introducing a considerable amount of diversification into the system. Likewise the middle farmers brought first the Green Revolution to Pakistan in the late sixties and then the second revolution which started in the mid-eighties and is still under way. The second agricultural revolution has introduced a tremendous amount of dynamism into the sector by diversifying its output and commercializing its operations.

The fourth happy occurrence for the Pakistani economy has been its openness to the outside world. This is the result of several factors, two of which need special mention. The emigration of millions of Pakistanis, first in the fifties and early sixties to Britain, then in the seventies to the Middle East, and, finally in the eighties to the United States has exposed the Pakistani economy and society to outside influences, most of which have been beneficial. The second type of openness was the result of the state's inability to enforce trade controls. This resulted in rampant smuggling, much derided by Pakistani officials and representatives of aid-giving agencies. However, extensive smuggling played an important role in improving the quality of industrial output; it forced the local producers of manufactured goods to compete with smuggled goods. Smuggling, therefore, served to open the economy to external competition; the premium paid by the consumers for smuggled goods over those produced locally represented a kind of tariff on imports. That the quality of most Pakistani goods, in particular those manufactured for domestic consumption, is better than those produced in India is in large measure the result of the state's permissive behavior in Pakistan with respect to smuggling.

There are other reasons for Pakistan's good economic performance since it achieved independence in 1947. In addition to the four happy developments I have discussed above, the list should also include the country's extraordinary agricultural endowment, particularly the availability of water that irrigates round the year and a very significant proportion of cultivable land. We should also include the modern skills brought by the millions of refugees who came over to Pakistan at the time of the partition of British India. The country's extraordinary good fortune, which helped it to find foreign savings whenever there was a squeeze on domestic resources, should also be counted among the factors that contributed positively to economic development. This list can be expanded almost endlessly but the important conclusion to highlight from this analysis is that there are readily identifiable factors at play which contributed to Pakistan's remarkable economic performance since 1947. There is no reason why the same set of circumstances cannot be marshalled again to produce a similar set of results in the future.

Failure of Government Policy

It is now the time to balance the picture presented above by reflecting on some of the failures of government policy since independence. Some of these failures, being well known, have been the subject of intense discussion for a long time. Some others are less well recognized and therefore have not received the attention either of the public at large or of the policy-makers. And then there is a third category of policy failure and the origin of this is in some of the recent initiatives, particularly of the present administration. The government in recent years -- especially the present regime -- has taken some steps that are moving the economy in the right direction. But some of these steps have produced consequences that could not possibly have been anticipated by the policymakers. As I will argue in the concluding part of this essay, the unhappy consequences of some of the recent social and economic policies will have to be addressed quickly if Pakistan is to realize its full economic potential.

I will pick two examples of policy failure under each one of the three categories identified above, thereby balancing the list of four happy developments with six instances of policy failure.

By far the most important failure that has gone virtually unnoticed is the inability of the political system to devise a legal framework for the conduct of economic business. A viable legal framework has to be defined in a broad sense: it does not only mean the presence on legal books of laws and regulations for governing economic behavior. Such laws exist in Pakistan. A legal framework also means that people have respect for the laws that govern all economic transactions and also have the confidence that they can have recourse to appropriate institutions -- courts, tribunals and bureaucratic organizations charged with the task of overseeing the implementation of economic laws and regulations. Such recourse for the resolution of disputes, if available at all, is often not used by the people. There is a lack of faith in the efficacy of the institutional arrangement for dispute resolution. As a reaction to this failure, people spend a great deal of time and energy in exploring other channels such as building contacts with officials placed in the right areas; or using elected officials to lend voice to their grievances; or depending on *safarish* (the use of personal favors and/or contacts) for getting their work done. This diminution of confidence in the legal framework for conducting economic transactions leads to a vicious cycle: as more importance is given to the development of contacts and to safarish, institutions progressively deteriorate. Corruption becomes rampant, for the contacts people use for getting favors from the bureaucracy usually charge a fee for the services they render. The society pays -- in fact, has already paid -- a heavy price for this failure.

Another important area of failure of public policy is the way public assets have been transferred for private use. The most egregious example of this comes from the land policy various governments have pursued since independence. The tradition of land grants goes back to the Mughul, Sikh and British periods. It took a nasty turn in the fifties and sixties when irrigation was introduced to large tracts of virgin land in the province of Sindh. A significant portion of this land was given to government functionaries -- mostly civil and military officers. We have now become familiar with the social and political consequences of this practice. The land grants in Sindh effectively resulted in the transfer of potential income from the province's indigenous population to new land colonizers. A similar form of income transfer is now occurring as a result of another practice that has become common in recent years. We are for the moment less conscious of this approach but its ultimate results could be equally troubling. I am referring here to the monopoly on the availability of information about the development plans of agencies such as the Karachi Development Authority, the Lahore Development Authority, the Capital Development Authority, and dozens of cantonments strung across the country. Where these development plans involve the acquisition of land on the periphery of cities, those with information about them can obtain vast windfall gains simply by buying land from those who own it -- generally poor peasants -- and then selling it at a multiple of the purchase price to the development authorities. The net result of all this is a sizeable transfer of assets and income from the less well-off segments of the society to those that are more privileged and are thus well placed to have access to critical information. The government's urban and rural land policy has therefore resulted in a serious worsening of income and asset distribution with all the economic and social consequences that such developments usually entail.

The two familiar examples of policy failure that I would like to emphasize are in the areas of social development and domestic resource generation. It is now well known that for a variety of reasons, most of which were the consequence of the policies pursued by the government, Pakistan has not been able to match its impressive economic performance in the last four and a half decades with an improvement in the social well-being of its people. Various indices of social development point to this paradox: at 103 deaths of infants per thousand of live births; with 600 maternal deaths per 100,000 births; with class enrollment rate of only 27 percent of girls of primary school age; with a population growth rate of over three percent a year, Pakistan ranks among the countries with one of the poorest levels of social development.[5] Better performance is expected from an economy with an impressive record of GDP growth and with per capita income that probably places it among the world's middle-income countries. There is a high cost associated with continuous neglect of the social sectors; it is now well known that a low level of social development translates into high levels of population growth. In its World Development Report for 1991, the World Bank estimated Pakistan's stationary population at 557 million in the middle of the twenty-first century. If this projection holds, Pakistan in the year 2050 will become the third largest country in the world after India with 1.8 billion people and China with 1.6 billion people.[6]

The second well-known policy failure concerns the inability of the economy to generate enough savings from within to provide for an adequate amount of investment. In fact, for the last several years Pakistan has been running a budgetary deficit even on the current account. This means that the country must not only borrow to pay for development, it must also go out and obtain resources to pay for a portion of government's current expenditure. I made a brief reference to Pakistan's extraordinary good luck in the past which made it possible to receive large amounts of foreign savings to finance a significant proportion of development expenditure. But with some very dramatic changes in its external environment Pakistan has lost the old leverage over the United States and other western countries. It seems very unlikely now that these countries will be generous in supporting Pakistan with their own savings to the extent they did in the past.[7] This is clearly an untenable situation; unless Pakistan makes a determined effort to mobilize domestic resources, its investment rate must decline, and if that happens the country will not be able to sustain the GDP growth to which it has become accustomed in the past.

My final list of failures of government policy includes items of relatively recent vintage: as already indicated, they are the consequence of some of the recent initiatives taken by the government. The first of these relates to the present administration's privatization program. The government's effort to place in private hands the assets acquired by the state in the early seventies is commendable. However, it must be recognized that privatization without attention to the creation of a regulatory framework within which the private sector must be obliged to work could create a very unhappy situation. The argument sometimes made with reference to Pakistan is that private greed when aggregated results in overall social good.[8] This argument rests on very dangerous ground. Unless the government creates laws, rules and regulations to guide the working of the private sector and sets up institutions to ensure that these laws and regulations are observed, it is inviting the kind of response from the people that produced the impulse to put the public sector on the commanding heights of the economy in the first place.[9]

The second failure of government policy that belongs to this category is again the outcome of a recent initiative with good intentions. I refer here to the decision taken during the period of President Zia ul-Haq to allow the private sector to establish educational and health facilities for use by the people who could afford to pay for them. This policy helped to meet the demand for these kinds of services on the part of a growing number of people in the middle and upper classes who were not happy with the quality of service provided by the state sector. The problem with this approach is that it is contributing in a significant way to the polarization of the Pakistani society. Private schools are providing western education in English medium to an increasing number of children from the middle and upper classes. New private universities are being set up to serve the same groups in the society. At the same time the state sector, partly because of political reasons and partly because of the paucity of resources, continues to furnish education of indifferent quality to its clientele. Urdu -- or sometimes one of the regional languages -- is the medium of instruction and a traditional curriculum is given preference over modern instruction. The initiative taken by the private sector in providing modern and relevant education needs to be applauded and encouraged. However, the state must find a way to open the facilities already created or being set up in the private sector to the less privileged segments of the population. Unless this is done, there is a distinct danger that considerable widening of the gap in the level of social development will occur between different income groups. Such a development will have unfortunate long-term implications for social and political stability.

Pakistan in the Year 2000

I now come to the final part of my chapter: to speculate about the future, to paint the picture of the Pakistani economy as it might look at the turn of the century. Two scenarios are possible: in one Pakistan is able not only to sustain but to better its past performance, in the other, the country finally succumbs to the large number of structural problems which could have weighed it down in the past. It is well within the capacity of the Pakistani economy to generate a growth rate of 6 to 7 percent a year in its GDP. If that happens the size of its economy could double from the present level of some $50 billion to about $100 billion in today's dollars. Since the rate of population growth cannot be reduced over the short run, even a 6 to 7 percent rate of increase in GDP will mean a rate of growth of no more than 4 percent in per capita income. Therefore, by the year 2000 Pakistan's income per capita, reckoned by using the conventional methodology, could reach $660 compared to about $420 in 1992. With this level of growth, Pakistan should be able to see a major restructuring of its economy. The manufacturing sector should become the most important one of the economy; the sector of services should see the growth of a number of sophisticated enterprises; urbanization will proceed at a rapid pace but should create livable conditions in towns and cities; the country should get further integrated into the global economic and social system; and, finally, Pakistan should begin to turn the demographic corner with a palpable decline in the rate of fertility.

The other scenario is considerably more grim in tone. Gross domestic product may increase at a rate little more than the rate of increase in population. If that were to happen there will be no improvement in the quality of life; if anything, mass poverty, banished in the seventies and eighties, will return again. Agriculture will remain the predominant sector of the economy and large cities will be unable to provide even the most basic amenities to their growing population. Pakistan would be left way behind by the countries of East Asia; it is not inconceivable that even some of the countries of South Asia will begin to overtake Pakistan. Some of them have already done that in terms of social development.

While I attach a relatively low probability to Pakistan actually taking the low road to development, it is useful to underscore that there are a number of clearly visible signs that point toward such a course. The initiative lies with the government; if it makes the right decisions now there is no reason why Pakistan should not see the high road, why the picture I have painted above about relative prosperity and modernization could not actually materialize. The failure to act on the part of the government will prove to be very costly indeed. While the emphasis being placed by the current administration on reviving the private sector and giving it a prominent role in the economy is appropriate, it must be recognized that the state must continue to play an important role in helping the economy to move in the right direction. The private sector, no matter how dynamic it is, cannot substitute for the state.

What types of government policies will help Pakistan to realize a bright economic future rather than turn up with a dark and somber outcome? The answer to this question is to be found in the analysis that I have already presented above: in the four happy developments I noted from Pakistan's history and the six failures of government policy I highlighted above. Adding all these together provides me with a ten point agenda for the future, which I will summarize as follows.

- Rebuild the capacity of the civil service to handle economic crises to which the country will remain as prone in the future as it was in the past. While it was correct to take away from the civil service the responsibility for economic policy making, an efficient civil administration is an essential element in any good strategy of sustained economic development.

- Abandon medium and long-term economic planning. There is little point in using the country's very scarce manpower capable of doing strategic planning in formulating five-year development plans. It has been the country's experience that these plans become irrelevant the moment they are approved by the government and published for the information of the public. Instead, this manpower should be used in pursuing for the state other functions identified in this agenda.

- Encourage the small industrial entrepreneurs and middle-sized farmers to perform even more aggressively in their respective sectors. The best way of doing this is the creation by the state of what, in today's language, is called an "enabling environment."

- Keep the economy open by permitting unlimited contacts with the outside world, moving toward a convertible currency, and introducing a trade regime that does as little as possible to inhibit exchanges of goods, commodities and services with the outside world. The past policy of allowing people to travel freely to foreign countries and to emigrate should be maintained.

- Create a legal framework for the conduct of economic transactions in which the people have confidence and which can protect the rights and obligations of all parties involved in economic exchanges.

- Introduce a transparent urban and rural land policy in which the land held by the state is auctioned to the highest bidder and in which the plans of urban development agencies including cantonments are made public well in advance of land acquisition.

- Commit public resources for improving the level of social development for the poorer segments of the population, in particular advancing the economic and social welfare of women.

- Improve the resource base of the government by taxing the more dynamic sectors of the economy including agriculture, small industry, construction, and internal commerce.

- Concentrate on creating a regulatory framework for the working of the private sector. This is particularly required to regulate the new financial institutions -- commercial and investment banks, leasing companies, and *mudarbas* (mutual funds that do not pay fixed rate of dividend but are run on the basis of profit or loss) -- that have recently been established.

- Provide mechanisms such as scholarship funds and subsidies that would make it possible for the deserving poor to gain access to the educational and health facilities that have been set up or are being established in the private sector.

Only one thing remains to be said before I conclude this presentation which is that this is an ambitious agenda which can be implemented only on the basis of a broad consensus among all segments of the country's social and political community. In an address delivered last year at the occasion of the annual convocation of the Lahore University of Management Sciences, I had proposed the negotiation of a new social compact aimed at moving the country toward modernization and prosperity.[10] I should perhaps urge once again that there is still time for the negotiation of such a compact.

The views expressed in this chapter are those of the author and do not necessarily represent those of the World Bank, where he currently works as the Director of the China and Mongolia Department.

Notes

1. This point was developed by me at some length in an article I contributed to a recent book on poverty in South Asia. See Shahid Javed Burki, "Alleviation of Poverty in Pakistan: Myth or reality," in T.N. Srinivisan and Parnab Bardhan, *Poverty in South Asia* (New York: Columbia University Press, 1988).

2. This estimate uses the Purchasing Power Parity methodology which is different from the conventional way of estimating and comparing incomes of different countries. For an explanation of the PPP methodology and estimates of national income of several developing countries based on it, see The World Bank, *World Development Report, 1992* (Washington, D.C.: 1992), 299-301.

3. See The World Bank, *World Development Report, 1992* (Washington, D.C.), Table 1, p. 218.

4. For a good and detailed account of the politics of economic decision making in India, see Francis Frankel, *India's Political Economy* (Princeton, N.J.: Princeton University Press, 1982).

5. These statistics are from The World Bank, *World Development Report, 1992* (Washington, D.C.: 1992), Tables 27, 28 and 32, pp. 270, 272 and 280.

6. See The World Bank, *World Development Report, 1991* (Washington, D.C.: 1991).

7. One illustration of the extent of support Pakistan received from abroad was revealed recently in *The Washington Post,* which published some estimates of the resources that flowed into the country during the Afghanistan war. See Steve Coll, "Secret CIA Escalation in '85 Tipped Afghan Balance," reprinted in *International Herald Tribune*, July 21, 1992.

8. In the context of Pakistan, this argument was first advanced by Gustave F. Papanek in his book, *Pakistan's Development: Social Goals and Private Incentives* (Cambridge, Mass: Harvard University Press, 1967). Mahbub ul Haq's seminal work on the Second Five Year Plan (1960-65) took the same approach. See his book, *Strategy of Economic Development: A Case Study of Pakistan* (Karachi: Oxford University Press, 1968).

9. This argument was developed by me in a paper presented at a seminar held in Lahore, December, 1991. See Shahid Javed Burki, "Privatization, Deregulation, and Good Government: A New Economic Development Paradigm for Pakistan." A paper presented at the seminar on Financing Pakistan's

Development in the 1990s, Lahore University of Management Sciences, December 15-17, 1991.

10. This address was published in full by *The Friday Times*, Lahore, December 21, 1992.

2

Growth Without Change: The Demography of Pakistan

Lee L. Bean

Future population estimates or projections are speculative at best, but the shorter the time frame the more likely they are to reflect reality because demographic variables producing change (births, deaths, and migration) modify slowly in the absence of catastrophic events. However, responding to the needs of planners for long-term estimates, demographers enter the realm of speculation and therefore seek to avoid the stigma arising from error while eschewing the aura of prophesy. They do so by presenting a range of future population estimates based upon "informed judgments" regarding future trends in birth and death rates.[1] Typical population projections made for developing nations in the 1960s included an assumed "worst case scenario." This was an estimate assuming constant high fertility and declining mortality, producing very rapid rates of population growth. Such estimates and reality rarely coincide. Pakistan, however, is one of those cases where speculation and reality are the same.

In 1968 the demographic section of the Pakistan Institute of Development Economics published a series of population projections for Pakistan, then West Pakistan, (Bean, Khan and Rukanuddin, 1968). Under the assumed "worst case scenario" of declining mortality and constant high fertility, it was estimated that Pakistan's population would total 83.4 million persons in 1980. The 1981 census reported 84.2 million. Using 1981 census data, the Pakistan Population Census Organization projected the 1981 population to 1991 assuming an annual rate of increase of 3.1 percent. The estimate was 114.3 million. The older PIDE 1990 estimate extrapolated to 1991 was 115.2 million. The difference between the projected and actual 1981 population was small, and the two projections for 1991 differ by only one percent when working with data collected 20 years apart. Although the results of the most recent census effort are not available at this time, most observers expect a population count of approximately 114 million.

The close approximation of the current population of Pakistan to the worst case scenario drawn in the mid-1960s raises three questions of interest. Why has there been no change in the projected high rate of population growth when for more than a third of a century (Aslam, 1991) Pakistan has supported efforts to curtail fertility rates and consequently rates of population growth? Are the social and economic conditions of the 1990s consistent with the problems assumed to be associated with rapid population growth? And finally, what can be anticipated in the future? These three questions will be the central focus of this chapter. However, before they can be addressed, it is necessary to provide a summary of the demographic patterns of the last two decades. It is these patterns which make the three questions interesting. Therefore the next section of the chapter summarizes recent demographic trends in Pakistan beginning with the question of how certain can we be about demographic information. Summaries of population growth, fertility, and mortality follow. The chapter then addresses the three questions noted above, sequentially.

Demographic Trends

Demographic Data: Certainty and Uncertainty

There is considerably more demographic information available for Pakistan than there was two decades ago, and a significantly greater capacity for the analysis of demographic data. A small group of demographers associated with the Pakistan Institute of Development Economics in Islamabad has produced high quality analyses. (See, for example, Shah 1986; Sather 1984, 1987, 1989; Sather and Kiani, 1986.) A second important contributor to our understanding of the demography of Pakistan is the National Institute of Population Studies in Islamabad, founded in March 1986. Its staff has provided excellent summaries of available demographic information (Rukanuddin and Farooqui, 1988), coordinated major demographic surveys (National Institute of Population Studies and Demographic and Health Surveys, 1991), and undertaken or cooperated in a number of special studies primarily focusing on family planning programs results and constraints. (See for example Rukanuddin et al., 1989; Michael Semple and Yemeema Mitha, 1986; Sotoudeh-Zand, N.D.; National Institute of Population Studies and Population Welfare Division, 1989.) This chapter draws heavily on the work of scholars associated with these two organizations.[2]

Since independence, Pakistan has undertaken five population censuses. The first in 1951 occurred only four years after independence when the government was short of trained personnel and financial resources to support such work. It provided limited information, and there was a rather substantial underenumeration. The 1961 census occurred under more favorable circumstances and was of reasonable quality given the difficulties of communication and transportation, compounded by working in two provinces, West and East Pakistan separated by 1000 miles of Indian (and hostile) territory. There was some under enumeration particularly of females, and other errors which have been identified in several publications. (See Bean, et al., 1968.) The 1971 census was postponed until 1972 because the civil war abrogated the religious binding of East and West Pakistan. The 1981 census was conducted more or less as scheduled, although there were serious questions regarding the validity of the count in parts of the nation because it was believed that certain ethnic groups attempted to inflate their numbers for representational purposes.[3] The 1991 census was also postponed because of the "law and order" situation, primarily in the Sindh.

All five of the censuses have been subject to problems of varying magnitude, but delays, undercounts, and overcounts are all simply part of the process of counting people. A census is, after all, a political process. Given the political instability of Pakistan since its independence, a completely reliable sequence of censuses is not surprising nor cause of great concern. A number of procedures are available to evaluate and adjust census data, and Pakistan's censuses have been supplemented with a surprisingly large number of demographic surveys.

The surveys are of particular importance in view of the fact that Pakistan has made absolutely no progress in establishing a valid and reliable vital registration system.[4] In the absence of vital registration data, the 1962-1966 Population Growth Estimation project (PGE, hereafter) was initiated to estimate fertility and mortality rates. This was followed by the Population Growth Surveys (PGS) in 1968-1971 and 1976-1979. Sample surveys which were designed to measure fertility, family planning, and other variables include the National Impact Survey (NIS) in 1968-69, the Pakistan Fertility Survey -- part of the World Fertility Survey -- in 1974-75, the Pakistan Contraceptive Prevalence Survey of 1984-85, and the recently completed Pakistan Demographic and Health Survey of 1990-91 (Rukanuddin and Farooqui, 1988, Table 5.1; and Bhatti, 1990). Other important surveys include the Population, Labour Force and Migration Survey of 1979-80, and the National Migration Survey of 1984.

As effective as the planning and execution of these surveys may have been, collecting information from a largely illiterate (and enumerate) population always involves some error. Moreover, there has been an emphasis on fertility surveys which often yield information on infant and child mortality, but less information on general mortality. Thus there is some variation in the quantity and quality of data on the vital statistics of Pakistan, but the trends are clear (Rogers, 1990).

Population Growth

As noted in the introduction to this chapter, the demographic hallmark of Pakistan is its rapid and recently accelerating rate of population growth. Independence in 1947 found approximately 32.5 million individuals in West Pakistan,[5] growing at a rate of 1.8 percent per annum. A total of 33.7 million was recorded at the time of the 1951 census, 42.9 million in 1961, 65.3 in 1972 and 84.2 in 1981. (See Table 2.1.) As noted above, estimates place the population at 114 million in 1991, a number yet to be confirmed by the delayed 1991 census. The annual percentage rate of increase was estimated to rise from 1.8 percent between 1947 and 1951 to 2.4 percent in 1961, to 3.0 in 1972 (assuming an adjustment for an undercount in the 1972 census), and to 3.1 percent in 1981 with probably the same rate since 1981 (Rukanuddin and Farooqui, 1988:4). It is believed that neither immigration nor emigration significantly effected the population numbers and rates of growth after partition, but there has been substantial short-term labor migration, primarily to the Gulf States, and temporary refugee migration from Afghanistan. There has been a high rate of internal migration. One consequence, as noted in Table 2.1, is that the rate of population growth has been substantially greater in the urban areas than in the rural areas although Pakistan remains a predominantly rural population.

Mortality Patterns

At the time of independence, it was estimated that the crude death rate in Pakistan was 25-30 per thousand, that is, 2.5 to 3.0 percent of the population died annually. As reported in Table 2.2, the first official measurements emerged from the Population Growth Estimates (PGE) project in 1962. Because PGE used two methods to collect data (registration and retrospective quarterly surveys) and combined the results for a composite measure based upon a procedure known by the name of its originators (Chandrasekar and Deming -- CD), the range of estimates for the crude death rate remained relatively broad (12-19). The aggregate of the data for three years (1962-1965) showed a similar range: 11 to 18. Shifting to a different methodology which makes it hard to be confident about comparisons across time, the retrospective Population Growth Survey (PGS) suggests a crude death rate of 12 in 1968, 11.5 in 1976, and 10.5 aggregated over 1976-1979. The survey of 1984-1986 reports a CDR of 10.7. Other mortality measures are generally consistent with the trend in the crude death rate.

Life expectancy at birth was estimated to be in the low 30s (32.9 years for males and 34.4 years for females in 1950-1952) shortly after independence. The first life table constructed from the PGE data of 1962-1965 reflected a life

TABLE 2.1 Population Size and Rates of Growth in Urban and Rural Pakistan, 1951-1991

Year	*Total Population (Thousands)*	*Average Growth Rate Per Annum (percent)*	*Urban Population (Thousands)*	*Intercensal Urban Growth Rate Per Annum (percent)*	*Rural Population (Thousands)*	*Intercensal Growth Rate Per Annum (percent)*
1951	33,370	1.8	3,109	4.1	27,487	1.4
1961	42,880	2.4	9,655	4.8	33,324	1.8
1972	63,309	3.6 (3.0[a])	16,594	4.8	48,727	2.6
1981	84,254	3.1	23,841	4.4	60,412	2.5
1991 (Est[a])	108,909	2.9[b]				
1991 (Est[b])	114,333	3.1[c]				

[a] The Intercensal rate of growth of 3.6 percent assumes no undercount in the 1961 census. The rate of 3.0 percent assumes an undercount of 7.5 percent.

[b] NIPS estimate.

[c] Population Census Organization/NEMIS projection.

[d] Document of the World Bank. Report No. 7522-PAK. Table 5.2.

Source: National Institute of Population Studies, 1988. Tables 1.2 and 2.3.

TABLE 2.2 Demographic Parameters, Pakistan, Various Years

	Fertility Estimates (per thousand)		*Mortality Estimates (per thousand)*			*Life Expectancy*	
Year	*CBR*[a]	*TFR*[b]	*CDR*	*IMR*[c]	*MMR*[d]	*Males*	*Females*
1951	43.1-62.4						
1962	43.6-51.7		17-19	152-159			
1963-65		6.1-7.9	16-19				
1962-65				136-143		52.4	48.7
1976	42.8		11.5	87			
1976-79		6.9		94		56.1	57.0
1984-86	36.6-42.8	6.9	10.7	112	6-8		

[a] National Institute of Population Studies, 1988. Table 5.1. The ranges represent alternate data sources.
[b] Ibid. Table 5.2.
[c] Ibid. Table 6.1. IMR = Infant Mortality Rate
[d] MMR = maternal mortality rate, death per thousand births.

expectancy at birth of 52.4 years for males and 48.7 years of females.[6] The 1976-1979 PGS produced estimates of 56.1 and 57.0 years for males and females respectively. These data imply that the greatest gains accrued to females, reversing the male-female differential of 1962-1965, which favored males. This represents a significant improvement in life expectancy for females, roughly eight years versus approximately only four years for males. The same type of sex specific improvements is reflected in the reported infant mortality rates. The 1962-1965 PGE reported an infant mortality rate of 137 for males and for females. By 1976-1979, according to the PGS results, the rates were 102 for males and 86 for females. These improvements in female mortality rates are somewhat surprising in view of the continuing high sex ratio (Weiss, 1990:238), high rates of childbearing, and the high level of maternal mortality. For example, the maternal mortality rate, estimated at 4 to 8 maternal deaths per 1000 live births (1984-1986), is about one-third higher than the estimated level for India, eight-times higher than the level in Sri Lanka, but about 20 percent lower than the rate in Bangladesh. (UNDP, 1990:148).[7]

It is difficult to argue that the trends reported for the crude death rate, life expectancy, and infant mortality are completely accurate, because the procedures used to collect the data have changed over the years. Some of the mortality changes may be due to variations in the methods of collecting data on mortality. However, the overall consistency of the trends indicates that there has been some improvements in mortality.

Fertility: Early, Often, and Late

Prior to the introduction of the one-child policy in 1979, the Chinese government encouraged limitation of fertility by stressing three principles: later, longer, fewer; that is, a later age at marriage, increased birth spacing, and termination of child-bearing with fewer children. The high rate of fertility in Pakistan results from a pattern which reflects the opposite forms of behavior. Marriage is relatively early and childbearing begins early; birth intervals are short; and women persist in childbearing until late in life.

One might argue that such a summary is far too pessimistic and that there are some indications of increased acceptance of procedures and methods to limit family size at the individual level and fertility rates at the national level. Some of the reports, however, are contradictory. For example, Karim summarizes data from several sources. He suggests that the crude birth rate has fallen from 51.0 in 1961 to 36.6 in 1985-86 and that the total fertility rate has fallen from 7.5 in 1965 to 6.0 in 1985-86. Of course, he also reports that the total marital fertility rate was 8.02 in 1974 and 8.02 in 1984 (Karim, 1989:12-13).[8] Rukanuddin and Farooqui also report a decline in the crude birth rate but little change in the total fertility rate. (See Table 2.2, above.) Preliminary results from the 1990-91 DHS survey suggest, however, that the total fertility rate has fallen to 5.5, but there are several reasons to suspect the accuracy of this preliminary report.[9] Moreover Jain and Nag cite 6.6 as the total fertility rate for 1990 (Jain and Nag, 1992:30).

The trends implied by various fertility measures may reflect actual differences without confirming that there are real changes in the patterns of childbearing within marriages. For example, there is general agreement that the crude birth rate has fallen in recent years. This index (births divided by the total population expressed as a rate per 1000) is insensitive to the distribution of the population by age. Some of the change may be due to the fact that the proportion of the population in the youngest age groups has increased because of the high fertility rate and increased infant and child survival, and therefore the relative proportion of individuals in the childbearing years of life has declined. This type of change in the distribution of the population by age would result in a decline in the crude birth rate even if marriage rates and fertility rates remained constant.

The total fertility rate (a summary of fertility rates by age of women typically over the age range 15-49) corrects for the insensitivity of the CBR to the age distribution, but it is insensitive to the proportion of married women in each age group. Consequently, an actual increase in the mean age of marriage for females could produce some decline in the average number of children women in Pakistan might expect to have at the end of their childbearing years of life (say age 49), i.e., the total fertility rate.

Studies indicate that there has been some increase in the mean age at marriage of females. Korson and Sabzwari found that in the city of Karachi between the period of 1961-1964 and 1980 the mean age of female marriage registrants had increased from 21.1 to 22.8 years in the highest rent district, from 19.9 to 20.5 years in the middle rent district, and from 18.8 to 19.7 years in the lowest rent district. Although the age of males at marriage is less important, they found that for male marriage registrants there was an increase from 27.9 years 29.6 years in the highest rent district, a slight decrease from 27.2 to 26.9 years in the middle rent district, and a slight decrease from 26.3 to 26.0 years in the lowest rent district (Korson and Sabzwari, 1984:257-279). Karim also showed an increase in the age of marriage for females from roughly 18 years of age in 1951 to 21 in 1985 (1989:15). (See also Alam and Karim, 1986.) Data from the 1990-91 DHS survey imply that the age of marriage has continued to increase. Part of the reason for the increase might be ascribed to the Family Laws Ordinance passed in 1961, which set the minimum age at marriage for females at 16 and for males at 18. As Sathar and Kiani have pointed out, between 1961 and 1981 the percentage of never-married women increased from 46.6 percent to 68.9 percent in the age cohort 15-19, and from 12 percent to 24.4 percent in the age cohort 20-24. This appears to offer some evidence that the Family Laws Ordinance making 16 the minimum age of marriage for females was taking effect (Sathar and Kiani, 1986:535). According to the results released in the first, preliminary report, 80.1 percent of women age 15-19 were married (ever married) while data from a 1975 survey indicate 98.0 percent of the women in the same age group were currently married.[10] Nevertheless, by age 30-34, over 96 percent of the females in 1990-91 had been married.[11]

The apparent increase in the mean age of marriage for females may have produced a decline in the total fertility rate, but is there any evidence that a substantial proportion of married women have adopted methods which would result in lower fertility rates?

In spite of the fact that Pakistan has supported some form of family planning effort since 1955, there is little evidence that the information program has encouraged women to adopt a set of reduced family size expectations or that the information and service program has produced a significant number of women practicing effective contraception. If Karim's figures are accurate there is little or no evidence of changing fertility behavior within marriages between 1974 and 1985.[12] Pullum's analysis of the Pakistan Contraceptive Prevalence Survey indicates some evidence of an emerging family size norm, but only among restricted population groups: primarily the educated, urban women of the Punjab. At the other extreme, he reports that "women in the oldest age group and belonging to Boluchistan are the subgroups showing the greatest evidence of fatalism or normlessness" (Pullum, 1990:1). The 1990-91 DHS survey shows, however, that 36.15 percent of currently married women want no more children, but these women are concentrated in the older ages of life; the percentage does not exceed 50 percent until age 35-39 (NIPS and DHS, 1991:16). Yet even if women indicate that they want no more children, few adopt methods to restrict future pregnancies. Sather reports that 9.1 percent of Pakistan women were currently using contraceptives in 1984-85, and only 11.8 percent had ever used contraceptives (Sather, 1989). According to the 1990-91 DHS survey, only 9 percent of currently married women age 15-49 were using contraceptives but 16 percent had ever used contraceptives. The conclusion reached by Sather in her analysis remains apt: "Variations are so minute that the size of the non-contracepting segment stays almost unaltered, suggesting failure of the population programme to make a demographic intervention" (1989:26). More recently the staff of the Population Institute at the East-West Center summarized the situation as follows:

> With one of the world's highest population growth rates, Pakistan faces great challenges to achieving fertility reduction. Policy makers in Pakistan have recognized the problem of population growth for years, but fertility remains high. Despite a national family planning program, contraceptive use remains very low. Most couples desire large families, and there are many cultural and religious objections to contraception (1991:1).

In summary, some decline in birth rates may have occurred in Pakistan over the past several years, but this change may be due primarily to an increasing age of marriage for females. There is a limited amount of evidence that some small proportion of women in Pakistan may have adopted procedures which would reduce family size. However, there is also evidence that it is a very small proportion of women who use contraceptives, and that proportion has not increased much, if at all, since the early 1970s.[13] While there may be a demand for family planning evidenced by the number of women who want no more children, that demand has not been translated into behavioral changes among Pakistan's female population.

The Demography of Pakistan in Comparative Perspective

The demographic picture which emerges from the brief summary presented above is bleak. There have been moderate improvements in mortality conditions and little change in fertility. Consequently, the population of Pakistan has been growing at a rapid pace. Is Pakistan unusual? That question may only be answered when Pakistan is placed in a comparative perspective. Therefore, in Table 2.3 data are presented on basic measures for Pakistan and other countries in South Asia and the Middle East. Note that there are some differences between the numbers in Table 2.3 and those reported above. All of the data presented in Table 2.3 are from the United Nations Development Program report for 1990 and therefore reflect a consistent set of procedures for evaluation and adjustment of demographic data. In the interest of preserving comparability, the UNDP estimates are used without correction. The figures for Pakistan are generally consistent with those presented in Table 2.2, but a higher crude birth rate is accepted by the UNDP as a better estimate than that reported in other sources.

Among the countries included in the data presented in Table 2.3, only five countries have worse mortality conditions than Pakistan. These are Afghanistan, Bangladesh, Nepal, and Yemen (reported as two countries in the late 1980s). Each of these countries also has a lower level of economic development as measured in terms of GDP per capita. However, according to the UNDP data, two of these five countries have slightly lower TFRs than Pakistan. Afghanistan and the then two Yemens have higher TFRs along with four pro-natalist countries: Kuwait, Oman, Syria, and Saudi Arabia. Jordan, also reports a higher total fertility rate, which only recently supported any forms of fertility limitation efforts, primarily in the private sector, also reports a higher total fertility rate.

Thus while Pakistan may not be described as the extreme case, it is clear that both mortality and fertility rates compare unfavorably with those of many other countries within South Asia and the Middle East. The absence of more significant changes has been somewhat surprising to some observers of Pakistan

TABLE 2.3 Mortality and Fertility, South Asian and Middle East Nations, Circa Late 1980s

	Mortality Measures			Fertility Measures	
Region and Country	*Life Expectancy at Birth (years)*	*Under Age 5 Mortality Rate (per thousand)*	*Infant Mortality Rate (per thousand)*	*Births Per Woman (per thousand)*	*Crude Birth Rate (per thousand)*
SOUTH ASIA					
Bangladesh	52	188	104	5.5	42
India	59	149	98	4.3	32
Nepal	52	197	127	5.9	39
Sri Lanka	71	43	32	2.6	23
Pakistan	58	166	108	6.4	46
MIDDLE EAST					
Afghanistan	42	300	171	6.9	50
Egypt	62	125	83	4.8	35
Iran	66	90	61	5.6	41
Iraq	65	94	68	6.3	42
Jordan	67	57	43	7.2	45
Kuwait	73	22	19	4.8	32
Oman	57	64	40	7.2	46
Syria	66	64	47	6.7	44
Saudi Arabia	64	98	70	7.2	42
Turkey	65	93	74	3.5	28
U.A.E.	71	32	25	4.8	23
Yemen, A.R.	52	190	115	7.0	48
Yemen, P.D.R.	52	197	118	6.7	47

Source: United Nations Development Project, 1990

in part because of the economic development which has occurred and because of the existence of a longstanding family planning program. Why has there been less demographic change than anticipated?

Growth Without Change

In this section we review selected interpretations arising from the observed minimal changes in mortality and fertility in Pakistan. At the outset it is important to note that there has been significant economic development in Pakistan, in spite of rapid population growth. For example, Burki writes as follows:

> . . .during Zia ul-Haq's eleven years in power, Pakistan added 29.2 million people to its population. What is of considerable significance is the fact that the much larger population that lived in Pakistan at the time of Zia's death was much better off in economic terms than was the population at the time he assumed political power. During the Zia period, Pakistan was able to rid itself in large measure of the worst forms of poverty. A vast majority of its people could better satisfy basic human needs for food, shelter and clothing than could the populations of other countries of Asia. (1991:87)

In addition to general patterns of economic development, there has been an extensive pattern of medical manpower development and expansion of the infrastructure for health care. As noted in Table 2.4, the number of doctors in Pakistan increased by 764 percent between 1971 and 1990. Somewhat less is the 347 percent increase in nurses, the 200 percent increase in hospital beds, and the 240 percent increase in public health facilities. Still, these are impressive figures. Given the growth of medical manpower and facilities, why has there not been more improvement in mortality rates? Several suggestions have been made.

First, the medical system appears to be poorly structured. In Pakistan there is approximately one nurse for every five doctors. In the developing nations the ratio is 2.8, and in industrial countries 4.2 nurses per doctor. (UNDP, Table 11, p. 149.) The emphasis on producing doctors at the expense of other types of health workers has resulted in an oversupply of physicians emerging from the 17 medical colleges in Pakistan; a significant number of doctors are currently unemployed or underemployed. However, there are inadequate supplies of nursing staff and other paraprofessionals.

Second, there are serious inequities in the distribution of medical manpower and facilities. Although over 70 percent of the population is resident in rural areas, reports indicate that 83 percent of employed physicians are in urban areas, as well as 85 percent of all hospital beds, 83 percent of all hospitals, 97 percent of all TB centers, and 58 percent of all MCH centers. There is no formal structure to provide health services below the Basic Health Unit designed to serve a population of 5,000 to 10,000. Consequently, 36 percent of the population, approximately 39 million rural residents, have no reasonable access to health care. There are also major provincial differences in medical resources: for example, the ratio of population per doctor is three times higher in Boluchistan (in 1990) than in the Sindh -- in part because of the concentration of doctors and health care facilities in Karachi.

Third, Pakistan's investment in health care is limited. UNDP estimates that all developing countries allocated 0.9 percent of GNP to health in 1960, increasing that investment to 1.4 percent in 1986. Pakistan's allocation fell over the same period from 0.3 percent to 0.2 percent. Pakistan has, of course, benefitted from foreign grants and aid to its health programs. Unfortunately, these funds are often tied to facilities development, capital equipment, and training of medical manpower. Recurring costs for salaries, supplies, and equipment maintenance or replacement falls to the provincial governments, which simply lack the resources to meet these needs.

Fourth, the development of the public health infrastructure has lagged. UNDP estimates that in 1985-87 only 45 percent of the rural population had access to safe water and only 6 percent to adequate sanitation facilities; the respective proportion in the urban areas was 83 and 51 percent.

Finally, it is important to remember that the low level of life expectancy in Pakistan is due in no small part simply to the high level of infant mortality. Inadequate pre- and postnatal care are important causes, but there is also a linkage between the patterns of fertility and the incidence of infant mortality. Early and late childbearing and short birth intervals are clearly linked to infant mortality (Sathar, 1985). Progress in changing one demographic variable may also have an effect on changing another. Therefore it is important to understand some of the underlying reasons for the absence of significant change in fertility in Pakistan.

Family planning has a long history in Pakistan, and yet it has not worked as anticipated. There are a number of reasons which might be cited, and these have been documented in so many reports that the causes need not be repeated in detail. Rukanuddin cites the following problems: poor accessibility of services, poor quality of services, ineffective management and administration, and the lack of political and administrative support at all levels (1990). Other reasons may be cited as well including irregular and ineffective supplies of contraceptives, inconsistent program policies marked by failed experimental efforts, and the absence of long-term personnel commitments. (See also Burki, 1988:167.)

TABLE 2.4 Trends in Health Sector Inputs by Province

	Year			*Growth Rate: 1971 = 100 Percent*		
Province and Resource	*1971*	*1981*	*1990*	*1971-81*	*1981-90*	*1971-90*
SIND						
Doctors (total)	2,620	3,850	21,854	145	574	834
Doctor/Pop. Ratio	5,240	5,022	1,136	96	23	22
Nurses (total)	1,102	1,886	4,021	171	213	365
Nurses/Bed Ratio	6	5	6	89	117	105
Hospital Beds (total)	9,749	15,097	23,954	155	159	246
Bed/Pop. Ratio	1,408	1,266	1,430	90	133	102
PHC Facilities [a](total)	689	1,633	2,366	237	145	343
PHC/Pop. Ratio	19,927	11,701	10,493	59	90	53
PUNJAB						
Doctors	3,727	7,200	23,171	193	322	622
Doctors/Pop. Ratio	9,788	6,593	2,663	67	40	27
Nurses	1,730	2,534	5,343	146	211	309
Nurses/Bed Ratio	6	6	6	100	103	103
Hospital Beds	16,530	23,729	32,962	144	139	199
Bed/Pop. Ratio	2,207	2,000	1,872	91	94	85
PHC Facilities	2,026	3,174	4,605	157	145	227
PCH/Pop. Ratio	18,006	14,956	13,399	83	90	74
NWFP						
Doctors	371	1,287	6,803	347	529	1,834
Doctors/Pop. Ratio	21,930	8,521	2,121	39	25	10

(continued)

TABLE 2.4 *(continued)*

NWFP						
Nurses	148	328	1,059	222	323	716
Hospital Beds	6,431	8,427	11,510	131	137	179
Bed/Pop. Ratio	1,265	1,301	1,254	103	96	99
PHC Facilities	717	1,298	1,737	181	134	242
PHC/Pop. Ratio	11,347	8,449	8,308	74	98	73
BALUCHISTAN						
Doctors	227	600	1,623	264	271	715
Doctor/Pop. Ratio	10,374	7,228	3,354	70	46	32
Nurses	97	190	345	196	182	356
Nurses/Bed Ratio	13	801	10	64	123	79
Hospital Beds	1,928	2,416	3,464	125	143	180
Bed/Pop. Ratio	1,221	1,795	1,571	147	88	129
PHC Facilities	253	609	843	241	138	333
PHC/Pop. Ratio	9,308	7,121	6,457	77	91	69
NATIONAL						
Doctors	7,000	13,322	53,451	190	401	764
Doctors/Pop. Ratio	8,982	6,336	1,991	71	31	22
Nurses	3,105	5,004	10,768	161	215	347
Nurses/Bed Ratio	8	606	7	89	106	95
Hospital Beds	36,033	51,552	71,890	143	139	200
Beds/Pop. Ratio	1,745	1,637	1,480	94	90	85
PHC Facilities	3,972	7,281	9,551	183	131	240
PHC/Pop. Ratio	15,830	11,593	11,141	73	96	70

[a]PHC = Public Health Center
Source: Government of Pakistan, GOP Director General of Health, *Annual Reports*. Ratios are computed.

The literature on declining fertility in developing nations has demonstrated that there are independent and interactive effects of family planning and economic development (Mauldin and Ross, 1991), but with some considerable variation. Seemingly, in the case of Pakistan the family planning effort has not had a major impact, and economic development measured in traditional terms which focuses on growth in GNP and GDP per capita has had little impact on fertility. Recognizing that development may be multi-dimensional, both the World Bank and the United Nations Development Programme (UNDP hereafter) have in the past few years devoted increasing effort to other aspects of development. For example, UNDP has been responsible for the Human Development Index, which in its 1990 form combines measures of literacy, life expectancy, and GDP. This index suggests minimal "human-development" in the case of Pakistan. Among the 130 countries ranked from low (worst) to high (best) on the human development index, Pakistan ranks 36th. Table 2.5 reports the values of the three measures included in the index for selected South Asian and Middle East Countries. If one used only GDP per capita, Pakistan's rank would increase to 50, but if one ranked on literacy alone its rank would drop to 15. It is perhaps that dimension, literacy/education, that is a major indicator of barriers to fertility decline in Pakistan.

Evidence linking literacy/education to fertility is apparent from the data presented in Table 2.5. Calculating simply zero order correlations (the relationship of literacy to the total fertility rate without statistical controls for other variables), we find an r^2 (or amount of explained variance) to be .134 and for the correlation between percent literacy and the crude birth rate, .213. The observed literacy-fertility linkage, however, requires further examination.

Whatever evidence one finds of fertility limitation in Pakistan it is generally observed among urban and educated women, and the literature indicates that the relationship between education and fertility is stronger for females than males. Moreover, I hypothesize that if the disparity in educational levels between males and females is large and if there are cultural norms which generally and explicitly relegate females to a secondary position (Weiss, 1990), then the influence of female education on fertility may be reduced. On the other hand, the greater the commitment to education in general and the greater the gender equality, the lower the level of fertility. There are two reasons for this presumed linkage. First, the higher the level of commitment to general education, the higher the level of government support to general welfare programs, thereby reducing the need for large numbers of children to support parents in their later years of life. Second, the lower the disparity between male and female educational levels, the more likely the female is to be exposed to information outside of the nuclear or extended family. It is through these channels that women are more likely to secure information about access to and use of family planning.

TABLE 2.5 Human Development Index Values and Rank, Circa Late 1990's

	Human Development Index			
Region and Country	*Life Expectancy (Years)*	*Adults Literate (Percent)*	*GDP/Capita (US $)*	*World Rank*
SOUTH ASIA				
Bangladesh	52	33	883	23
India	59	43	1,053	37
Nepal	52	26	722	17
Sri Lanka	71	85	2,000	83
Pakistan	58	30	1,585	36
MIDDLE EAST				
Afghanistan	42	24	1,000	9
Egypt	62	45	1,357	45
Iran	66	51	3,300	61
Iraq	76	89	2,400	76
Jordan	67	75	3,161	73
Kuwait	88	70	13,843	88
Oman	57	30	7,750	48
Syria	66	60	3,250	62
Saudia Arabia	64	55	8,320	64
Turkey	65	74	3,781	72
U.A.E.	71	60	12,191	77
Yemen, A.R.	52	58	1,000	25
Yemen, P.D.R.	52	42	1,000	31

Source: United Nations Development Program, 1990. Table 5, pp. 190-197.

To estimate the effects of male-female educational differences, I have calculated a weighted disparity index, the educational disparity index or EDI. The index is constructed by first of all calculating the difference in the percentage of adult male and female literates. It is then weighted by a factor indicating the overall commitment to education expressed as the difference between 100 percent and the proportion of literate males. If there is a general investment in at least male education the weight is small. Symbolically, the index is as follows:

$$EDI = (M_1 - F_1) * (1.00 - M_1)$$

Where M_1 is the proportion of adult male literates

F_1 is the proportion of female literates

The EDI values for various South Asian and Middle East countries are presented in Table 2.6. Suggestive of the linkage is that r^2 increases to .280 in the case of EDI and TFR, and to .442 in the case of EDI and CBR: that is, the correlation between EDI and the two measures of fertility is more than twice the value of the correlations between percent literate and the two fertility measures.

Although the finding linking the EDI index and fertility are preliminary at this stage, it is indicative of the fact that the absence of significant educational development coupled with the persistence of gender differences in educational opportunities may be very important. The relationship between education and fertility has been extensively documented, and therefore the failure to extend the education of women as well as men may be a major constraint on changing fertility behavior.

Education and literacy in particular have been major goals of the Pakistan government for years -- now decades. As Berstecher has noted, "Ever since the Pakistan Educational Conference of 1947, literacy has been high on the public agenda. Neither the National Education Commission of 1959, nor the series of education policy pronouncements which marked the 1970s failed to mention literacy as an important priority" (1991:17). Like family planning priorities and goals, literacy and education goals have not been achieved. "The country's literacy ratio and school enrollment rates are among the lowest in the world. With 26.2 percent literacy ratio in 1981, Pakistan is placed at 111th position among the 125 countries of the world" (Rukanuddin and Farooqui, 1987:125).

No pride may be taken from the fact that the literacy rate (percent literate age 10 and over) increased from approximately 18 percent in 1951 to 26.2 percent in 1981. With the high rate of population growth, the actual number of illiterates in Pakistan more than doubled in three decades, increasing from 20.7 million in 1951 to 42.7 million in 1981 (Rukanuddin and Farooqui, 1987). There are enormous disparities in literacy levels by residence and region as well as sex. Consider the extreme cases. In the Sindh 58 percent of the males above age 10 were literate, and 42 percent of the females -- in the urban areas. In the rural areas the rates were 24 percent and 5 percent. In Boluchistan, 42 percent of the urban males and 18 percent of the urban females were literate, but only 10 percent of the rural males and 2 percent of the rural females. Overall, in 1981 only 7 percent of rural females in Pakistan above age 10 were classified as literate, and if there were a significant undercount of young unmarried females, the picture would be considerably worse because the missing women are more likely to be illiterate (Government of Pakistan and UNICEF, 1988; see also Siddiqui 1990). Enrollment ratios at each level of education mirror the illiteracy problem. Many students enroll in primary schools and may remain long enough to be classified as literate, but they leave the educational system before achieving any significant formal level of completed education (GOP and UNICEF, 1988:60 and 61).

TABLE 2.6 Percent Literate by Sex and Educational Disparity Index, South Asian and Middle East Nations, Circa Late 1985

Region and Country	*Educational Disparity Index (EDI)*	*Percent of Population Age 15 and Older Literate*[a]		
		Male	*Female*	*Differences*
SOUTH ASIA				
Bangladesh	1.20	43	22	21
India	1.20	57	29	28
Nepal	1.65	39	12	27
Sri Lanka	0.07	91	83	8
Pakistan	1.26	40	19	21
MIDDLE EAST				
Afghanistan	1.89	39	8	31
Egypt	1.19	59	30	29
Iran	0.87	62	39	23
Iraq	0.03	90	87	3
Jordan	0.31	87	63	24
Kuwait	0.31	76	63	13
Oman	1.86	47	12	35
Syria	0.79	76	43	33
Saudi Arabia	1.16	71	31	40
Turkey	0.34	86	62	24
U.A.E.	N.A.			
Yemen, A.R.	2.03	42	7	35
Yemen, P.D.R.	1.39	59	25	34

[a] United Nations Development Program, 1990. Table 5, pp. 136-137

Source: United Nations Development Program, 1990.

In summary, the slow achievements in improving mortality and reducing fertility in Pakistan have no simple cause. There is an unbalanced, poorly distributed supply of medical manpower. An effective health institutional structure has not been developed. Health care fails to reach large numbers of the population, and the absence of a complete and comprehensive public health infrastructure exposes much of the population to health risks leading to illnesses which are treatable but untreated. A major problem remains infant and child mortality which have some linkage with high fertility rates. Failure to reduce fertility arises not simply from a family planning program that lacks continuity, resources, and commitment, but also from social constraints that limit the development of interest in and commitment to fertility limitation. Data suggest that an important constraint may be the continuing low level of educational achievement in Pakistan, which is accentuated by the gender differences in educational attainment in Pakistan.

Growth Without Crises

In spite of the high rates of population growth, Pakistan has not encountered the crises which were predicted during the 1960s, in part because the population of Pakistan has served as a significant resource for economic groups. The population of Pakistan was an export commodity during the late 1970s and early 1980s. As a consequence of the phenomenal growth in income among the oil-producing Gulf States, particularly following the oil-embargo of 1973, large numbers of Pakistani workers were recruited to work in the Gulf region. The numbers of Pakistani workers never rivaled those of Egypt, nor did the percentage ever rival that of Jordan. Still the numbers were significant: 1.7 million or about 2 percent of the population in 1981 (Rogers, 1990). The remittances from these workers provided a substantial and significant flow of hard currency into Pakistan (Burki, 1988:175). Such employment opportunities and the resultant flow of hard currency are becoming a matter of history. Even before the Gulf war and its consequent economic disruptions, the flow of labor had started to decline in Pakistan. Many of the massive infrastructure developments had been completed; patterns of recruitment shifted to turn-key projects involving Koreans, Malaysians, and Filipinos. And the decline in oil prices reduced the opportunities to fund and develop new projects which would provide labor opportunities. While the Gulf war resulted in the exclusion of certain population groups from employment in the Gulf (especially the Palestinian-Jordanians and other Jordanians as well as Yemenis and Iraqis), there is no indication that new opportunities will reverse the decline in labor opportunities for Pakistani workers in the Gulf. While some opportunities will continue, the numbers will decline and the remittances fall.

It is difficult to fully measure -- or overestimate -- the importance of migrant labor and the remittances. Burki's analysis indicates that worker's remittances increased from $578 million dollars in 1976-77 to a peak of $2,886 million dollars in 1982-83. Since then the amount of remittances has declined by about one-third to $1,987 million dollars in 1988-89 (1991:107), and the repatriation of Pakistani workers from Kuwait and Iraq during the Gulf war caused a further, significant decline (Khan, 1992:200). Few of these funds were used for investment. Quibria's study of remittances from Asian workers to their home countries indicates that much of the worker remittances went to consumer goods,

90 percent in the case of India and 62 percent in the case of Pakistan with the balance (22 percent) allocated to real estate and 16 percent for physical and financial investment (1986:91). Consequently, it would appear that whatever reduction of massive poverty occurred during the Zia years might be attributed to worker remittances and not to governmental policies and programs. Burki notes, for example, that "if the worst forms of poverty were alleviated and if income distribution improved during the Zia period, it was not because of deliberate policy. It was the consequence of the large amount of capital that came into Pakistan from the workers who had gone to the Middle East." (1988:106-7.)

The large labor supply of Pakistan generated by its high rate of population growth is central to other explanations of economic growth in Pakistan. Pyatt argues that the labor supply of Pakistan has been instrumental in maintaining a seven percent per annum growth in the purchasing power of the gross domestic product between 1960 and 1988. He notes that "both in agriculture and manufacturing, Pakistan has relied heavily on an abundant supply of cheap unskilled labour which remains plentiful" (1992:4). He also identifies two other important factors: natural resources (essentially expansion of irrigated land) and an unregulated informal economic sector including "illegal activities which generate considerable income" (1991:5). Such an economic system is, of course, fragile, and as a consequence, Rais A. Khan argues that "Pakistan's economy in 1991 remained basically vulnerable" (1992:200). Indicators of the vulnerability of the economy include a 1990-91 unemployment rate of 13.45 percent and an inflation rate of 12.29 percent. Khan reports that the Minister of Finance stated in May of 1991 that during 1991-92 debt servicing would consume 53 percent and defense expenditures 47 percent of revenue receipt, and ". . . expenditures on development programs, public administration, and social sectors such as health and education would have to be met from external sources" (1992:200).

Future Implications: More of the Same?

In short-run terms the demography of Pakistan is relatively simple to describe. The population will grow rapidly, but probably no more rapidly than it has for the past decade because the resources and capacity to reduce mortality quickly and significantly are not present. Abid Aslam states that Prime Minister Nawaz Sharif was the first head of state in Pakistan in a quarter of a century to make a commitment to family planning, and "it is on this statement of urgency that programmes are pinning their hopes of breathing life into a moribund population programme" (1991:30). However, there is no momentum which will force a rapid reduction of fertility, and in the absence of such force the large proportion of the population under age 15 will soon begin to marry and the females to bear children. With larger numbers of women in the childbearing years of life, the number of individuals added to the population will continue to increase, accelerating the investments required to educate and nurture the population. Absent continuing and rising demands for expatriate labor in the Gulf states, increasing numbers of employment opportunities must be created (Hashmi, 1990) to avoid the expansion of a large, disaffected, volatile labor supply. How these things can be achieved is unclear at this time, but the persistent conflict over political power and the resources that such power can control will not provide the basis of stability necessary for effective implementation of social, demographic, and economic development programs.

Notes

1. Migration is often ignored or assumed to be constant because its effect is often trivial relative to births and deaths or because information on migration is less reliable than measures of other demographic processes.

2. NIPS (National Institute of Pakistan Studies) publishes a range of analytical reports, and has recently initiated a new journal *Pakistan Population Review*, which complements *The Pakistan Development Review*, a major outlet for demographic research in Pakistan.

3. The demography of ethnicity has been a matter of major concern in a wide range of countries. For a discussion of the implications of differential rates of growth among various groups in Pakistan, see Kennedy, 1991.

4. In the 1950s foreign consultants argued that Pakistan should initiate a survey system for recording births and deaths because it would take "a quarter of a century" to develop an efficient vital registration system. Consequently the Population Growth Estimation Project was initiated, to be followed by a sequence of large, and often expensive, surveys, all of which have been funded in large part by external donors. One must wonder whether all of these efforts have simply postponed the development of a vital registration system for yet another quarter of a century.

5. All data cited for the period 1947-1972 refer to the former province of West Pakistan or contemporary Pakistan.

6. The life table constructed from the 1971 PGS data by Yusuf and Hussain yielded a life expectancy at birth of 51.8 years for males and 49.5 years for females (1985).

7. Rogers has calculated that if the maternal mortality rate in Pakistan is 7, that is, within the range of 4 to 8, "then about 28,000 Pakistani women die in childbirth annually, and 80 children lose their mothers at birth daily. Slightly less than 33 percent of all female deaths in the age group 15 to 49 years are directly or indirectly related to maternity. . . ." (1990, p. 453).

8. The total fertility rate (TFR) is the number of children women might expect to have had by the end of the childbearing years of life defined as age 49. The marital total fertility rate (MTFR) is similar but includes only married women while the TFR is based upon age-specific fertility rates (births divided by women in each age group) regardless of marital status.

9. It appears that the DHS questionnaire was overloaded with every possible optional module, i.e., sets of questions related to specific topics such as breastfeeding and marriage to relatives, among others. The length of the questionnaire may have led to less effective probing to ascertain all live births. Further analysis may clarify the strengths and weaknesses of these survey results.

10. The implied changes in age at marriage may reflect not only real changes in age at marriage but also other normative changes. The sex ratio (males relative to the number of females) is quite high in Pakistan, suggesting a failure to report the presence of females in the household as well as high levels of female mortality. Both conditions probably influence the sex ratio. With higher levels of education and increased urbanization one might anticipate that the failure to record the presence of females, particularly young unmarried women, would have decreased. However, even now there seems to be an unusual sex ratio pattern in Pakistan which has led some observers to speak about "eight million missing" females -- the number which would have to be added to the Pakistan population to "correct" the reported anomalous sex ratio.

11. The traditional role of females -- marriage -- persists, and traditional patterns of arranged marriages remains dominant. For example, according to the 1990-91 DHS survey, 62.7 of ever-married women had married a relative and 50.5 percent of all ever-married women had been wed to a first cousin (NIPS and DHS, 1991).

12. Like all other data, one must accept the data on marital fertility rates cautiously. The statistics for the two dates come from surveys using different procedures to solicit information on fertility. Moreover, the pattern of change at specific ages raises several questions. The age-specific marital fertility rates in 1984 were lower than the 1974 rates for ages 15-19, 20-24, 25-29, and 30-34, but higher for ages 35-39, 40-44, and 45-49. This suggests a pattern of fertility limitation quite different from what one would predict. One would anticipate that some decline might occur across all age groups as women adopt methods to increase birth intervals. However, one usually expects to find that women in the older age groups will reduce fertility by a larger amount than younger women because they have a larger number of births and more surviving children.

13. There is some evidence that there may have been a decline in the knowledge and use of contraception over the past quarter of a century. Ahmed writes that "in 1968-69 a 'modern' contraceptive method was known to 83

percent wives 15-49 in West Pakistan, any method to 98 percent. . . ." (1989, p. 1). The knowledge of any method dropped to 61 percent in 1985.

References

Alam, Iqbal, and Mehtab S. Karim. 1986. "Marriage, Remarriage and Divorce in Pakistan and Their Effect on Fertility." In Nasra M. Shah (ed.) *Pakistani Women: A Socio-economic and Demographic Profile*. Islamabad: Pakistan Institute of Development Economics.

Aslam, Abid. 1991. Pakistan's Renewed Commitment to Family Planning, *Populi*, 18: 29-35.

Bean, Lee L., Masihur Rahman Khan, and A. Razzaque Rukanuddin. 1968. *Population Projections for Pakistan 1960-2000*. Monographs in the Economics of Development, No. 17. Karachi, Pakistan, Pakistan Institute of Development Economics.

Berstecher, D. 1991. Human Development in Pakistan: Issues in Basic Education. Unpublished paper, UNESCO.

Bhatti, Mansoor-ul-Hassan. 1990. Pakistan Demographic and Health Survey 1990-91. Pakistan Demographic and Health Survey. *Pakistan Population Review*, I: 1, 72-76.

Burki, Shahid Javed. 1986. *Pakistan: A Nation in the Making*. Boulder: Westview Press.

-------------------- 1991. Pakistan's Economy Under Zia. In Shahid Javed Burki and Craig Baxter, *Pakistan Under the Military: Eleven Years of Zia ul-Haq*. Boulder: Westview Press.

Cleland, J., and Z. Sathar. 1984. The Effect of Birth Spacing on Childhood Mortality in Pakistan. *Population Studies*, 38: 401-418.

Government of Pakistan and UNICEF. 1988. *Situation Analysis of Children and Women in Pakistan*. Karachi: UNICEF, Elite Publishers, Ltd.

Jain, Anrudh K., and Moni Nag. 1992. South Asia. In Susan Greenhalgh et al., Population Trends and Issues in the Developing Countries: Regional Reports. The Population Council, Research Division, Working paper No. 35.

Karim, Mehtab S. 1989. South Asia Study of Population Policy and Programmes: Pakistan. Islamabad, *United Nations Population Fund*, pp. 12-22.

Kennedy, Charles H. 1991. The Politics of Ethnicity in Sindh. *Asian Survey*. XXXI: 938-955.

Khan, Rais A. 1992. "Pakistan in 1991: Light and Shadows." *Asian Survey*. XXXII: 197-206.

Korson, J. Henry, and M.A. Sabzwari. 1984. "Age and Social Status at Marriage, Karachi, Pakistan, 1961-1964 and 1980: A Comparative Study." *Journal of Comparative Family Studies*, XV, 2, pp. 257-279.

Mauldin, W. Parker, and John A. Ross. 1991. "Family Planning Programs: Efforts and Results, 1982-89." *Studies in Family Planning*. 22: 350-367.

National Institute of Population Studies and Population Welfare Division. 1989. *Effects of Rapid Population Growth on Social and Economic Development in Pakistan*. Islamabad, Pakistan, National Institute of Population Studies and Population Welfare Division.

National Institute of Population Studies and Demographic and Health Surveys, 1991. Pakistan Demographic and Health Survey, 1990-91: Preliminary Report. Institute for Resource Development/Macro International.

Population Institute, East West Center. 1991. "Asia's Demographic Future: the Next 20 Years." *Asia-Pacific Population & Policy*. No. 14.

Pullum, Thomas W. 1990. "Evidence for and Against the Emergence of Family Size Norms in Pakistan." *Pakistan Population Review*, I: 1, pp. 1-11.

Pyatt, Graham. 1992. Towards Balanced Development in Pakistan. Discussion Paper 108, Development Economics Research Centre, University of Warwick, England.

Quibria, M. G. 1986. "Migrant Workers and Remittances: Issues for Asian Developing Countries." *Asian Development Review*. 4: 78-99.

Rukanuddin, Abdul Razzaque, 1990. "A Country Strategy Paper on Population Welfare Programme in Pakistan." Unpublished paper prepared for UNFPA, Pakistan.

Rakanuddin, Abdul Razzaque, and M. Naseem Iqbal Farooqui. 1988. *The State of Population in Pakistan, 1987.* Islamabad, Pakistan: National Institute of Population Studies.

Rogers, Tom. 1990. "Population Growth and Movement in Pakistan: A Case Study." *Asian Survey.* XXX: 446-460.

Sathar, Zeba. 1984. "Does Female Education Affect Fertility Behavior in Pakistan?" *Pakistan Development Review*, pp. 573-590.

------------ 1985. "Infant Mortality in Pakistan: Some Trends and Differentials." *Journal of Biosocial Sciences*, 17: 351-359.

------------ 1989. "Demand for Children and Family Planning." UNFPA, *South Asia Study of Population Policy and Programmes: Pakistan.* UNFPA, Islamabad, Pakistan, pp. 23-31.

Sathar, Zeba, and K. Kiani. 1986. "Delayed Marriages in Pakistan." *Pakistan Development Review*, p. 535.

Nasra M. Shah (ed.) *Pakistani Women: A Socioeconomic and Demographic Profile.* Islamabad: Pakistan Institute of Development Economics.

Siddiqui, M. 1990. *Education: Past, Present, Future.* Rawalpindi.

United Nations Development Program. 1990. *Human Development Report: 1990.* New York: Oxford University Press.

Weiss, Anita M. 1990. "Benazir Bhutto and the Future of Women in Pakistan." *Asian Survey*, XXX: 433-445.

Yusuf, Farhat, and Mazar Hussain. 1985. "Abridged Life Tables for Pakistan Based on the 1971 Population Growth Survey." *Journal of Biosocial Sciences* 17: 91-96.

3

The Plural Medical System and Women's Health in Pakistan: What the Health Statistics Do Not Reveal

Anne T. Sweetser

Anyone interested in learning about health conditions in Pakistan would probably start by reviewing the published health statistics. Impressive numbers of hospitals and doctors, and rapid growth in facilities and personnel in the past decade would be obvious. The researcher might conclude that improving conditions were at the root of the increased life expectancy and improved infant and overall mortality rates. However, comprehension of health conditions and health care cannot be gained from these data, for ultimately health conditions refer to whether or not people perceive that they are well and health care refers to the kind of assistance they seek when they feel poorly.

The basic concepts of health and illness that Pakistanis employ differ from those common in the West, as do the available treatment options and the criteria people use when they select a treatment source and later evaluate the care they received. Fundamentally, these differences are rooted in the fact that most Pakistanis view the world from a predominantly religio-moral as opposed to secular-scientific perspective. Their sense of welness is holistic, including emotional and spiritual as well as physical dimensions; their search for treatment is ultimately a search for contact with healing power conceived primarily in Islamic terms and understood through reference to the hierarchical structures of power they experience in society.[1]

This chapter is limited to exploration of two subjects: the plural medical system and the particular health problems women face in Pakistani society. After reviewing the available health statistics, I will describe the practice of biomedicine, discuss the main alternatives, Yunani Tibb and religious healing, and comment on the nature of choices individuals or families make when seeking care. In the discussion of women's health, I report on some very disturbing realities about women's health and access to care, and describe the way in which popular and purportedly Islamic notions about their identity and proper social role severely constrain their opportunities for full and healthy lives. My observations are based upon two and a half years of anthropological research in the early 1980s, including several months in Lahore and twenty months of intensive field study in Kaghan Valley, North West Frontier Province. I visited public and private hospitals and clinics of many types from major cities to remote mountain villages, compiled articles about health from the press, participated in daily life and listened to casual conversations in the village, and conducted formal interviews at the end of my residence.[2]

During the 1980s, the population of Pakistan grew at a high annual rate of 3.1 percent, increasing from 82.58 to 112.05 million.[3] Life expectancy increased dramatically, from 52.0 years for men and 51.0 for women to 59.3 years for men and 60.7 for women.[4] In this period also, the crude death rate fell significantly from 16.2 deaths per thousand to 11.6, and the infant mortality rate continued a striking pattern of improvement, dropping from 124.0 to 104.0 infant deaths per thousand. The crude birth rate increased slightly, from 43.7 births per thousand to 44.4 per thousand.[5]

From these data one might properly conclude that the nation has recently entered the demographic transition from high to low fertility and mortality rates. In a period of very rapid population growth, death rates fall first and some years later birth rates also decline, possibly as a result of people realizing that their children have a much greater chance of surviving to adulthood than before. A slight drop in total fertility rate[6] from 7.0 to 6.7 starting in 1982 through 1987[7] would support this conclusion.

In the same decade, the number of physicians increased from 10,777 to 51,883 reducing the number of patients per physician from 7,549 to 2,127. The number of nurses rose from 5,336 to 16,948 and the number of dentists increased from 928 to 2077. Also, the number of hospitals increased from 4,068 to 4,447, while the number of beds in them expanded from 47,412 to 71,897. From 1980 through 1987, the number of pharmacists increased from 1,673 to 3,153 and between 1980 and 1988 the number of midwives grew from 3,537 to 12,011.[8]

One might hypothesize that the reductions in mortality are a reflection of the increased numbers of trained health workers and facilities, and conclude that health conditions are improving significantly in Pakistan. But this would be overly hasty, in part because the statistical information reviewed thus far is minimal, revealing nothing about the distribution or quality of personnel and facilities. More important, the inference of causal relationship between health conditions and demographic statistics is fallacious. Where the demographic transition is an abstract statistical model about large populations and can therefore be demonstrated with such data, human response to disease is extremely complex and cannot be reduced to an enumeration of personnel and facilities -- availability cannot be used to predict utilization, efficacy or satisfaction.

Review of additional statistical data in itself raises doubts about the suggested relationship between health care and demographic change. For example, the number of people for each hospital bed was only slightly reduced from 1,716 to 1,535 during the 1980s despite the very significant increase in the number of beds.[9] Also, in reporting the number of hospitals in 1980, the United Nations appears to have combined the number of hospitals (602) and dispensaries (3466) (excluding those operated by the armed forces and private doctors), but had not added the numbers of maternity and child welfare centers (812) reported by the Government of Pakistan.[10] The total (4068) thus included many ill-equipped and poorly-staffed health stations as well as small hospitals in rural areas. Financial data raise additional questions. GNP per capita was only US$350 and the total (public and private) per capita expenditure on health care was US$8.46 in the mid-1980s. Only one percent of the national budget, or US$0.81 per capita, was allocated to health.[11] It seems improbable that the significant improvements in mortality rates could be attributed to health care at a time when such small allocations had to cover the great expansion of facilities and personnel, as well as the cost of actual health services.

No data are available on morbidity, though the National Health Survey of Pakistan is now preparing a baseline health profile for the country.[12] No data are published concerning the distribution of facilities and trained health workers between urban and rural areas and among various regions within the country, other than by province.[13] No data are given about the numbers of male and female doctors and nurses, nor the percentage who are actively practicing. Nothing is reported about the allocation of bed space for men and women in hospitals, or about the availability of health care for women outside urban areas. Nothing is revealed about private clinics, care provided by practitioners of non-biomedical traditions, or about public health and sanitation programs. Finally, and of great import, no information is available concerning the quality of medical training, the facilities, or the available medicines, either as assessed by international health specialists or by those who rely upon the health care system.

A more fundamental problem with these statistics is the fact that they are motivated by pervasive assumptions about the possibility of accurately assessing social behavior through quantifying selected information. One assumes not only that a hospital is a building of significant size, but that it is supplied with specialized equipment, stocked with an array of medications, and staffed by various qualified workers, including fully trained doctors and nurses, who provide services day and night. Further, one assumes that the men and women who seek care there respect and trust the institution and its employees to treat their maladies competently and completely. Therefore, one assumes that by counting the number of hospitals, one is obtaining an estimate of the available health care, and that if one had utilization data, one would know a great deal about the health of the population in the area. Unfortunately, these assumptions amount to an arbitrary imposition of cognitive and affective meanings from one cultural milieu to another, for the buildings, equipment and supplies are poor or missing; the workers, mostly paramedics in rural areas, are frequently absent; and the quality of their work is distrusted.

Full appreciation of the nature and dimensions of contemporary health problems of Pakistan requires understanding the manner in which Pakistanis themselves conceptualize and feel about health, illness and proper treatment, and choose among and evaluate sources of care, and regard the health conditions in their country.

Plural Medical System

Pakistanis rely on many folk, religious, and professional sources of health care, not just upon physicians and hospitals. They commonly seek help from practitioners of several different types of therapy simultaneously or serially. The alternatives include home treatment with herbs and diet, Yunani Tibb (Galenic medicine resystematized and elaborated by Muslim physicians), and an array of religious therapies, from sole reliance upon prayer to use of amulets, exhalation of blessings following recitation of the Qur'an, visits to shrines, and exorcism rituals. The concepts and vocabulary Pakistanis employ to analyze and describe the body in health and illness, while primarily those of Yunani Tibb, include elements of the Ayurvedic humoral system as well. Homeopathy is also taught and practiced by some practitioners too. Popular expectations of the structure of clinics and the interaction between practitioners and their patients; of the significance of signs and symptoms; of the types of prescriptions and other advice healers give; and of the speed and efficacy of treatment, are variously derived from and applied to experience with different types of medicine.

Home Treatment

Much attention is lavished upon someone who is considered sick in Pakistani society. In villages relatives, friends and neighbors discuss someone's ailment and offer numerous remedies. Women readily share suggestions about foods to eat or avoid and about herbs (prepared in various ways, singly or in combination) that are thought to be efficacious. They also discuss the practitioners they have had experience with, when the possibility of moving outside the home and the immediate community are considered. Men likewise converse about health problems, and speak with women in their own families. As urbanization and literacy increase, people are much more likely to know and repeat the names of specific medicines, but the pattern of attention in the form of suggested treatments and referrals to specific healers is the same.

Throughout the country there are people whose recommendations of herbal remedies are respected and sought out. Some older women are revered for their knowledge of herbal treatments. I noticed that it was from men, including widely famed *hakims* (practitioners of Yunani Tibb), rather than from women, that I heard the greatest praise for these older women's skills and how these were gleaned through years of trial and error treatment of sick children. Women themselves tend to denigrate home based herbal treatment and are very modest about their abilities. Some are very reluctant to discuss the topic and deny any knowledge of herbal medicines, apparently because of their association with some forms of evil magic. I concluded that the manner in which adult men lauded older women's skills reflected not only the women's knowledge but a more tolerant attitude toward older women.

The Biomedical System

Within the biomedical system, services are available at many levels from different types of institutions. Hospitals range from large general hospitals in provincial capitals and other major cities to regional hospitals in smaller cities and towns and institutions with very few beds in more isolated areas. Small dispensaries are scattered throughout remote regions of the countryside in major villages. In addition there are specialized hospitals at which treatment for TB or mental illness may be obtained. The government also maintains a network of military hospitals that serve the armed forces and some government officials. Christian missions also run hospitals, some general and some specializing in the treatment of specific ailments such as leprosy and eye diseases. The Agha Khan also sponsors numerous community clinics, and one of the country's most modern hospitals located in Karachi.

In rural areas biomedical care is often most readily available through private sources, starting with shopkeepers who stock a few aspirin tablets. In larger villages and towns there are often pharmacies that are run by men who have served the required time as dispensers or worked as medics in the army. Physicians who serve in government hospitals often work outside clinic hours in private practice, and others who have completed the required national service have established private practices, primarily in cities.

Dispensers have one or two years of training following matriculation at the end of ten years of school. Some, at least, are very competent at handling routine problems, suturing wounds, giving basic medicines and referring patients when they require more sophisticated treatment. Dispensers are not permitted to charge for the services they provide, but some villagers reported that they did pay a small fee, possibly for the medicines they receive. Like the doctors in small hospitals, they are responsible for supervision of the stock of medicines, and reports of missing supplies were common at both levels.[14]

After five years in a rural post, a dispenser may compete for licensing as a pharmacist. Those who succeed may establish lucrative businesses, so ambitious if not-too-well-connected young men are attracted to becoming dispensers. Older pharmacists served in the armed forces, as apprentices or had other types of training. Pharmacists diagnose and prescribe as well as sell medications, though their licenses permit only the latter. Many compete to demonstrate their competence or power, so they tend to dispense broad spectrum antibiotics and pain killers, as well as vitamins, iron supplements and laxatives liberally. A few also prescribe homeopathic remedies, which, though popular in India, are commonly regarded as Western medicine for those too poor to pay for biomedical prescriptions. Seeking immediate relief of symptoms, patients may see a series of pharmacists and receive an assortment of medications, all in improper dosages, over a short period of time, for pharmacists do not inquire about prior treatments and their patients would be unable to give useful responses in any case. The pharmacist's shop in the bazaar often has a counter or display case, posters distributed by pharmaceutical companies, and a side room where truncated examinations, especially of women, may be conducted.

"Doctor" is the term used for anyone who appears to have competence with biomedicine. The dispenser, the pharmacist, the itinerant trader with a supply of iron tablets to sell, like the physician, are all honored with this title. Physicians in Pakistan hold the MBBS degree, the equivalent of the MD in the British system. To qualify for this five year program, a student must first do Cambridge A-levels (requiring one year of classes following matriculation), and an F.Sc. (a two year preliminary degree in sciences).

Admission to medical schools is widely known to depend upon cash and *safarish*, connections or influence (which may also depend in part upon cash). It is very rare that a student performs so well on examinations that his position cannot be given to a better-connected candidate. Thus, being in medical school is primarily evidence of prior and future family influence rather than of unusual intelligence or dedication to helping people. When political activity is permitted only in colleges and universities under martial law regimes, medical schools become highly politicized. I was told that one year in the 1970s medical students were not tested in anatomy or physiology because their political protests severely threatened the stability of the government. Under the administration of Zulfikar Ali Bhutto, several new medical schools were opened, and complaints that these were set up in locations to reward supporters or appease opponents were common in the early 1980s. (President Zia ul-Haq chose to support Yunani Tibbia Colleges, see below.)

Consciousness of status difference generally pervades the work of most physicians, and they are widely viewed as greedy and inhumane. The disadvantaged complain bitterly that doctors would not treat those who could not pay, and that they would only give weak medicines to the poor and uninfluential who could never repay favors with further introductions.

While doctors are reassigned after some years, functionaries in hospitals are poorly-paid members of the local communities. They chafe under the attempts by successive physicians to establish proper bureaucratic order in the smaller hospitals and demand fees from patients for every service they perform.[15] The lack of comfortable, family-based patterns of relationship in government clinics fosters discord and contributes to the distrust patients feel toward these institutions.

For the physician, assignment to a rural area poses special problems as well. He envies those of his classmates who arrange a better position, again through connections. The appointment means that he must leave family, including his wife and family, behind, because living conditions are so unsatisfactory in rural posts. Transportation may be so difficult that days are required for a round trip. He loses out on opportunities to build and expand his social network in an urban area, and these connections are essential for continued influence and future opportunities for himself and his children. He is isolated from colleagues, expected to work with limited equipment and supervise a resentful staff. He may well not speak the same language as his patients who often come so late in their illness that he is unable to do much to help, and he may not have the supplies that would allow him to try. Even salaries in rural areas are (or were) much lower than in cities.[16] Small wonder that absenteeism is high! Yet the losses for citizens the physicians are intended to serve are far greater.

Women physicians, or "lady doctors," whose training emphasizes obstetrics and gynecology, face particular problems. Their professionalism is subordinate to their roles as women in the families into which they marry (see below). Responsibility for their choices and safety rests with their husband's family, so few ever practice far from home, or at all after starting to bear children. In a sense, the greatest benefit of an MBBS degree for a woman is that her marriage prospects improve and the opportunities for her children may be enhanced. Though there were three positions for female physicians in the districts of Mansehra and Kohistan in the early 1980s, only one of these was ever filled, to the best of my knowledge. Thus, up to three million women were dependent upon a single female physician in the public system and she, obviously, could not begin to fulfill their needs. Fortunately a few female MDs were on the staff at a regional Christian missionary hospital, but they were also overburdened with patients.

Throughout the biomedical care system, non-availability of soap and water for hand washing between patients is the rule, and carelessness with sterilization of syringes and other equipment, for example, repeated use of needles and auriscopes with little or no cleaning, probably leads to spread of infection among patients. In 1981 there were no proper storage facilities for blood in the country, so only 20 percent of the amount needed was available and reputedly 80 percent of that was defective.[17]

Drugs are purchased by the central government for the entire country using the British formulary rather than a simpler generic list. Several international drug companies operate local plants where medications are produced and sold throughout the countryside by networks of salesmen. Nonetheless, the Minister of State for Health and Social Welfare reported that 20 tons of medicines had been wasted during 1980 because there was no adequate system for their distribution.[18] The information about activity, dosaging, counter-indications etc. supplied with the medications was negligible if present at all. Medicines in Lahore General Hospital were said to be either sub-standard or expired,[19] and I often found old medications in pharmacies. Patterns of prescribing are also problematic. Typically, several medications are given simultaneously, including some to control the side effects of others. For example, rather than recommending oral rehydration for a diarrhea patient, a doctor will prescribe one medicine to quell peristalsis, an antidiuretic, a pain killer for cramps, medication(s) to control the nausea that is caused by the first three, and perhaps an injection of streptomycin. Part of the reason for this is that patients expect such polypharmacy and suspect that they have not been treated fully if they are not given an array of substances. Also, improper dosages of antibiotics are commonly prescribed for insufficient periods of time. Patients rarely complete the courses that are prescribed before seeking new prescriptions from other healers as noted above, so they may receive several different antibiotics in improper amounts, and possibly all for a condition for which they are not required in the first place. Biomedical substances are prescribed by untrained or undertrained persons, from itinerant traders to pharmacists. Like these practitioners, some Yunani Hakims, those from the Delhi school rather than the conservative Lucknow school that advocates reliance solely upon native herbal (*desi*) treatments, substitute biomedicines for tonics for particular organs, apparently without knowledge of potentially dangerous interactions among them, and also give herbs to counteract their heating effects. Many are concerned about the side effects of the strong medications.

Hospitals are distressing places in Pakistan; many people think of them as places to go to die, or at least as places to be avoided if you are not willing to risk dying. A small percentage of beds is generally reserved for women, and others may be set aside for members of one or another branch of government service. Much of the nursing and care is provided by family members who may stay there around the clock. When someone is hospitalized, it is incumbent upon the patient's friends to visit, so family members must entertain these guests and worry about the cost of providing tea and sweets. Hospitals are notorious for serving only those who can pay and reports of atrocities were common in the Urdu press during the August, 1981. I found three reports of family members having to run around hospitals to locate physicians to treat patients who were left unattended while bleeding seriously in emergency rooms.[20] One author titled his piece "Hospitals or Slaughterhouses?"[21] and others called for shutting down hospitals if they were intended solely for the profit of physicians.[22] There were complaints that sewage and filth was left to fester in clogged drains,[23] of food so dreadful as to be inedible,[24] and reports of operations being done on the wrong patients![25]

In short, the statistician's assumptions about the meaning of "hospital," "doctor," and "nurse" are all inappropriate for Pakistan. While it would certainly be wrong to assume that no physicians are conscientious and work hard to help their patients, the career pressures under which many struggle, the quantity and quality of equipment and supplies available to them, the conditions of the hospitals, and the problems they face in supervising permanent staff make their profession a very different one than that of medicine in the West. Most corrosive perhaps are the difficulties they have communicating with patients who commonly mistrust their profession and the government sponsored services, speak different languages, and employ different concepts to analyze health problems, and their expectations of care.

Yunani Tibb

Yunani Tibb (Greek medicine or wisdom), or Islami-Tibb, is Galenic medicine, itself a revision of the system of Hippocrates and Aristotle, augmented and resystematized by Muslim scholars. The most influential text in this tradition, still in use today in Pakistan, is *al-Qanun fi al-Tibb* (Canon of Medicine), written by the Persian, Ibn-Sina (Avicenna) during the 13th century. Derived from an analogy with the separation of blood that has been heated in a crucible into four parts, Yunani medical theory centers around the notion of four humors which constitute the body: blood, phlegm, bile, and black bile or *sauda*. These are constituted of the four elements earth, air, fire and water, which are composed of the four fundamental qualities of heat, cold, dryness and moisture. Each is associated with a temperament or personality type as well: sanguine, phlegmatic, bilious or choleric, and melancholic, respectively.

Individual health is conceptualized as proper balance among the humors and the qualities they represent. Every person has a unique point of balance that represents health, and hence a unique constitution or temperament. This varies with age and sex, occupation, etc. Imbalance, due to excess or deficiency of one or more humors, is the equivalent of disease, and the restoration of balance is the aim of treatment. The system is allopathic: when an individual suffers from excess heat, for example fever, proper treatment consists of consumption of foods and herbal medicines that have a cooling effect on the body. Cooling (or sun-) baths, bloodletting or cupping, and herb-induced purging are other main forms of remedy.

Causation is also split into four categories. First the material cause, the substance itself; second the efficient cause, which moulds the material, including age, sex, mental and physical activity, sleep, habits, etc.; third, the formal cause which determines the shape and quality of a thing; and fourth the final cause, that which governs the function of the material in question.[26] Yunani Tibb is thus a holistic medical system that recognizes innate and environmental, congenital and acquired, organic and functional, and physical and emotional dimensions.[27]

Diagnosis depends upon careful observation of mental function, pulse and respiration, stools and urine, and the appearance of every part of the body including tongue, skin, hair, eyes, etc. Questions about likes and dislikes, sleeping, occupation, dreaming, emotionality, etc., also are asked.[28] Symptoms are identified and the underlying imbalanced state determined. Diseases may be internal or external, and simple or complex (affecting simple or complex organs) depending upon the number of underlying disturbances.

In the first centuries of Islam there was controversy about the acceptability of Greek medicine within the religion, due to the notion of vital force as the fundamental motivating factor for life. Theologians distrusted this concept because it appeared to contradict the primacy of divinity. In recent years in Pakistan, however, precisely this factor has contributed to the renewed acceptance of this medical system. The fact that a non-physical force or entity is held responsible for life itself in Yunani Tibb means that it is not perceived to be in contradiction with religion in the way that secular biomedicine is. Soon after taking power in 1978, Zia ul Haq announced as part of his program to Islamicize the country that he would be promoting Yunani Tibb because it was better suited to the Muslim temperament of the people of Pakistan.[29]

Pakistanis speak highly of hakims, stressing that they treat the whole person, not just the patient's body, and that they give personalized treatment. They are aware that hakims are motivated by human sympathy, *hamdardi*, rather than greed, and point to the fact that they accept no payment for their services, though they may sell the substances they prescribe for their patients. These beliefs are propagated by hakims themselves, in part, at least, in their competition with biomedicine. The hakims generally inquire about a person's residence and occupation as well as their physical complaints, but their examinations were so short[30] in popular city clinics that, even though much might be deduced from this information, a comprehensive understanding of the patient's personal situation and individual temperament could hardly have been attained. Those who practice in villages and are well acquainted with those who seek their help probably do have a good sense of their individual patients. The verifiability of the hakims' claims about their work is not essential; rather, the function of the claims is to assert the moral basis of Yunani Tibb and legitimate its practitioners as healers in this society where religious consciousness and awareness of dangerous side effects of (often misprescribed) biomedicines are both increasing.

Religious Healing

Belief in religious healing, in one form or another, is ubiquitous in Pakistan. Few would question the idea that birth and death are the responsibility of Allah, and many assume that much of what occurs during life is predetermined. The existence of a hierarchy of beings, including some who may be responsible for illness or misfortune, is set forth in the Qur'an, so the truth of their existence cannot be questioned by the faithful. Also, the Prophet Mohammed recommended certain preventive practices and herbal remedies, and sometimes healed by praying over a supplicant, as recorded in the Hadiths. Thus, medicine is undeniably a dimension of religion.

A variety of forms of practice are encountered under the rubric of religious healing: reliance upon prayer; prophetic medicine; and numerous types of popular practice. Those who propound exclusive reliance upon prayer generally reject the legitimacy of the latter forms, claiming that by relying upon mundane substances, from herbs to ink and paper, while attempting to manipulate blessing power, people are demonstrating lack of faith in Allah or even being idolatrous. Similarly, biomedicine is commonly regarded as non-religious and impure and thus denigrated in comparison with religious healing and Islami Tibb. Those who support Prophetic medicine argue that if Mohammed employed certain techniques to prevent or cure disease, they must be acceptable within Islam. Others who sanction the use of all forms of treatment note that even though certain remedies were not discovered until recently, they were part of Allah's creation and must therefore be acceptable to Him.

Prophetic Medicine

The Hadiths, the recorded sayings and actions of the Prophet, include commentary on the nature of health and illness, the responsibility people bear for nursing the sick, and relevant ideas about purity and pollution, as well as a record of specific treatments the Prophet used. Care of the seriously ill is a compulsory religious duty (*farz*). Failure casts responsibility upon the entire group, just as widespread calamity reflects the degradation of society because people forget to exchange moral advice.[31] In the case of routine sickness, care is less compulsory but in accord with the actions of the Prophet (*sunnat*) and will be rewarded by angels who pray for the care giver.[32]

The Prophet recommended moderation in all things to preserve health of the body and mind.[33] He ate honey every month and had cupping (bloodletting) done every season to maintain internal purity. He also stressed diet for good health, as the stomach is the fountain of health. For treating various ailments he prescribed black nigella (presumedly black cumin), for several others he suggested sea costus. Henna and juice of truffles had limited use. Branding or cauterization was mentioned but condemned for all but treatment of wounds.

Popular Religious Healing

The line between Prophetic and popular healing is quite blurred. Preparation of amulets (*tawiz*) based on passages in the Qur'an, exhalation of blessings immediately after recitation from the Qur'an (*dum* or *dua*), and multiple repetition of certain Qur'anic phrases for an extended number of days (*wazifa*) are among the most common methods of popular religious healing. Certain passages in the Hadiths condone such practices, but others that appear to reject them have been stressed by theological conservatives in the recent past. Similarly, visits to shrines, formerly much more common (or at least publicized), are condemned as heretical.[34] The line between medicine and 'magic' -- the deliberate manipulation of nonhuman force -- is very slim.

The concept of *jinns* is syncretized with varieties of indigenous spirits in each society where Islam has been adopted. In Pakistan *bhootna* or ghosts are recognized to be just like jinns but less powerful. *Churrail* are vengeful spirits of women who died in childbirth. They are recognized by their vertical eyes and are known throughout North India. In the Himalaya, powerful *perian*, or fairies, dwell in remote high places above communities that they previously ruled, notably Hunza. They generally leave people alone, but they have been propitiated by the Shina peoples of Gilgit as part of their ancient religion.[35] Also in the Hindu Kush and Himalaya, people acknowledge the existence of wild, aggressive bestial women (like a *ghuul* or male *yeti*) who may apprehend a lone male and attack him fiercely.

Religious healing, in its various forms, provides explanations and remedies for a variety of common, chronic physical and psycho-social problems. It permits attribution of cause, displacement of responsibility from the victim, and the opportunity for actions to be undertaken to counteract the situation, and these are among the major elements of healing.

Discussion: Choosing a Healer

The search for competent help when one is sick involves multiple discussions among family and friends about possible causes and explanations for the problem, use of home treatments, and complicated decision making about whom to consult. People view health and illness holistically and seek resolution of both physical and mental aspects of distress by consulting practitioners of different types of medicine. To address various possible etiologies and to maximize the possibility of obtaining the appropriate countermeasure which will result in immediate relief, people seek help from practitioners of different therapies simultaneously or serially.

The individual practitioner, rather than the medical theory to which he subscribes, is paramount in most decisions people make about where to seek help. The familiar (family-based) structure of the hakim's clinic, and its strong religio-moral legitimation contribute to the appeal of this type of practice, but the practitioner's reputation for piety, generosity, and success are most important. For some problems, notably physical presentations of psycho-social conflict and convulsions, religious forms of healing are recognized as the only correct ones. But in another sense, religion is always the sole appropriate form of treatment for all health and other problems in life, and few would challenge the idea that without the blessing of Allah no one will be healed by any form of treatment. Secular, scientific medicine is thus devalued as a theory, and physicians are commonly thought to be greedy and inhumane, and terrible hospital conditions are openly deplored. Yet people, particularly men (see below), flock to pharmacists and doctors their friends have recommended hoping to receive through biomedicine the power that will restore them to proper, balanced functioning.

Women and Health

Full comprehension of the health and health care issues facing women in Pakistan requires an understanding of the way women are viewed, the significance of Islamic precepts in popular perceptions of them, and the roles they occupy in social life. Wide class differences separate a very small number of well-off, educated women in urban centers from the vast majority who have little or no education, virtually no independent mobility, and extremely limited control over property or productive resources. Economic and social constraints result in great restrictions on women in much of the North West Frontier Province, Boluchistan, and the poor in rural areas and urban slums in other parts of the country.[36] These class differences aside, women throughout the country are affected by widely shared notions about the nature and capacities of women.

Women are believed to be fundamentally different from and in many ways inferior to men. In what might be seen as a subconscious yet deliberately self-fulfilling prophecy, men regard women as intellectually and emotionally weak and thus incapable of making reasonable decisions or exercising responsibility for them. I was told "women are unable to think!" by a man who insisted that it was unnecessary, inappropriate, and useless to have women respond to a felt-needs survey in a rural development project intended for their benefit. For him, any participation in public life was by definition male, so the prospect of women's involvement broached a categorical as well as a moral impossibility.

In his quite typical view, if women were to learn to speak Urdu in addition to the local dialect, to read and write, and to handle money, they would become like men in having the tools required for life outside the home; in some insidious manner they would cease to be women, and an incomprehensibly disastrous dissolution of all order and propriety might ensue. Some stated that if women were to be capable of functioning outside the home, there would be no food to eat. Others seemed to fear that women's pollution would contaminate the entire world. Men were unable to countenance the notions that role might be separated from structure, that intellect might be distinct from body, and that domesticity might be analytically distinguished from physicality. So women are not permitted or encouraged to learn any mundane, non-domestic skills, and do in fact remain largely ignorant of and incompetent in responsible action and decision making in the public domain. Men are unaware, or flatly deny, that women's limitations are a consequence of socialization rather than a reflection of fundamental (in)capacity tied to their physical structure.

On the other hand, men staunchly assert the absolute equality of women in Islam. All souls will be greeted in the same way on the fearsome Judgment Day. Neither men nor women will be favored, and Islam is (and was historically) the corrective to all those religions that espouse the contrary. That women's equality is limited to salvation, and contradicted in social life, is never seen to diminish the totality of their equality. In the world view of those with whom I spoke, the categorical abyss between ideology and practice on this issue was unbridgeable. For them, Islam could never be touched by all the social and historical aberrations created by its followers. Though the religion might have been used to legitimate or justify rapacious wars or brutal regimes, its purity could never be tarnished. Similarly, whatever local customs, such as those concerning the role and treatment of women, might be practiced by a society espousing Islam, the sanctity of the ideology would never be fouled, even though the practices might contradict basic principles of the religion.

Women's sexuality is commonly perceived to be insatiable and thus threatening to men and the public order they strive to maintain. Where a woman simply meeting the eyes of a man outside the immediate family is often understood to be blatantly promiscuous, supervision of women's movements and contacts is felt to be necessary to ensure their obedience and chastity, and preserve the *Izzat* (honor) of the men and the family. Purdah, or concealment of women, correlates with social status, for the very poor rely upon women participating in agricultural or other work which precludes complete seclusion. The upwardly mobile stress concealment of women is an indicator of sufficient wealth to afford their release from labor. Highly educated urban women have superficially greater freedom. Women's personal names are not used outside the most intimate circles, and reference to women in another man's family is scrupulously controlled, or might precipitate fighting. To protect their identity and family dignity, men expend great effort to make sure that all other men know that they are properly controlling the women in their families. At the same time, consciousness of sexuality is pushed to the foreground, and opportunity for illicit contact is sought as ardently as effort is made to preclude it.

Expectations of women are primarily determined with reference to their bodies. It is a woman's duty to care for her husband and his home. Production of children, especially sons, for his family is her most important task, and hence her most treasured goal. Ability to become pregnant, to deliver a healthy baby, to have a son, and to keep children alive through childhood all reflect on the quality and character of the woman. In an infertile marriage the woman is most abjectly miserable, for she must personally bear responsibility for a situation that may not be her fault. Pseudocyesis, false pregnancy, was reputedly common where I conducted research, suggesting that the psychological pressure on women to reproduce is intense. Grown sons who remain emotionally dependent on their mother permit a mature woman to achieve some status and power in life. She may exercise considerable control over her sons' wives, but is unlikely to ever control productive resources or exercise authority outside the home. An older, post-menopausal and thus no longer threatening, woman may be highly respected as an idealized, caring, motherly figure by many men in a small community who yearn for the special closeness they had with their own mothers.

A woman's health is likewise thought to depend largely upon her sexuality. Postpartum depression and related disorders are often attributed to misalignment of the uterus. Hysteria is conceptualized as a woman's emotional disease related to the condition of her reproductive organs, much as it was in late 19th century Europe. Stress and strain are thought to make a woman irritable and sick, so strenuous physical exercise or mental exertion is best avoided. Thus in the early 1980s, many conservatives argued against permitting girls to study math and physics on the grounds that their fragile health, specifically proper hormonal balance, might be disrupted by the effort required. Again, the possibility of influence from 19th century Europe, where women were required to take rest cures to force them into docility, is evidenced.[37] Menstruation is referred to as sickness and widely believed to require rest because the loss of blood is thought to induce weakness at the time. In the long run, *khun-ki-kami*, or insufficiency of blood, is a great concern of women. The humoral notion of lost heat contained in this important humor, is central to understanding a common Pakistani view of woman's bodies and their reproduction-dominated dynamics.

In the village where I conducted field research, it took me a long time to be accepted and trusted by both women and men. At first women retreated to their homes when I approached; after their husbands came from the bazaar to deal with the intruder, recognized me, and attested that I was acceptable, the women were in fact anxious to converse with me. Many months passed before I was regarded as a potential source of help for health problems with which they were suffering. Constrained by great shame, they were very reluctant to seek advice about common reproductive and other internal illnesses. Slowly I learned of some of the most miserable conditions I could imagine. In a small area, I spoke with five women who had been bleeding for several years. After years of uninterrupted reproduction, starting in their teens, these women's reproductive systems had deteriorated. One was in such intense pain that she could barely speak. At least two others, I discerned, were nearing death. Only one of these five had received care at a hospital; she reported that doctors had told her the tumor they removed had 113 roots. Other women came to me in grievous tears because they believed they were not permitted to pray due to prolonged leukorrhea. The greatest concern of all of these women was the punishment they would suffer following their deaths as a consequence of not being able to pray regularly. They were unaware that the Prophet had stipulated that vaginal discharge continuing past ten days, or post-partum discharge continuing past forty days, was illness, and that a woman suffering from such a condition could pray immediately after ablutions.[38]

Women in remote areas must typically perform demanding physical tasks such as carrying all the family's water up steep hills in heavy containers even in severe weather conditions. Those in families with greater resources may be forced to stay within the compound walls, and get far too little exercise. Early and frequent pregnancies, widespread severe iron deficiency and generally poor nutrition seriously undermine many women's strength while they are still young. Thus, women are typically either drawn, hollow-cheeked, and grey-skinned with deep lines from worry and exposure to sun and wind, or very plump, flaccid and unfit.

Women's access to health care is very limited due to standards of family honor and economic constraints. Purdah places constraints on interaction between women and care givers. Depending on the status of the family, the type of complaint a women has, and the closeness of the healer to the family, she may or may not be permitted to seek help. If an amulet (tawiz) is sought from a close relative, the patient, in the company of another close female relative, may be able to directly ask for help. If her ailment is internal, especially reproductive, she will not be able to consult any male practitioner anywhere near her home. Instead her husband may purchase medicines from a doctor or at a pharmacy at a distant location when on a trip for some other purpose. The expectation that a competent doctor will be able to identify the problem without seeing the patient or asking many questions facilitates prescription under these circumstances.

Only when it is apparent that special help is required, often far too late for minimally comfortable travel or successful treatment, and only if the family can afford to arrange and pay for the trip, will the woman be seen by competent biomedical personnel. At least one other woman must accompany the patient to be present during the examination and help care for her if she must stay in the hospital. For each woman who travels approximately one man must accompany the group to ensure the safety and honor of the women. Thus, for residents of remote regions, a trip to a hospital when a woman is severely ill requires that many family members leave home and is thus often prohibitively costly. A healer closer to home may be too close to the community to be allowed to learn about the woman's problem. The result is that women frequently are denied access to medical care by circumstances that are considered to be beyond the control of men.

Other locally available care for women is poor or underused. Though the dispenser had ferric and folic tablets for pregnant women, propriety prevented him from educating men about their advisability. Men might have been offended that their wives were being obliquely referred to in conversation, and very probably would have been reluctant to request the tablets because that would have amounted to an inappropriate public announcement of their wife's condition. Pregnancy is not regarded as a special health condition in any case; people rarely mention it when seeking medication for apparently unrelated complaints, so women undoubtedly consume dangerous drugs while pregnant. Birth control pills are available through a completely separate network of offices. My efforts to obtain pills at the request of older village women who generally already had ten living children were met with grossly offensive ridicule from the men in these offices.

Whereas the dispenser was very competent at suturing wounds and providing care for many routine ailments, there was no one with the knowledge to provide postoperative care for those who did receive biomedical treatment outside the valley. One woman ran through fields of tall corn after me as I walked along on the road in a community some distance from my main field site. She showed me a suppurating hysterectomy scar, complained that she was suffering from pain because her periods were about to recommence, and hoped I would give her pain medication. All I could do was write a discreet note that a member of her family could give to a pharmacist with the hope that she would receive a full course of broad spectrum antibiotics, and urge her to really rest for many days.

Doctors sometimes vacationed where I worked and I asked them about their perceptions of the health conditions. Since they were approached for help only by men, they were aware of the great problems villagers faced, but they remained oblivious to the difficulties encountered by the women who were unable to seek their help. They realized that men sometimes complained about problems they would expect to encounter during the winter, for example, chest pain and cough, in order to obtain medicine for use when needed. Their comments suggested that, perhaps naturally, they regarded women's health problems in a similar light -- as potential or abstract rather than pressing and severe.

Improving the availability of women health-care workers would seem to be an obvious remedy. However, a woman who agrees to serve away from her home is viewed with great suspicion by the men in the region where she is sent to work. Since they would never permit the women in their own families to train as nurses or midwives and thus be involved with the defilement of childbirth or dealing with people's bodies, or to work out from under their supervision and away from home, they readily conclude that the woman who does so is from such a dishonorable family that they would permit this, or personally of such reprehensible moral character that the men in her family have thrown her out. A "lady doctor" whose education evidences high family status who serves in a rural area is in some ways even more perplexing. The woman's presence proves her disrespectability, men consider her a fair target for sexual advances, and her opportunities to help women are limited. I was taunted with lewd hilarity and derision when I purchased medication for leukorrhea at a pharmacy in a regional town at the request of a woman friend; a female health care worker would have been unable to make this or any purchase. Her requests for resupply through appropriate channels might be greeted with similar responses.

Nonhuman agents are often considered responsible for women's problems. Hot flashes and other symptoms of menopause are commonly attributed to jinns. At least in the area where I conducted field research, women seemed unaware that menopause was a normal part of life. Instead some told stories of repeated episodes of possession, and others begged me for medicines to restore their periods. Since knowledge about menstruation, pregnancy and childbirth as well as menopause is not disseminated but only learned through experience, their lack of awareness was plausible. They were also reluctant to accept my assertion of its normalcy, for, as an unmarried woman, I could not be expected to know such things. The women's tendency to suspect nonhuman causation was often derided, publicly if not privately, by men who overlooked women's lack of access to other forms of explanation and treatment and claimed that this further proved that women were superstitious or less rational than men.

In sum, I found there to be a rigid conception of womankind in which body type was assumed to define intellectual capacity and emotional character, and to dictate social role. Men most earnestly declared it to be their religiously-defined responsibility to ensure the perpetuation of moral order, including overseeing of the appropriate activities of women, even though local customs might in some ways deviate from religious prescriptions in some details. As a whole, the entire nation seems to diminish, conceal or ignore women's health issues. Like women themselves, they are largely kept out of sight and public consciousness lest anyone's honor be offended. Very few hospital beds are reserved for women, and very few highly trained women health workers are stationed outside urban areas. Islam, rather than being cited as a compelling force for social policies that will ensure the well-being of every citizen, is instead referred to as the source of honor-indexed constraints on public speech, mobility, and access to care that result in great suffering for the half of humanity that gives birth, prepares food, and stays out of the public domain lest their pollution contaminate and disrupt the world.

Conclusion

The uninformed researcher who depends upon published statistics for information about health and healing in Pakistan is easily misled into believing that good and improving services are amply provided in the nation. This is primarily a consequence of uncritically transferring assumptions about the definitions of health, doctors, and hospitals, and about standards of quality from Western society when interpreting the available data. Instead, health conditions and the accessibility of health care are severely prejudiced against half of the population on the basis of sexual identity, and the quality of services and supplies is often poor.

More fundamental is the fact that many different types of health care based on widely divergent medical theories are available in Pakistan. People make judgements about the nature and severity of health problems, defined holistically to include psycho-social as well as physical conditions, and then seek treatments simultaneously or serially that will address all of the contributing factors -- from practitioners of Yunani Tibb and religious healing as well as biomedicine. They are most comfortable in clinics with a familiar hierarchy in which the healer exercises paternal authority over subordinates. The concepts and vocabulary they most commonly use when analyzing the body and its well-being are primarily derived from Greco-Islamic humoral theory. They evaluate the care they receive and the practitioners with whom they have interacted largely in religio-moral rather than secular, scientific terms.

Notes

1. See Anne T. Sweetser, *The Power to Heal: Medicine and Society in the Pakistani Himalayas*, Ph.D. dissertation, Harvard University, 1992.

2. For help with selecting and translating materials from the Urdu press, I am grateful to Qamar Jalil of the Berkeley Urdu Language Program in Pakistan. For assistance with formal interviews during the last few months of my research in Kaghan, I am grateful to Azra Parveen, Naseem Akhtar, Amirzada Asad, and Munir Qureshi.

3. United National, *Statistical Yearbook for Asia and the Pacific, 1991*, p. 293. The World Bank gave slightly higher numbers than the United Nations for 1988, so they would no doubt indicate a somewhat greater total population in 1990 as well (The World Bank, *World Tables, 1989-90 Edition*, p. 437).

4. United Nations, *Statistical Yearbook for Asia and the Pacific, 1991*, p. 293. World Bank figures show a higher life expectancy at birth in 1980 of 53.0 years for both sexes combined, and also a higher figure in 1987 (the last available year) of 56.5. For that year, the United Nations figures were 53.7 for males and 51.9 for females (The World Bank, *World Tables, 1989-90 Edition*, p. 439). Except for Nepal and Bangladesh, Pakistan was the only nation where male life expectancy at birth exceeded that for females in the late 1980s (The World Bank, *Women in Pakistan*, 1989, p. xv, note 6).

5. United Nations, *Statistical Yearbook for Asia and the Pacific, 1991*, p. 293. The World Bank shows a steady drop from 144.0 infant deaths per thousand in 1968 to 109.0 in 1987 (The World Bank, *World Tables, 1989-90 Edition*, pp. 438-439).

6. The total fertility rate is the number of children women might expect to have by age 49.

7. The World Bank, *World Tables, 1989-90 Edition*, pp. 438-439.

8. United Nations, *Statistical Yearbook for Asia and the Pacific, 1991*, p. 307.

9. United Nations, *Statistical Yearbook for Asia and the Pacific, 1991*, p. 307.

10. Federal Bureau of Statistics, Statistics Division, Government of Pakistan, *Pakistan Statistical Yearbook, 1985*, p. 310.

11. Griffin, Charles C., *Health Care in Asia: A Comparative Study of Cost and Financing*, World Bank Regional and Sectoral Studies, 1992, pp. 158-9.

12. See Malik, Iftikhar, Gail Fisher, Gregory Pappas, and Akhtar Qureshi, "Prospects for the National Health Survey of Pakistan: Goals and Objectives," in *The Pakistan Journal of Medical Research* special supplement devoted to the survey, forthcoming, 1993. (The present author has an article in this supplement about survey methodology, "Getting the Right Answer by Asking the Right Way: The Importance of Speech Patterns for Eliciting Accurate Survey Responses.")

13. Federal Bureau of Statistics, Statistics Division, Government of Pakistan, *Pakistan Statistical Yearbook, 1985*, p. 311.

14. Theft of medicines by staff in Lahore General Hospital was reported as common in *Mashriq*, July 7, 1981.

15. Similar complaints appeared in the Urdu press, for example, *Nawa-i-waqt*, August 8, and 14, 1981 and *Mashriq*, August 18, 1981.

16. In the early 1980s, physicians posted to rural assignments received half the salary of their urban counterparts and no travel allowance. There was discussion of raising their salaries so that they could afford to visit their homes without losing their entire income.

17. *Mashriq*, July 31, 1981.

18. *Mashriq*, June 21, 1981.

19. *Mashriq*, July 7, 1981.

20. *Nawa-i-waqt*, August 8 and 14, 1981 and *Mashriq*, August 18, 1981.

21. *Nawa-i-waqt*, August 14, 1981.

22. *Mashriq*, August 18, 1981.

23. *Nawa-i-waqt*, August 8, 1981.

24. *Mashriq*, August 18, 1981.

25. *Nawa-i-waqt*, August 14, 1981.

26. Shah, Mazhar H., *The General Principles of Avicenna's Canon of Medicine*, Karachi, 1966, Naveed Clinic, p. 19.

27. Shah, *Avicenna's Canon*, p. xxviii.

28. Shah, *Avicenna's Canon*, pp. 213-216.

29. F. No. 5-2/80-NCT, National Council for Tibb, 46 Bazaar Road, Islamabad, paragraphs 2 and 3.

30. In one clinic I timed the consultations for several hours. I found there to be a bimodal pattern of 40 seconds and 110 seconds per patient!

31. Karim, *Al-Hadis*, Vol. 1, p. 281.

32. Karim, *Al-Hadis*, Vol. 1, pp. 281-2.

33. Karim, *Al-Hadis*, Vol. 1, pp. 656-7 and 424-426.

34. This echoes the positions taken by schools of Islam that developed in India approximately a century ago. The Barelwis accepted local practices, the Ahl-i-Hadiths rejected all but strictest adherence to the Shari'at, and the Deobandis, while stressing restoration of Shari'at law, were willing to accommodate their followers' desires for spiritual counsel in the indigenous manner. Today in Pakistan the term "Wahhabi" (from the early 19th century fundamentalist movement in Arabia) is used for religious and political conservatives, including the Jama'at-i-Islami. Many who espouse Deobandi interpretation are in fact closer to the latter than to the original Deobandi formulations.

35. Jettmar, Karl, *Der Religionen des Hindukusch*, Kohlhammer, 1975, especially p. 219 ff. I read a draft English translation prepared by Adam Nayyar.

36. The World Bank, *Women in Pakistan: An Economic and Social Study*, 1989, p. xxii.

37. See Barbara Ehrenrich and Deidre English, *For Her Own Good: 150 Years of the Expert's Advice*, Doubleday Anchor, 1978.

38. Karim, *Al-Hadis*, Vol. 1, p. 734.

4

Education in Pakistan: Past Dilemmas and Future Prospects

Nasir Jalil

There is a wide consensus that education plays a critical role in promoting the cultural, social, economic and political development of a country. As Lockheed and Verspoor et al. state:

> education forges national unity and social cohesion by teaching common mores, ideologies, and languages. It also improves income distribution, increases saving and encourages more rational consumption, enhances the status of women, and promotes adaptability to technological change. Although most analysts agree that the process of education imparts not only knowledge and skills but also important attitudes, behaviors, and personal characteristics, consensus on this point is recent.[1]

They further point out that:

> a diverse body of literature demonstrates that the adults in developing countries who have higher levels of educational attainment have more paid employment, higher individual earnings, greater agricultural productivity, lower fertility, better health and nutritional status, and more 'modern' attitudes than adults who have lower educational attainment. They are also more likely to send their children to school. These characteristics are dimensions of development.[2]

The prevailing picture in Pakistan presents a sharp contrast to the characteristics summarized above. Pakistan is an agrarian country where a large section of the population is illiterate. Low participation rates pervade the educational system. The country has a low average educational attainment, and a high fertility rate -- poor indicators of health and nutritional status.

One of the critical areas of neglect in Pakistan in the past has been education and training. Development plans have laid heavy emphasis on economic growth and accumulation of physical capital. Resources were invested in sectors known to yield quicker returns than education which, while it has the potential to yield a higher rate, has a long gestation period.

Of the meager resources allowed to trickle down to education, tertiary education commanded the largest share, perhaps because of the ability of this subsector to produce skills and knowledge needed by the growing economy but also because of the political power of the middle and upper classes. Owing to inadequate funding, state-subsidized education in Pakistan reached only a small fraction of the population. This strategy was seemingly successful in achieving limited goals, but unfortunately led to the under-utilization of the vast human potential in the country.

The low priority given to education, along with the chronic shortage of resources constitutes one of the core dilemmas of education in Pakistan. Other issues include: the imbalance between different subsectors of education; school access, especially the wide gender gap; urban-rural disparity;and the problems of adult illiteracy. Despite numerous past attempts, these critical issues continue to plague Pakistan's education system.

This paper will attempt to present a brief overview of the recent theoretical and empirical literature on the relationship between education and various aspects of development with a view to highlighting the benefits and returns from investing in education (human capital), and its relevance for Pakistan. In the second section, a few key issues of education in Pakistan will be discussed focusing on the efforts being made to address them. The policies and programs implemented during the Zia regime; those now being proposed and contained in the Educational Policy 1992-2002; the Social Action Program 1992-1995, and the Eighth Five Year Plan 1993-1998 will be examined.

Education and Development: Theory and Empirical Findings

Dimensions of Development

Over a period of time, development has come to be recognized as having more than one dimension. According to one source, the notion of development may be understood as change in a desirable direction which could encompass different dimensions, in particular the expansion in the support of the basic needs, and greater participation for all segments of society.[3] The core assumption is that education cuts across three important dimensions: the economic, the cultural-ideological and the political. The emerging consensus in theory has been substantiated with empirical findings which seem to validate the assumption that education and training of people are key to balanced development.

The first dimension of development is useful only when defined in terms of economic growth. It assumes that education increases the efficiency of the production system of a society commonly measured by Gross Domestic Product (GDP) or Gross National Product (GNP). Other measures of growth are the levels of industrialization and technology. Pakistan's past development strategy was largely designed to pursue this dimension of development of economic growth.

The second dimension of development seeks the satisfaction of the population's basic needs. Fagerlind and Saha believe there has been a general recognition that the living conditions of a population may be a better indicator of the level of development than the economic indicators.[4] These life conditions are sometimes divided into basic human needs of a material nature and those related to satisfaction. Food, water, energy, shelter, on the one hand, and education, security, recreation and communication, on the other, are included in the material and psychosocial categories.

While the notion of basic needs is not incompatible with economic growth, to measure development in terms of them is to place stress on the distributive aspects of society. Thus, indicators of the satisfaction of human needs, for example, education and health, show the extent to which societies are distributing their resources and thus raising the level of the quality of life. Pakistan's development plans gave prominent position to this ideal but failed to deliver beyond the rhetoric.

The third dimension of development involves the attainment of objectives sought by various groups in a society, which are linked to the use of scarce resources.[5] In addition to the focus upon economic growth and the equitable distribution of the society's resources in meeting human needs, attention must also be directed to the levels that determine the distribution of these resources.[6] The more developed the society, the greater is the participation in the decision-making process; and no one group should dominate another. The most common indicators of political development, such as participation and access to political positions lead to the development of national integration and cohesion.

Education and Economic Development

Education and training have been recognized by economists as an investment in human capital. Thus investment in education has traditionally been justified by optimistic assumptions, the first being that an educated population contributes to the socioeconomic development of the society as a whole, and the second, that education contributes to the well-being of individuals within the society.[7]

In many countries the correlation between national investment in education and economic growth is striking. Lockheed et al. have cited several empirical studies, noted below, which provide a basis for making the argument that "there is a relationship between education and economic growth."[8] Among them, Benavot in his study for the period 1930-1980 found that primary education had a significant positive effect on the economic growth of 110 developed and developing countries, and for the period, 1945-1980, Lau et al. found economic growth greatly affected by primary education in twenty-two East Asian and Latin American countries and by secondary education in fifty-four East Asian, Latin American, African, and Middle Eastern countries.

Virtually all the newly industrialized economies that experienced dramatic growth in the past twenty-five years, such as Hong Kong, Israel, Japan, South Korea, and Singapore, achieved universal or almost universal primary enrollment by 1965. The most successful of those economies also had high enrollment in secondary school and a labor force that was almost universally literate just before rapid and sustained industrial growth began.

Earnings provide an indirect measure of productivity, but productivity is the best measure of education's economic impact. Workers and farmers with more education are more productive than those with less education, and the rate of return is high (Lockheed et al., 1991:3). Psacharopoulos estimated that the returns to completed primary education are 27 percent and the returns to secondary education are 15 to 17 percent.[9] An individual's benefits from education are significantly higher than social returns, reaching 49 percent for primary and 26 percent for secondary education.[10] The returns to education in developing countries are higher than those in more advanced countries, although they appear to diminish over time.[11] Education remains profitable, and its social rate of return still exceeds that of other investments by a considerable margin.

According to Bowman and Anderson, a literacy rate of about 40 percent is necessary but not sufficient for a sustained level of economic growth.[12] However, they further contend that industrialization and more rapid economic expansion cannot occur until 70 to 80 percent of any population is literate.

While it is impossible to argue that raising levels of literacy would directly result in increased economic development, the correlation between the two is clearly apparent (Table 4.1).

TABLE 4.1 Percent Literacy for Countries at Different Levels of Development

Countries	*1960*	*1975*	*1985*	*1990*
Low Income	29	38	32	60
Middle Income	54	71	72	88
Industrialized	—	99	98	96

Source: World Bank, *Education,* World Development Report, 1980, Washington, D.C. 1980, Table 23, pp. 154-5; UNESCO Office of Statistics, *The Current Literacy Situation in the World.* Paris, 1985, cited in Fagerlind and Saha, 1989, p. 44, and: World Bank, *World Development Report, 1992,* Washington, D.C., 1992, Table 1, pp. 218-9.

Education and Political Development

It is generally agreed that education acts as an agent for change in the political system, and as Coleman argues, the educational system can be viewed "as the master determinant of all aspects of change."[13] The most widely accepted definition of political development is the following:

> Political development can be regarded as the acquisition by a political system of a consciously-sought and qualitatively new and enhanced, political capacity as manifested in the successful institutionalization of . . .new patterns of integration regulating and containing the tensions and conflicts produced by increased differentiation, and. . .new patterns of participation and resource distribution adequately responsive to the demands generated by the imperatives of equality.[14]

For Fagerlind and Saha, the key concepts are clearly those of integration and participation. Integration refers to the extent to which a society is able to create unity and solidarity among its people, and to bring about a sense of national identity over and above that generated by family, tribe, village or region.[15] In Pakistan, the problem of integration relates to the blending of various ethnic or social identities into one of national unity. The concept of participation is almost self-explanatory. The underlying assumption here is that a population in which there is extensive political mobilization, either through voting, interest in, or reading about political matters, is preferable to one in which the masses are politically inactive or stagnant.

Benefit from Women's Education

There is a strong case for educating women because of the several benefits that accrue to mothers, children and the society.[16] Elementary education improves hygiene and nutritional practices, which improves child survival. Education further highlights the advantages of controlling family size.[17] Children of educated mothers live healthier, longer lives. Apparently, the more education women attain, the more likely they are to seek professional health care, which also lowers child mortality. In Africa, a difference of one percentage point in the national literacy rate is associated with a two-year gain in life expectancy.[18]

Pakistan is a perfect example of a country where rapid population growth and high fertility rates continue to adversely affect maternal health and child survival. A growing population of young people has strained education budgets, and an increasingly large number of young people, often the children of rural and low-income families, receive little or no education.

Conclusion

Education is a cornerstone of economic growth and social development and a principal means to improve the welfare of individuals. As discussed above there is a positive though intricate relationship between education and development in its various dimensions. It presents a strong case for heavy investment, both public and private, in education. Specifically, Pakistan needs to increase school access at all levels, particularly at the primary level since it lays the groundwork for further education and produces a literate and numerate population, which helps to eradicate the widespread illiteracy in the country.

Past Dilemmas and Future Prospects

Education is one of the keys and integral components of human resource development and has faced serious problems in Pakistan in the past. Starting with a very low base since the nation's birth in 1947, Pakistan's educational infrastructure has grown tremendously, yet the educational enterprise continues to be characterized as one of the weakest, most inefficient and inequitable systems in the world. The gravity of the situation, however, seems to have been recognized, as indicated from an official statement that:

> during the past three decades, Pakistan's social sector development has lagged far behind. . .its economy which during this period grew at a rate of around 5.5 percent. In the past decade, Pakistan had been the fifth fastest growing economy in the world (excluding small countries with population under two million). Yet Pakistan exhibits, perhaps, the greatest discrepancy in the two-way relationship between human development and economic growth.[19]

One of the critical problems in Pakistan's education system is the low funding in education.

Financing Education in Pakistan

Countries differ in terms of the importance they give to education and training. Several Asian countries, particularly Japan, South Korea, Singapore, Hong Kong, Taiwan and Malaysia, give high priority to investment in human resources. The ratio of expenditure for education to total public expenditures is a rough indicator of the relative importance accorded to this sector. And educational expenditure relative to Gross National Product (GNP) or Gross Domestic Product (GDP) is a measure of a country's effort to support education.

Historically, Pakistan has accorded a low priority to education. During the Ayub regime (1958-1969), education was given a back seat both in terms of effort and relative importance since the regime had devoted itself to pursue economic growth. The Bhutto regime (1971-1977) accorded a higher relative importance to education but the level of effort registered only a marginal increase over the Ayub period. Under the Zia regime (1977-1988), education's relative importance and the level of effort given to education registered improvement over the previous two regimes. The Sixth Five Year Plan (1983-1988) made investment in human resource development a part of its basic economic framework, and during this Plan the ratio of education expenditure to GNP increased to 2.02 percent from an annual average of 1.5 percent during previous regimes.

Within the overall objectives of the Sixth Plan, a significant boost was given to the social sector of the Plan, especially the part designed for the rural areas under the Prime Minister's Five Point Program (1986-1990). A number of strategic policy decisions were taken to enhance the resource base for education. For example, the *Iqra* (literacy) surcharge for education was levied on imports which yielded additional resources of Rs 13.1 billion. The recurring expenditure of the provinces on education was over and above the 1982-83 level, which was treated as development expenditure and reimbursed to the provinces. This amounted to Rs 14.3 billion and helped them to expand their education system. The foreign funding earmarked for education projects was passed on to the provinces in addition to their normal share in the Public Sector Development Program (Planning Commission, 1990:160). These policies could be only partially implemented.

Today, in terms of effort, Pakistan spends a comparatively low percentage of its GNP on education. For instance, in 1989 Pakistan had the lowest expenditure on education (2.6 percent) as compared to several countries in the Asian region, such as Malaysia (5.6 percent), Iran (3.1 percent), Sri Lanka (3.0 percent), Thailand (3.2 percent), India (3.2 percent), Singapore (3.4 percent), Bhutan (3.7 percent) and Nepal (2.8 percent). Only Myanmar (2.2 percent), and Bangladesh (2.2 percent) were lower.[20] For the year 1989, the average education expenditure as a ratio of GNP for all developing countries was 3.6 percent. UNESCO calls for a minimum of 4.0 percent expenditure of a developing country's expenditure for education.

In terms of relative importance, or the proportion of budget given to education, during 1987-88 Pakistan was spending 5 percent of its national budget on education, which was one of the lowest in the region. The ratio for other countries was higher: Malaysia (16.9 percent), Iran (18.1 percent), Sri Lanka (7.8 percent), South Korea (26.6 percent), Thailand (16.6 percent), Philippines (10.3 percent), Singapore (11.5 percent), India (8.5 percent), Nepal (10.8 percent) and Bangladesh (10.3 percent) (UNDP, 1991:148-9).

During the initial four years of the Seventh Plan (1988-1992) for which data are available (see Table 4.2), the total expenditure on education as a ratio of GNP achieved an annual average of 2.32 percent.[21]

During the Seventh Five Year Plan (1988-1993), Pakistan allocated Rs 23.11 billion or 6.6 percent of the total public sector development outlay for education (Planning Commission, 1988:328), an amount 66 percent higher than the allocations made during the Sixth Plan. However, according to the tentative estimates available, the actual total expenditure on education during the Seventh Plan was Rs 25.25 billion (including Rs 4.0 billion from foreign aid). Thus the actual utilization during the Seventh Plan appears to be over 100 percent, which shows a tangible increase of over 72 percent utilization during the Sixth Plan. The higher financial utilization of the Plan allocation has been attributed to the smooth implementation of six foreign-aided primary education projects, the allocation of funds for the Education Foundations in the Provinces and payments of arrears of salaries to ex-teachers of *Nai Roshni* or (New Light) Schools.

During the Seventh Plan, foreign aided projects and private sector investment in education have strengthened the resource base for education. However, the user charges (tuition, room and board) of higher education, intended for expanding the resource base could not be increased as desired in the plan. In a bid to attract the private sector in the field of education, the Government announced a 50 percent matching grant in the budget for 1991-92 for new schools and educational institutions opened by the private sector (Finance Division, 1991:146).

TABLE 4.2 Public Expenditure on Education in Pakistan During 1988-1992 (Current prices,Rs Million)

Year	*Development Expenditures*	*Non-Development Expenditures*	*Total Expenditures*	*Total Expenditures as Percent of GNP*
1988-89	3,981.8	15,501.0	19,482.8	2.4
1989-90	4,644.8	16,239.6	20,884.4	2.3
1990-91	4,067.4	19,500.0	23,567.4	2.3
1991-92[a]	3,701.3	24,090.0	27,791.3	2.3

[a] Budget Estimates

Source: Planning and Development Division, quoted in *Economic Survey 1991-92,* p.149.

The present government has acknowledged the need to accelerate progress in the area of human development as its major challenge and among the highest priorities (Finance Division, 1992:xiii), as reflected in the various actions taken. The most important actions taken thus far include: (1) the formulation of the Social Action Program (SAP) 1992-1995, with special emphasis on the expansion and upgrading of educational facilities; (2) establishing a committee to oversee and coordinate the preparation and implementation of the Social Action Plan; (3) encourage the private sector to play a greater role in the provision of education and health services with the help of matching grants; and (4) by raising the budgetary allocation for the social sectors and strengthening the implementation capacity.

The Social Action Program 1992-1995, has provided the development outlay of Rs 53.04 billion for this three year program.[22] Of this allocation, the total share for education will be Rs 21.45 billion to be distributed as Rs 6.512 billion, Rs 7.145 billion and Rs 7.793 billion for the years 1992-93, 1993-94, and 1994-95 respectively.[23]

The allocations made for education under the SAP are mainly for primary education, teacher education, adult literacy and the Education Foundation. The fear of increasing the burden of recurrent expenditures has been stated as one of the causes that has thwarted educational expansion in the past. Keeping in view this prohibiting factor, the SAP provides that "the accelerated development funding will be fully supported by providing the required current financing, not only to sustain physical facilities and provide salaried staff, but also to increase non-salary components to improve and maintain the quality of services."[24] Therefore, beside the development outlay, a total of 39.147 billion has been earmarked for recurrent expenditures in education during 1992-1995.[25]

Providing fiscal incentives to increase private investment in education is an encouraging feature of the government policy, which declared that "all educational institutions established between July 1, 1991 and June 30, 1995, have been granted a "five year tax holiday." In reality the tax incentives are for companies and individuals which donate funds for educational purposes. It is an effort to improve the system by offering tax abatements either by abolishing (for individuals) the existing ceilings on donations or relaxing them for companies.[26]

On December 20, 1992, the Government of Pakistan announced its Education Policy 1992-2002 "to make education compatible with the demands of prospective economic activity, and social-cultural and political development in an egalitarian Muslim Society."[27] To achieve the targets of the education policy, Pakistan's Education Minister announced the estimates and projections for the next ten years. A total of Rs 143.368 billion has been earmarked for educational development during 1992-2002, which includes Rs 36.078 billion for the private sector. The policy has also made provisions for recurrent expenditure: Rs 264.87 billion (the current annual recurrent expenditure of Rs

26.487 for the next ten years), and an additional Rs 78.184 billion resulting from the implementation of the proposed education policy. The private sector is expected to raise Rs 13.184 billion for its own annual expenditure requirements.

According to these projections, with the annual average of Rs 10.07 billion, the development expenditure on education in Pakistan during the next 10 years may reach an unprecedented level. However, these seemingly large numbers warrant a cautious interpretation, since the level of effort or the ratio of these expenditures as the percentage of GNP remain at an average of 2.56, which is still lower than the 4 percent prescribed by UNESCO. If the past record of educational expenditure in Pakistan is kept in mind, it may not be easy to dispel fears of a shortfall in these projected expenditures. Similarly, the prospects of private sector investment in education to the tune of Rs 50 billion during 1992-2002 have not met the test of experience.

The initial thinking of the Eighth Five Year Plan 1993-1998 reiterates the increasing appreciation for education development in the country, and seeks to democratize educational opportunities so that it becomes equally available to every citizen of Pakistan rather than being limited to elites only. Addressing the need for greater equity and increased social mobility the Eighth Plan lays more emphasis on improving rural and especially female education along with strengthening the technical capability of the work force.

The initial estimates for the Eighth Five Year Plan 1993-1998 proposed Rs 69 billion (includes Rs 40.13 billion allocated for education under the Social Action Program 1992-1995). To broaden the resource base for education, the Plan proposes to organize the Iqra surcharge as a separate fund to be used solely for the literacy program, and to provide fiscal incentives (including tax exemptions and loan facilities) as well as the matching grants to the private sector for establishing new educational institutions at all levels. The Plan is expected to propose a gradual increase of user charges at the post-secondary level and other income-generating activities (such as creating endowment funds) at higher education institutions.

The measures proposed in the Educational Policy, the Social Action Program and the Eighth Five Year Plan have great potential to transform the country and could set Pakistan on its long journey towards "Education for All." But it may not be possible to reach this goal without raising the share of education to at least 4 percent of the GNP and increasing the annual expenditure on education to 20 percent of the annual budget.

Financing Education Subsectors

The expenditure share is the percentage of total educational expenditure spent on a particular level of education. The expenditure shares reflect a country's decision regarding the relative amounts to be invested at different stages of the educational structure. In Pakistan, within education, development outlay as well as the actual expenditures in the past have largely favored the tertiary level. From the Fifth Plan on, primary education began to claim a relatively higher share.

The Bhutto regime nationalized all private schools, with the exception of those operated by foreign governments.[28] There was also a general policy shift away from exclusive economic growth towards equity-influenced education development in Pakistan. More emphasis was given to primary education, as indicated by the sharp increase in the actual expenditures which reached 12 percent of the total expenditure on education during 1970-1978. Technical education suffered a drastic cutback when the expenditure fell from 14.3 percent (during the Second and Third Plans) to 7.7 percent of the total expenditure on education during 1970-1978.[29] The level of allocation and expenditure for higher education showed a moderate increase over those made in the previous plans. The Bhutto regime, therefore, must be credited for setting the tone and funding for a shift towards basic education, which successors found difficult to reduce.

It was under the Zia regime, during the Sixth Plan 1983-1988, that primary education received relatively greater emphasis for the first time, both in terms of political commitment and willingness to fund this subsector -- particularly under the Prime Minister's Five Point Program 1986-1990. The actual expenditure for primary education during this Plan reached only 26.31 percent of the total expenditure in education. This was less than its share of 37.17 percent in total outlay for education, but it was a good start.

The primary subsector made further gains during the Seventh Five Year Plan 1988-1993 when, of the total development outlay of Rs 23.110 billion for education, Rs 10.128 billion were allocated to the primary subsector, raising its share to 43.83 percent, followed by secondary education with 28.30 percent. Thus, primary and secondary school education claimed almost 72 percent of the total allocation for education.

According to the tentative evaluation of the Seventh Plan, the actual expenditure in education of Rs 25.246 billion (including foreign aid to education) had exceeded the original outlay of Rs 23.110 billion, raising the level of utilization of the plan allocation to the tune of 109 percent. Utilization in the primary sector amounted to 116 percent. The actual expenditure was Rs 11.766 billion against the plan allocation of Rs 10.128 billion, and in college education it was 308 percent. The actual expenditure in this subsector was Rs 1.8922 billion compared to its original allocation of Rs 615 million. Thus, the Seventh Plan provides evidence of the latent high absorption capacity in the primary education subsector, which has been under-utilized in the past.

Despite some progress, the subsectoral allocations and expenditures in education in Pakistan continue to reflect an imbalance. For instance, in 1988, of the total expenditure in education, the share of higher education was 18.2

percent, which was the highest among several countries in Asia. For instance, the percentage in India was 17, Bangladesh 8.7, Sri Lanka 6.5, Myanmar 13, Malaysia 14.9, South Korea 7 and Iran 10.5, respectively (UNDP, 1992:156). In contrast, a share of 36 percent for primary education in Pakistan in the year 1987-88 was the lowest in the region. Sri Lanka had the highest ratio, 93.5 percent, followed by India 41.8, Bangladesh 46.4, Malaysia 37.9, South Korea 43.6, and Iran 41.5 percent (UNDP, 1991:148). For 1985, the average public allocation in Asian countries was 48 percent for primary education, 31 percent for secondary education, and 19 percent for higher education (Tan and Mingat, 1992:26). This declining pattern is similar to that found in Latin America, where the corresponding shares of public spending are 51, 26, and 24 percent, respectively (Tan and Mingat, 1992:26).

The government has announced that the share of primary education in education spending is likely to improve during 1992-2002. The public sector will assume the entire responsibility to finance the development of primary education to the tune of Rs 51.3429 billion. This would raise the share of this subsector to 47.85 percent of the total outlay. Similarly, the share of secondary education is expected to increase to 24.24 percent during this period.

Education Policy 1992-2002 has estimated a total of Rs 4.511 billion to be spent during the next 10 years for the promotion of literacy in the country. Of this only Rs 1.227 billion or 27 percent is expected to come from the public sector and the rest, 73 percent is expected to be mobilized by the private sector. Low public sector allocation for literacy reflects the government's approach toward this issue as will be discussed below. The estimates/projections for development expenditure during 1992-2002 in respect to the various subsectors is given in Table 4.3.

Mobilization of public and private resources needed for education development is the key for the success of new programs. Major responsibility lies with the public sector not only to demonstrate its own willingness to provide the earmarked resources but also to ensure that the incentives are in place to facilitate the private sector's investment in education. A gradual increase of user charges at the post-secondary level may prove helpful but may not be decisive in redressing the needs of the education sector. The setting up of the Iqra Fund to use the Iqra surcharge, levied on imports, exclusively for literacy education is an extremely important measure.

Access to Education in Pakistan

Since Pakistan's inception, despite several efforts made to increase the number of schools and colleges to enhance the participation rates at all levels, progress remains slow. The data for the year 1990, presented in Table 4.4 give a comparative position of Pakistan. In terms of enrollment ratios, Pakistan's lowest position reveals a dismal picture and also points to the size of the challenge facing it.

TABLE 4.3 Education Development Expenditure in Pakistan by Subsectors During 1992-2002 (Rs Billions)

	Total Outlay	*Public*		*Private*	
		Allocation	*Percent Share*	*Allocation*	*Percent Share*
Primary	51.34	51.34	100.00	0.00	0.00
Literacy	4.51	1.23	27.27	3.28	72.73
Secondary	38.99	26.00	66.68	12.99	33.32
Higher Secondary	9.08	7.24	79.74	1.85	20.37
Higher Education	6.06	2.42	39.93	3.58	59.08
Technical/Vocational	9.44	3.73	39.51	5.71	60.49
Technical Training	1.70	1.70	100.00	0.00	0.00
University [a]	10.16	5.23	51.48	4.93	48.52
Education Foundation [b]	7.48	3.74	50.00	3.74	50.00
Scholarship	2.43	2.43	100.00	0.00	0.00
Miscellaneous	2.42	2.42	100.00	0.00	0.00

[a] Including Agricultural Universities

[b] Including Recurring Expenditures

Source: Ministry of Education, *Education Policy 1992-2002*, Govt. of Pakistan, Islamabad, December 20, 1992. p. 15.

TABLE 4.4 Percent Enrollment Ratios in 1990: An International Comparison

	Enrollment Ratios (Percent)		
Country	*Primary*	*Secondary*	*Tertiary*
Pakistan	39	19	3.6
India	99	41	9.7
Bangladesh	70	18	4.2
Iran	116	53	6.3
Egypt	90	68	18.8
Turkey	113	50	10.6
Korea (S)	104	87	36.2
USA	100	98	63.0
Canada	105	105	67.3

Source: UNESCO, *World Education Report 1991*. Paris, 1991.

The issue of access to education in Pakistan arises both from the supply-side and the demand-side. The supply of education in Pakistan has been historically limited relative to the size of the school-going population, which means a shortage of schools and teachers. The lack of resources has been a constant constraint for the provision of additional schools and teachers, and has adversely affected school access.

The demand for education, an important determinant of school access, has certainly been less strong to compensate the weak state response. Under similar circumstances, communities in other developing countries have mobilized their own resources to build schools and provide for teachers, but this has not been the case in Pakistan. Poverty has discouraged poor parents from using their limited income to educate their children. The school access issue is not confined to the total supply of education and the demand for it. It also involves a careful analysis of how opportunity for education is distributed among different groups in society.

Primary Education

In Pakistan in 1948-49, the participation rate at primary level age group 5-9 was about 19.8 percent. There were only 9,073 primary schools for a total school age population of 4.2 million, of which only 0.83 million were enrolled in primary schools. Beginning with the clarion call from The Education Conference of 1947 through the deliberations of various Education Commissions and education policies, the nation has repeatedly declared its goals to achieve universal primary education. Recently, on the occasion of the world conference on "Education for All" held in March 1990, Pakistan committed itself to enter the 21st century with universalization of primary education, with a target of an 80 percent literacy rate (Finance Division, 1991: 142). The Education Policy 1992-2002 also seeks to achieve these goals by the year 2002. At present, Pakistan has a 63.5 percent enrollment at the primary level.

The most notable shift in the state policy favoring basic education (including primary education and adult literacy) was witnessed during the Sixth Plan 1983-1988. The Prime Minister's Five Point Program was launched to increase the participation rate at the primary level from 48 percent to 75 percent. However, by the end of the plan period only 63.5 percent could be achieved (79.5 percent for boys and 45.7 percent for girls). The lack of success has been attributed to low funding since only 50 percent of the plan provision of Rs 7,000 millions was made available. Other important reasons were lack of proper motivational campaigns for parents, social and religious taboos for girls' education and the non-availability of school facilities in certain localities (Planning Commission, 1990:160). According to the Planning Commission, by the end of the Sixth Plan, primary education facilities were available to only 60 percent of the children in the age group of 5-9 years. Primary schools lacked physical facilities; about 29,000 primary schools had no buildings and 16,000 schools had only one class room (Planning Commission, 1988:243).

The Seventh Plan 1988-1993 also declared its ambitious programs for primary education. The Plan aimed at providing school facilities for every child living within a distance of 1.5 Km, so that no child is deprived of basic education due to the lack of a school near their home. Table 4.5 provides the benchmark participation rates at the end of the Sixth Plan, the Seventh Plan targets, and a tentative estimate of achievements by the terminal year of the Plan (1992-93).

According to these estimates, the total participation rate at the primary level by the end of the seventh plan (1993) is likely to reach 75 percent, thus show an increase of 11 percent during 1988-1993, or 2.5 percent per annum, which is less than the annual 3 percent achieved during the Sixth Plan. Although the target for the boys' increased participation rate will be achieved as planned in the Seventh Plan, there will be a shortfall of 10 percent in the case of girls. Also at this average annual increase, Pakistan may not be able to enter the twenty-first century with a 100 percent participation rate at the primary level as recently announced by the government.

TABLE 4.5 Participation Rates in Pakistan by Education Levels 1987-92 (percent)

Level	*Benchmark (1987-88)*			*Targets (1992-93)*			*Likely Achievement in (1992-93)*		
	M	*F*	*T*	*M*	*F*	*T*	*M*	*F*	*T*
Primary	80	46	64	89	70	80	89	60	75
Middle	41	19	30	53	29	42	60	26	43
High	24	10	17	33	15	24	37	14	26
Second [a]	36	15	24	44	22	33	49	20	35

[a] Participating for Secondary level is the average for Middle and High school participation rates.
Source: Planning Commission. Government of Pakistan, 1992.

Gender Gap and Urban-Rural Disparity

The national rates of participation at various levels of education conceal the discrepancies prevailing within the education sector. For instance, in 1987-88, the total enrollment ratio for primary level in Pakistan was 63.5 percent (Table 4.6). But the participation rates separately for boys and girls respectively were 79.7 and 45.7 percent, indicating a gender gap of 33.8 percentage points. Similarly, the participation rate for urban areas was 19.2 percent higher than the rate for the rural areas. Again, within urban and rural areas, the enrollment ratios for boys and girls were different.

In general, the enrollment ratio at the primary level for urban boys (86.7 percent) is 9.7 percent higher than the corresponding ratio for rural boys, 77 percent, but 60 percent higher than the ratio for girls in rural areas, 37.2 percent. Therefore, the real challenge in improving the enrollment ratio at primary education in Pakistan lies in targeting girls and boys in rural areas.

TABLE 4.6 Pakistan Primary Education Enrollment Ratios

	Enrollment (Thousands)		*Enrollment Ratio (Percent)*	
	Benchmark 1987-88	*Target 1992-93*	*Benchmark 1987-88*	*Target 1992-93*
Total	9310	13876	63.5	79.7
Boys	6123	7951	79.5	88.5
Girls	3187	5925	45.7	70.3
Urban				
Total	3100	4155	77.4	86.7
Boys	1800	3200	85.7	93.1
Girls	1300	1855	68.3	80.0
Rural				
Total	6210	9721	58.2	77.0
Boys	4323	5651	77.2	86.8
Girls	1887	4070	37.2	66.6

Source: Planning Commission, *Seventh Plan 1988-93 and Perspective Plan 1988-2003*, Islamabad, 1988, p. 246

To improve the overall participation rate at the primary level and in order to bridge the gender and the urban-rural gap, the present government's emphasis on the effective implementation of the Social Action Program 1992-1995 is correct. The SAP strategy seeks to target the female group, and projects an acceleration of its annual participation rate by 8.8 percent as compared to 2.5 percent for boys and 4.9 percent for the country as a whole. It is expected that the participation rate for girls may increase from 49.2 percent in the benchmark year 1991-92 to 63.3 percent in the year 1994-95. The corresponding increase for boys is estimated to be 6.3 percent so that by the terminal year of SAP, this rate for boys may reach 89.3 percent. For the country as a whole, it could increase to 76.5 percent by the end of 1995 (Planning Commission, 1992:37).

The SAP strategy is to increase enrollment capacity through creating 2.892 million new seats, 1.660 million of which will be for girls, by opening new primary schools, mosque schools, and by adding classrooms in existing schools. The funds needed for these program have been allocated under the SAP as noted above.

Based on the past experience of low utilization, the government also intends to ensure the utilization of the increased enrollment capacity through several measures such as: (1) effective legislation to control child labor, and, (2) the introduction of compulsory enrollment in all areas, as facilities become available at a reasonable distance. To achieve the accelerated targets for girls' enrollment, the proposals under consideration seek to provide incentives where feasible, such as school feeding programs for 2 million girls, plus security, and transport.

The retention problem is quite serious, particularly in the rural areas. About 60 percent of the children drop out before acquiring the competence to read and write. Poverty, poor motivation, shortage of trained and qualified male and female teachers, shelterless schools, poor teacher attendance in rural areas, an urban-oriented curriculum irrelevant to rural life and an unattractive school environment, have resulted in a high drop out rate. The government plans to reduce these rates by providing an improved environment in schools such as buildings for the shelterless schools, hygienic latrines, clean water and boundary walls wherever necessary. A factor which is constraining the expanded access to female education is the non-availability of land for primary schools in congested urban localities and in the heart of rural areas. In the case of female primary schools, the Government plans to buy land -- if the community is not able to provide free land.

The Education Policy undertakes the task of universalizing primary education in Pakistan with a sense of urgency. The policy statement in this regard states, "Primary education shall be recognized as a fundamental right of every Pakistani child. Primary education shall be made compulsory and free so as to achieve universal enrollment by the end of the decade. . .for this transitory period, the minimum norm will be a two-room primary school with 5 teachers" (Ministry of Education, 1992:21). In order to achieve these goals of increased access at primary level, the Education Policy plans the following:

1. Construction of 106,957 new primary and Mosque schools.
2. Two-room primary schools for the 24,750 shelterless schools.
3. 20,000 existing primary schools will be provided an additional room.
4. Major repairs will be carried out in 50,000 schools.
5. 265,000 primary teachers will be trained.

Issue of Adult Literacy

There is no doubt that literacy plays a very significant role in the overall growth and development of a country. Pakistan has an extremely low literacy rate. Neighboring countries in Asia have made more progress in improving their literacy than Pakistan. For example, for the year 1990, the highest adult literacy rates existed in Maldives (95 percent), Sri Lanka (88 percent), and Myanmar (81 percent). Whereas Pakistan's adult literacy rate (including even those who could only write their name) is estimated to be 35 percent, which is even lower than that of India, which has a 48 percent literacy rate (UNDP, 1992).

In terms of the overall size, of Pakistan's population of an estimated 120 million for the year 1992, at least 43 million are unable to read and write. This places Pakistan within the group of ten countries in the world which account for three-quarters of the world's illiterate adult population. Among these ten countries, in terms of illiteracy rate, Pakistan has one of the highest rates, 65 percent, exceeded only by Sudan with 73.9 percent. However, Bangladesh (64.7 percent), India (52 percent) and Egypt (51.6 percent) have lower adult illiteracy rates than Pakistan.[30]

During the Zia regime, the Sixth Five Year Plan sought to improve the literacy level by means of a two-pronged attack, by accelerating primary education and by launching a functional literacy program for adults. Given the large size of the illiterate population, and the five-year duration of the literacy program, a selective approach was proposed to determine the target groups. In view of the vital significance of the younger age group and because they would yield the maximum returns, it was proposed to cover 15 million persons, 5 million males and 10 million females, of the cohort 10 to 19 years under the functional literacy program. In view of the catalytic role of women and the need to reach the rural population, a higher priority was given to women in rural areas. As the Economic Survey 1985-86 put it, under the Prime Minister's Five Point Program, substantial emphasis was placed on primary education to attain the objectives of mass literacy -- up to 50 percent by 1990.

By setting up the Literacy and Mass Education Commission (LAMEC) in 1981 an attempt was made to institutionalize the search for strategies to eradicate illiteracy and to promote functional literacy in Pakistan. During 1987-88 LAMEC was provided with a budget allocation of Rs 960 million, compared to Rs 50 million allocated in 1984. In the initial stages the Commission produced primers and literacy materials; launched a vigorous campaign for literacy; adopted a number of governmental measures for encouraging literacy activities; sponsored a number of radio and television programs and publicized the President's 10-point literacy program. However, it failed to establish an infrastructure which could start a chain reaction in the provinces and take the country forward on the path of literacy (UNESCO, 1991:10).

LAMEC launched its 'Nai Roshni' or 'Drop-in' school program (1986-1990) in 1986 that included the opening of 22,000 schools, with a view to offering a second chance to dropouts and an opportunity to those of the 10-14 year cohort who never attended a school. It provided them a free education with flexible timing and an informal environment in "open" school-like literacy centers. But this scheme collapsed before 1990 because of unfavorable factors such as: (1) its overly centralized and heavy bureaucratic structure; (2) lack of full participation of the provinces and the community as a whole in promoting and strengthening the system, (3) uncertainty about its future after 1990, and the likely discontinuance of financial resources (UNESCO, 1991:10).

Most of the literacy programs in Pakistan have failed due to:

1. The sporadic nature of efforts made to promote literacy.
2. Insufficient financial allocations.
3. Lack of proper planning and programming, i.e., non-coordination among different agencies and institutions carrying out literacy programs.
4. Rapid population growth which has continuously offset the meager efforts provided to promote literacy.
5. The extremely low level of motivation of adults to become literate.

By and large several efforts launched to promote literacy in Pakistan have achieved only marginal success.

With this experience of the past, the Seventh Plan changed its strategy to combat illiteracy in Pakistan. The new approach was summed up as follows: "The Sixth Plan experience has shown that a short cut to literacy is not only expensive but is hard to monitor. There is no substitute for formal education. The options available are: (1) to divert maximum resources for converting illiterates into literates with uncertain results. This would probably deny primary education to half of the new generation, or (2) to provide one hundred percent of the resources to primary education for the new generation and let the illiterates be phased out or taken care of largely by the Non-Governmental Organizations, or NGOs on a demand basis. Therefore, the Seventh Plan relies mainly on the expansion of compulsory education in the primary grades and the

Table 4.7 provides the recent estimates of literacy rates in Pakistan for the year 1990, which also points out the existing gender and urban rural disparity. In a population of 115 million in 1990, only 32 percent of its people are literate. The literacy rate of 22 percent for the female population is very low, which means that more than three-fourths of the female population (around 57 million) in Pakistan is illiterate. Similarly, there is a wide gap between urban and rural areas. In terms of interprovincial variation, the literacy rates in the most populated province, Punjab, are above the national average both for urban and rural areas as well as for the males and females. The only other high literacy rate is that of urban Sindh which is close to the national average for urban areas. Urban Sindh includes Karachi -- the cosmopolitan city of Pakistan with a population nearing 10 million. The literacy rates for rural Sindh, NWFP and Boluchistan are woefully low at 5, 7 and 2 percent respectively.

The Education Policy has set the year 2000 to achieve a literacy rate of 70 percent. The policy further declares "this formidable challenge cannot be met by the government alone. The whole nation needs to be mobilized for launching a campaign against the scourge of illiteracy and put on a war footing basis. The provincial governments, NGOs, and local institutions shall be actively involved both in planning and implementation" (Ministry of Education, 1992:21). The federal government will assume the role of coordination, monitoring and evaluation and also provide technical support for the development of materials and training.

TABLE 4.7 Percent Literacy in Pakistan by Province and by Gender (1990)

	Total			*Urban*			*Rural*		
	MF	*M*	*F*	*MF*	*M*	*F*	*MF*	*M*	*F*
Pakistan	32	41	22	54	61	45	21	30	11
Punjab	36	47	26	56	64	48	27	38	17
Sindh	33	40	24	54	61	46	14	22	5
NWFP	19	28	9	38	49	24	16	28	7
Baluchistan	11	16	4	34	42	18	7	10	2

Source: Ministry of Education, *Basic Education for All: Statistical Profile 1981-2000.* Government of Pakistan, Islamabad, 1989, p.16.

The initial thinking of the Eighth Plan (1993-1998) in relation to the eradication of illiteracy more or less echoes the policy statement of the Education Policy. The Eighth Plan includes the following approaches for increasing the literacy profile in Pakistan: (1) achieving the new goals of literacy by universalization of primary education and elimination of the early dropout rate through various measures, including legislation for compulsory primary education wherever it is accessible; (2) encouraging the NGOs to develop and launch community-based literacy programs on the basis of local demand, to be created by them through a motivational campaign and by linking the literacy programs with the socio-economic development of the learners, (3) including the literacy component in integrated rural development and urban community development programs of various departments and organizations, and (4) encouraging publication and circulation of special newspapers and reading material for illiterates.

The Eighth Plan estimates that by 1997-98, the population of the 10-plus age cohort will rise to 96.68 million, and through various efforts to be taken during the plan period, 46.51 million persons will be literate by 1997-98, giving a literacy rate of about 48 percent. These estimates are much lower and more realistic than the projections provided in the Education Policy which seeks to raise literacy in Pakistan to 70 percent by the year 2000. Given the experimental nature of non-formal education initiatives in Pakistan, and the predominant emphasis both in the Education Policy and the Eighth Plan, future prospects for improvement in literacy seem to hinge on successful implementation of the programs for universal primary education.

Secondary Education

At the secondary education level, the gross enrollment ratio for Pakistan during 1989 was 20 percent. The same ratios for other countries in Asia were: India (43), Sri Lanka (74), Nepal (30), Malaysia (59), Iran (53), and South Korea (86), respectively (World Bank, 1992:274). The Planning Commission estimates the total enrollment ratio for secondary education in Pakistan will reach 25 percent by the terminal year of the Seventh Plan, which would mean an achievement of 37 percent for males and 17 percent for females (see Table 4.5). Even if we accept the liberal estimate, a 25 percent enrollment ratio for secondary education in Pakistan is very low.

Efforts to improve access to and the quality of secondary education in Pakistan date back to the Education Conferences held during 1947 and 1951 when recommendations were put forth to diversify the curriculum at the secondary level by including courses in agriculture, commerce and industrial arts to suit the needs of the students on the basis of age, ability and aptitude.

In 1988, the Seventh Plan observed that, although significant expansion has taken place in secondary education, it remains inequitably distributed among income groups and regions in the country. The long distances involved in the availability of middle or high school facilities is another important factor which is responsible for the low enrollment ratio, especially in the case of girls. Every education policy and plan had recommended that classes XI and XII be added to secondary education. Not much has been done in the actual implementation (Planning Commission, 1988:243).

The Seventh Plan envisaged expansion of secondary education facilities to absorb the expected increase in primary school graduates. "During the Seventh Plan the participation rate will increase from 30.4 percent to 41.6 percent at the middle stage and from 17.2 percent to 24.1 percent at the high stage. The overall participation rate for classes VI to X will rise from 25.7 percent to 35.3 percent. It is expected that girls' enrollment will increase more rapidly than that of boys" (Planning Commission, 1988:247).

In terms of expansion, the plan called for upgrading a large number of primary and middle schools for girls. Construction of additional classrooms and improvement of existing buildings of middle and high schools will be carried out to accommodate the additional enrollment coming from the primary schools. In urban areas, a second shift in secondary schools will be introduced wherever feasible (Planning Commission, 1988:247). Incentives will be provided to attract good science and mathematics teachers. The ongoing project of the improvement of science education will be expanded to cover more schools, together with in-service training of teachers, construction of laboratories and an adequate investment in science equipment (Planning Commission, 1988:248). A small hostel for students will be provided in secondary schools which would serve several villages not within commuting distance. Efforts will be made to locate new secondary schools so that these facilities are available to the maximum number of students in all districts and tehsils (Planning Commission, 1988:248).

The Education Policy 1992-2002 envisages the diversification of secondary education into general and vocational tracks in the middle and high schools. Major targets set for the period 1992-2002 include: a 49.87 percent participation rate at the secondary level; an increase of about 17 percent over this ratio for 1992 assumed at 32.64 percent; an increased number of schools from 19,000 for year 1992 to 48,487 to accommodate the enrollment that is expected to rise from 4.75 million in 1992 to 9.15 million in 2002. The corresponding increase in teachers has been projected from 130,000 in 1992 to 338,586 in 2002. Computer education is to be made a part of the curricula at the secondary school level (Ministry of Education, 1992:9).

According to the initial thinking of the Eighth Plan 1993-1998, and in order to absorb the additional students from primary schools, it is planned to create 2.4 million additional seats in classes VI to X by upgrading primary and middle schools; establishing new high schools; and adding class rooms in the existing schools and the improvement of existing buildings. During the Eighth Plan period, it is proposed to review and revise the existing curricula, particularly science and mathematics, with the provision of additional laboratories, equipment and better trained teachers. By the end of the Eighth Plan, each district will have a model school for boys and for girls in the public or private sector. The private sector will be encouraged to establish high quality educational institutions.

Research findings in other developing countries support the expansion of secondary education, but there are mixed views about the diversification of the curricula. In its policy paper on vocational and technical education and training, the World Bank maintains that "the extra resources used in many countries would be better invested in improving student achievement in the academic curriculum or in increasing access to such education than in a few vocational courses to replace part of the academic curriculum" (World Bank, 1991:9). This poses a question about the relevance of current efforts to diversify secondary education in Pakistan into general and vocational tracks.

Tertiary Education

Compared to other levels of education, there has been a phenomenal expansion in Pakistan's higher education system during the past four decades. In comparison with primary level enrollment, which has multiplied 12 times between 1948-1988, and secondary level enrollment, which has grown 16 times, the college level increase is 30 times, the professional college level 18 times, and university level 98 times (The World Bank, 1990:22).

When compared to the 142 Arts and Science colleges, 19 professional colleges and two universities in Pakistan in 1948-49, the estimated number of these institutions in the year 1991-92 are as follows: 643 colleges (of which 231 colleges are for females), 99 professional colleges (8 exclusively for females) and 23 universities (three of which are in the private sector (Finance Division, 1992:261). The total enrollment at the tertiary level in Pakistan, estimated for the year 1991-92 is as follows: in Arts and Science Colleges, approximately 527,000, including 199,000 female students; in professional colleges 78,796 including 21,776 female students, and in universities 82,040, including 10,887 females.

In spite of the considerable increase in the number of universities, students and teachers, higher education is available to only 4.6 percent of the relevant age group (18-23) years (Table 4.4).

In 1977 the Federal Government took over the responsibility of financing expenditures in universities. This was done to ease the financial situation of the universities which had shown persistent deterioration over the earlier decades (Ministry of Education, 1984:53).

The government is taking a keen interest in the promotion of higher education and more funds are being provided to the universities for improving teaching and research. It has also provided a rolling fund of Rs 60 millions for supplementing research in the universities and the Research and Development Institutions under the National Scientific and Research Board (Finance Division, 1991:145).

The Education Policy 1992-2002 plans a more than 100 percent increase in the enrollment of university education by opening 4 universities in the public sector and 16 universities in the private sector. The total enrollment will be almost doubled from the present 86,000 to 186,000 and the total number of universities will have increased from 23 to 43. The increased enrollment will push the present participation rate of 0.9 percent to 2.0 percent in the year 2002. Universities will be encouraged to generate funds by various means and will be provided a sizeable endowment, to enable them to move towards financial self-sufficiency and financial autonomy. More powers will be given to the University Grants Commission to oversee the academic standards, financial management and development of universities. More funds will be provided to universities for research. The performance of Area Study Centers, Pakistan Study Centers and Centers of Excellence will be reviewed, and new centers of advanced studies in modern disciplines of science and technology will be established.

At the degree college level, the Education Policy calls for an increase in the number of colleges from 359 in 1992 to 795 in 2002, and for an increase in the present enrollment from 0.142 million to 0.267 million. This will increase the present enrollment ratio from 2.8 percent to 5.0 percent. Degree level education will be restructured and diversified. Degree level colleges will be made more autonomous and the feasibility of setting up a separate Funding Council for Colleges in each Province will be considered.

A National Council of Academic Awards (NCAA) will be established to regulate academic affairs of those degree-awarding institutions which are not affiliated with the universities. At the higher secondary level, 400 intermediate colleges are expected to be added to the present 545 colleges in order to raise the present level of enrollment from 0.45 million to 0.832 million by the end of 2002 thus raising the participation rate from 7.3 percent in 1992 to 14 percent.

Education is on a gender-separated basis in almost all schools through the college level. At the graduate level, universities are coeducational. For more than three decades conservatives have demanded that separate universities for women be established. The issue reached a crescendo in 1982 when President Zia, the Chief Martial Law Administrator, came out in support of separate universities for women. Several plans were developed by Dr. M. Afzal, Chairman of the University Grants Commission, but the matter was temporarily resolved when the Ministry of Finance failed to include funds in the budget for the opening of new women's universities. The matter has been highly controversial from the start, with many women leaders strongly opposed to the idea, feeling that such institutions would, at best, be second rate. Since then, the issue has become moot.[31]

Conclusion

The prevailing condition of education in Pakistan warrants the conclusion that education has a priority claim over the scarce national resources for several reasons: (1) there is enough evidence that education has a positive impact on socioeconomic and political development of a country; (2) in Pakistan, basic or elementary education has remained severely neglected in the past, (3) the issue of development of education must be approached with a sense of urgency or 'crisis' if Pakistan seeks to emerge from its current condition of poverty and ignorance to compete with the new realities of a twenty-first century world that will be much more complex than what we have today and awash with scientific and technological sophistication accessible only to the societies which are at least 'literate'. Therefore, the challenge facing Pakistan is not only to change the largely uneducated masses of this country into a literate nation by the turn of this century but also to lay the foundations for a truly prosperous and egalitarian society equipped with scientific and technological knowledge to face the future. The recent plans and policies are filled with comprehensive schemes with innovative features, which, if effectively implemented, may potentially transform Pakistani society from its less developed and illiterate status to a literate and prosperous nation.

The views expressed in this chapter are those of the author and do not represent those of the Government of Pakistan, where the author works as Assistant Educational Advisor in the Federal Ministry of Education.

Notes

1. Lockheed, Marlaine E., Adriaan M. Verspoor et al. *Improving Primary Education in Developing Countries*. The World Bank, Oxford University Press, New York, 1991, p. 2.
2. *Ibid.*
3. Fagerlind, Ingemar, and Lawrence J. Saha, *Education and National Development: A Comparative Perspective*, 2nd edition, Pergamon Press, New York, 1989, p. 29.
4. Fagerlind and Saha, p. 30.
5. *Ibid.*
6. *Ibid.*

7. Fagerlind and Saha, p. 3.
8. Lockheed, et al., p. 3.
9. Psacharopoulos, George, "Returns to Education: A Further International Update and Implications," in *Journal of Human Resources*, 1985, Vol. XX, pp. 583-604.
10. Lockheed, et al., p. 3.
11. *Ibid.*
12. Cited in Fagerlind and Saha, p. 43.
13. Coleman, James S. (ed.), *Education and Political Development*, Princeton: Princeton University Press, 1965, p. 3.
14. Coleman, p. 15.
15. Fagerlind and Saha, p. 124.
16. Lockheed, et al., p. 4.
17. *Ibid.*
18. *Ibid.*
19. Planning Commission, Social Action Program 1992-1995, Policy Planning Section, Planning Commission, Government of Pakistan, Islamabad, April 1992, p. 7.
20. *Human Development Report 1992*, United Nations Development Program (UNDP), New York, 1992, Table 15,pp. 156-7.
21. The public expenditure figures are derived from *The Pakistan Economic Survey, 1991-92*, p. 149.
22. Planning Commission, *Social Action Program, 1992-1995*, Policy Planning Section, Islamabad: Government of Pakistan, 1992, p. 47.
23. Planning Commission, 1992: 89.
24. Planning Commission, 1992: 47.
25. Planning Commission, 1992: 96.
26. Planning Commission, 1992: 120.
27. Ministry of Education, *(Draft) Education Policy, 1992-2002*, presented by the Minister of Education on December 20, 1992. Government of Pakistan, Islamabad, p. 2.
28. Korson, J. Henry, "Bhutto's Educational Reform," in J. Henry Korson, ed., *Contemporary Problems of Pakistan*, (Leiden: E.J. Brill, 1974), pp. 119-146.
29. World Bank, *Pakistan: Education Sector Strategy Review*, Washington D.C.: The World Bank, 1988, Report No. 7110-PAK.
30. Unesco, Education for All, 1992.
31. Korson, J. Henry, "Higher Education and the Status of Women in Pakistan," unpublished paper given at the Association for Asian Studies Meeting, Washington, D.C., March 19, 1989. See also, J. Henry Korson and Michelle Maskiell, "Islamization and Social Policy in Pakistan: The Constitutional Crisis and the Status of Women," *Asian Survey*, XXV, 6, 1985.

References

Coleman, James S. (Ed.), *Education and Political Development.* (New Jersey: Princeton University Press, 1965).

Fagerlind, Ingemar, and Lawrence J. Saha, *Education and National Development: A Comparative Perspective.* 2nd Edition, (New York: Pergamon Press, 1989).

Finance Division, *Economic Survey 1990-91* (Islamabad: Government of Pakistan, 1991).

Finance Division, *Economic Survey 1991-92* (Islamabad: Government of Pakistan, 1992).

Korson, J. Henry, "Bhutto's Educational Reform," in J. Henry Korson, ed., *Contemporary Problems of Pakistan*, (Leiden: E.J. Brill, 1974).

Korson, J. Henry, and Michelle Maskiell, "Islamization and Social Policy in Pakistan: The Constitutional Crisis and the Status of Women," *Asian Survey*, XXV, 6, 1985.

Lockheed, Marlaine E., Adriaan M. Verspoor et al., *Improving Primary Education in Developing Countries.* The World Bank (New York: Oxford University Press, 1991).

Ministry of Education, *Action Plan for Education Development 1983-1988* (Islamabad: Government of Pakistan, 1984.

Ministry of Education, *(Draft) Education Policy 1992-2002*, presented by the Minister of Education on December 20, 1992. Government of Pakistan, Islamabad.

Planning Commission, *Seventh Five Year Plan and Perspective Plan 1983-2003*, (Islamabad: Government of Pakistan, December 1988).

Planning Commission, *Final Evaluation of the Sixth Five Year Plan (1983-1988*), (Islamabad: Government of Pakistan, 1990).

Planning Commission, *Social Action Program 1992-1995.* Policy Planning Section, (Islamabad: Government of Pakistan, 1992), p. 47.

Psacharopoulos, G., "Returns to Education: A Further International Update and Implications," in *Journal of Human Resources*, 1985, Vol. XX, pp. 583-604.

Tan, Jee-Peng and Alain Mingat, *Education in Asia: A Comparative Study of Costs and Financing*, World Bank Regional and Sectoral Studies (Washington, D.C.: The World Bank, 1992).

UNESCO, *National Studies: Pakistan, Asia-Pacific Program of Education for All (APPEAL)*, UNESCO Principal Regional Office for Asia and the Pacific (Bangkok: UNESCO, 1991).

United Nations Development Program (UNDP), *Human Development Report 1991* (New York: Oxford University Press, 1991).

United Nations Development Program (UNDP), *Human Development Report 1992* (New York: Oxford University Press, 1992).

World Bank, *Financing Education in Developing Countries: An Exploration of Policy Options* (Washington, D.C: The World Bank, 1986).

World Bank, *Pakistan: Education Sector Strategy Review* (Washington, D.C: The World Bank, 1988). Report No. 7110-PAK, p. 91.

World Bank, *Higher Education and Scientific Research for Development in Pakistan*, Vol. II, (Washington, D.C.: The World Bank, February 1990), Report No. 8231-PAK.

World Bank, *Vocational and Technical Education and Training: A World Bank Policy Paper* (Washington, D.C.: The World Bank, 1991).

World Bank, *World Development Report 1992* (New York: Oxford University Press, 1992).

5

The Transformation of the Women's Movement in Pakistan

Anita M. Weiss

There are many things that a state may do to raise the ire of its people: it might increase taxes, it might imprison moral men, or it might make alliances with a recent enemy. Rarely in history has a state's actions against its *women* caused political turmoil and widespread unrest. But such was the result of the implementation of General Zia ul-Haq's Islamization program in Pakistan which facilitated the transformation of the women's movement in the country.

Women in Pakistan have banded together only recently to emerge as an important political movement. While there has been a collective voice through which women have been speaking in the public realm throughout this century, the nature of this voice changed in the 1980s due to shifting power relations within both the family and the state. The women's movement was finally able to broaden its scope beyond social welfare orientations and being a "moral conscience," to materialize also as a viable political movement. While elite women were at the forefront initially, the movement's base of support gradually has become more widespread concomitant with its extent.

Many stereotypes regarding women's roles and power in Pakistan exist in the west. Images of women living within veils, wholly dependent on men for sustenance cloud the reality of the lives of some Pakistani women, particularly elites. Gender inequity, while just one more type of inequity confronted by the "have-nots" in Pakistan, is not a major issue within wealthier families. Of course, this is not to say it does not exist, but rather its power within elite families is relatively weak.

For example, we can argue that because of gender inequities, 51 percent of all primary school age boys are enrolled in classes but only 28 percent of females in that age group are, a ratio of about two to one. The inequity becomes even greater when we look at who attends secondary school: 26 percent of eligible boys versus only 11 percent of eligible girls, a ratio of almost three to one (World Bank, 1988:280). However, when we look at tertiary education -- who attends colleges and universities in Pakistan -- gender discrepancies are lessened as the majority are elites, and the ratio again becomes two to one (UNDP, 1990:152).

In South Asia, there have been a number of reforms and movements which have affected Muslim women in the last century. These have been largely in the realm of family and inheritance law, and in promoting women's education and improved access to health care. The reality of their implementation has mostly affected elite women, those whose families either aspire to be "western" or "modern," and have had minimal impact on the lives of the majority of Pakistani women.

One link which ties most of the older reform movements together is that their most vocal advocates were men. We must remember that the pre-independence Muslim women's movement began as an offshoot of both the larger social reform movement in British India and of the growing Muslim nationalist movement. Muslim women in the nineteenth century did not have to contend with such social issues as abolishing *sati*[1] or promoting widow remarriage as did Hindu reformers, easing some of the extreme restrictions on women's activities associated with *purdah*, restricting polygamy, and ensuring women's legal rights under Islamic law.

Sir Syed Ahmad Khan's Mohammedan Educational Conference, which began promoting modern education for Muslims in the 1870s, included many of the earliest proponents of female education and of raising women's social status in the wider society. As tended to be the case in many other parts of Asia at the time, these advocates for social reform were men. Girls' schools, such as those opened by the Anjuman-e-Himayat-e-Islam (Society for the Promotion of Islam) in Lahore in 1885, were initially introduced to preserve "the Islamic values of life" and promoted female education within a religious framework that included tailoring and cooking courses as compulsory subjects (Mirza, 1969:16-21). It wasn't until 1896 that a woman's section of the Mohammedan Educational Conference was formed, followed three years later with the opening of the first girls' teacher training school (Mumtaz and Shaheed, 1987:36). More Muslim girls' schools were opened in the first decade of this century, but the progress was slow. By 1921, only four out of every thousand Muslim females had enjoyed the benefits of education (Mirza, 1969:26).

It was in the context of promoting education that a Muslim woman's words addressed a public gathering for the first time in the subcontinent. In 1903, a Parsi woman read aloud a paper by Chand Begum to the Mohammedan Educational Congress in Bombay. In it, Chand Begum had urged support for the fledgling female education movement and for its followers to spurn the ideas of *maulvis* who opposed it.[2] In their book, *Women of Pakistan: Two Steps*

Forward, One Step Back?, Khawar Mumtaz and Farida Shaheed, founding members of the Women's Action Forum, argue that:

> it is interesting to note that then (in 1903) as now (in 1985), Muslim women distinguished between Islam and what was being usurped or denied by religious orthodoxy in the name of Islam (1987:40).

But this move in 1903 did more than support women's education; it was a symbolic move outside of the bonds stipulated by traditional views of purdah. It was a small step in transforming the very idea of purdah, of that symbolic curtain which separates the world of men from the world of women. Indeed, many writers and social groups ostensibly came to promote female literacy while in effect they were advocating enhancing women's rights.

The nationalist struggle also tore at the threads in that curtain. Two important groups were soon established: the politically-oriented All-India Muslim Ladies Conference consisting of elite women who were, by and large, wives of leaders active in the Muslim League, and the social reform-oriented Anjuman-e-Khawateen-e-Islam, which was the precursor for other social welfare-oriented women's groups.

The Khilafat movement and the role of women in it -- specifically that of Abadi Begum (better known as Bi Amman) as spokeswoman for her imprisoned sons in 1917 -- began to tug at that curtain further. Bi Amman would address male crowds as her brothers and sons, skillfully using acceptable notions of kinship for a political cause. Sarfaraz Hussain Mirza (1969:32), in documenting the role played by women in the Pakistan movement, regards Bi Amman:

> as the only woman leader in the subcontinent who played a major role in awakening the Muslims and especially women in the country. . . .It was on account of her active participation in the movement that the masses resorted to follow her footsteps.

The Muslim nationalism advocated by the Khilafat movement spoke to all Muslims -- *men and women alike* -- for the first time. While remaining within the bounds of tradition, the precedent was being established to challenge purdah itself.[3] Begum Jahan Ara Shah Nawaz further advanced this sentiment in a memorandum that she and Mrs. Subbarayan of Madras submitted at the first Round-Table Conference in 1930-31 (Mirza, 1969:35), imploring that:

> the question of women's political status would receive consideration by the Conference. . . .They wanted the assurance of equal rights and obligations for all citizens without any bar on account of sex.

Although there was some dissent, the Muslim League agreed to support this demand the following year.

What we have seen is that in the gradual building up of support for a Muslim homeland, women's roles were being questioned and their empowerment was being linked to the larger issues of the education and advancement of the entire Muslim community, as well as nationalism and independence. Another assertion of the Muslim community's right to determine the family laws under which they would live was realized in 1937 with the enactment of the Muslim Personal Law. This reversed earlier attempts by the British to anglicize many civil laws which had resulted in the loss of certain rights, such as the right of Muslim women to inherit property, as ordained in the Qur'an.

Elite women remained an important part of the independence struggle, writing and demonstrating as members of the Women's Section of the Muslim League, partaking in civil disobedience as members of the Women's National Guard, and as candidates in the 1946 elections. Lady Maratab Ali, the matriarch of a powerful Punjabi family, is quoted as having said in 1942:

> The days have gone when Punjab's Muslim women were considered fit only for cooking food and minding children. It is now essential for them to take an equal share of responsibility with their menfolks in the field of politics. (as quoted in Mumtaz and Shaheed, 1987:45)

Mohammed Ali Jinnah also actively urged women to support the nationalist movement. Such public activities -- in the wake of the immediate crisis at hand -- were barely questioned by anyone. These women's actions, however, had important consequences for societal norms and values, and enabled women's activities outside the home to be regarded as acceptable. Mumtaz and Shaheed (1987:47) argue that:

> the nationalist struggle provided the environment in which Muslim women broke through traditional rules and restrictions, cast off their veils, left their homes, approached strangers, confronted the police, and entered politics.

We see a significant shift at this juncture, when women began to advocate for female education and question the social institution of polygamy. After independence was achieved in 1947, elite women, particularly those holding political positions, continued to advocate women's political empowerment through such efforts as their successful mobilization of support for the Muslim Personal Law of Shariat (1948), which recognized a woman's right to inherit all forms of property, and their futile attempt to have the government include a Charter of Women's Rights in the 1956 Constitution. Women's groups actively championed the most important sociolegal reform empowering women, the 1961

Family Laws Ordinance regulating marriage and divorce, which was enacted during Ayub Khan's martial law government.

After the creation of the State of Pakistan, the women's movement came to be associated with social reform activities. In particular, until the early 1980s, it was strongly identified in the public eye with APWA, the All Pakistan Women's Association, headed by the late Begum Ra'ana Liaquat Ali, the widow of the country's first Prime Minister.

Begum Ra'ana initially founded the Women's Voluntary Service in 1948, which channeled women volunteers' energies into relief work (such as medical aid and food distribution to refugees coming from India) and social welfare projects. In February, 1949 in Karachi, she convened a conference, attended by over a thousand active Women's Voluntary Service workers, which culminated in the formation of APWA. It was to be a voluntary, non-political organization for adult Pakistani women, encouraging their participation both as facilitators and as beneficiaries. Its goals were to create:

> educational, social and cultural consciousness amongst [Pakistani women] and improving opportunities for participation in economic development. (Mumtaz and Shaheed, 1987:52)

It was -- and remains -- largely urban-oriented and concerned with establishing specific projects such as health and family planning clinics, hospitals, industrial homes and related income-generating activities, schools and colleges. APWA's popularity as a viable, important and legitimate organization enabled it to become acceptable for middle and upper class women to participate in its activities. A part of APWA's mandate is to work to raise women's status and rights, and this occasionally led its members to participate in lesser known politically-focussed activities. For example, in 1953, APWA recommended that ten seats for women be reserved in the National Assembly and in each Provincial Assembly, and it actively supported the passage of the 1961 Family Laws Ordinance.

Begum Ra'ana also took the initiative to form other women's organizations after independence, including the Karachi Business and Professional Women's Club (1954), and the Pakistan Federation of University Women (1956), both of which became affiliated with APWA and later expanded. The Federation of University Women was instrumental in establishing a degree college for women in Karachi. These and other women's organizations were oriented toward women's personal empowerment, and specifically that which could be achieved through education and income-generating activities. Small numbers of women were involved, but larger political issues were rarely addressed. APWA's concerns were oriented toward social welfare and it essentially took no political sides, which enabled it to remain virtually unaffected by changes occurring in the national government.

I feel it is important to note here that a woman, Fatima Jinnah, unsuccessfully ran against Ayub Khan in Pakistan's 1965 presidential elections. This, however, was not the result of the mobilization of women's support, but was rather due to the Combined Opposition Parties' decision that she, the sister of Quaid-i-Azam Mohammed Ali Jinnah, was the candidate most likely to defeat Ayub Khan. Maulana Maududi, leader of the very conservative Jama'at-i-Islami and an outspoken political opponent of Ayub Khan, supported Fatima Jinnah's candidacy by issuing a *fatwa* (religious edict) that under "extraordinary circumstances" a woman could hold such a political office.[4] Although Fatima Jinnah was a national female candidate, she was not associated with women's issues nor actively supported by an organized women's movement.

The 1970s was an important decade for women's organizations when women and other previously disenfranchised groups became politicized in larger numbers. Begum Nusrat Bhutto was one of the co-introducers of the Convention for the Elimination of Discrimination against Women at the United Nations in 1973, an act symbolizing that Pakistan saw itself at the forefront of initiatives empowering women worldwide.[5] Pakistani women began entering the work force and government service in unprecedented numbers (albeit still marginally compared to men). Few women then could have imagined that less than a decade later a basic right -- the right to testify when a lone woman observed a person commit a crime -- might legally be taken away from them with the passage of the *Qanoon-e-Shahadat*, the Law of Evidence.

The Zia ul-Haq government implemented an Islamization program in February, 1979 which was to have a strong effect on mobilizing women, virtually forcing them to become social activists in order to defend their fundamental rights. The early 1980s witnessed the emergence of grassroots women's groups organized in response to the potential harshness and repression which many of the proposed laws could have on women. Cries of discrimination against women were initially raised in response to the 1979 "Enforcement of *Hudood* Ordinances," when women lifted the veil of silence which had fallen over Pakistan since the 1979 execution of former Prime Minister Zulfikar Ali Bhutto. Fledgling women's groups contended that the Ordinance failed to distinguish between adultery (*zina*) and rape (*zina-bil-jabr*) and that its enforcement was discriminatory.

This was followed by unprecedented protests organized in 1983-84 by such groups as the Women's Action Forum (WAF) and the Pakistan Women Lawyers' Association (PWLA) against the then-proposed Qanoon-e-Shahadat, which many felt did not give equal weight to men's and women's legal testimony. Protesters feared that women might be restricted from testifying in certain kinds of hudood cases (such as when they were the sole witness to their father's or husband's murder), and that their testimony in other matters would be irrelevant unless corroborated by another woman. Responding to the debate,

Begum Syeda Abida Hussain, Chairman of the Jhang District Council and the sole directly elected female member of the National Assembly, said that women in Pakistan were in the midst of fighting the biggest *jihad* (holy war) in history, and that "Islam enjoins rights and responsibilities on Muslim women which are not subject to any dispute."[6] [Begum Syeda Abida Hussain is currently the Pakistan Ambassador to the United States.] The ensuing protests delayed promulgation of the Qanoon-e-Shahadat for nearly two years, and resulted in the final version which called for the testimony of two women being equal to that of one man in financial cases. In other instances, acceptance of one woman's testimony has been left to the discretion of the presiding judge.

An important break with the past occurred when women themselves organized (or expanded) groups such as the *Khawateen Mahaz-e-Amal* (Women's Action Forum, WAF), the Pakistan Women Lawyers' Association (PWLA) and the Business and Professional Women's Association in the early 1980s. This was followed by the establishment of research-oriented activist groups, such as the Aurat Foundation, Simorgh and Shirkat Gah. These groups -- headed by women -- prompted unprecedented private and public discourse about the position of women in Islam and women's roles in a modern Islamic state. Significantly, they revealed the inherent controversy emerging in Pakistan's rapidly changing society: whether or not women and men were to be regarded by the state as equal economic actors and the extent to which parliamentary and civil rights found in the West are applicable in a modern Muslim context.

Perhaps the most important women's group which has facilitated the transformation of the larger women's movement in Pakistan is the Women's Action Forum (WAF), or Khawateen Mahaz-e-Amal. The WAF was organized in 1981 by women in Karachi, Lahore and Islamabad on the principal of collective leadership, specifically in response to the Hudood Ordinance and other potentially discriminatory laws and to strengthen women's position in the society. It provided a venue for women, most of them from elite families, to band together and formulate policy statements as well as engage in political action to safeguard women's legal position.

The WAF Charter begins with a 1944 quote from Pakistan's founding father, Quaid-i-Azam Mohammed Ali Jinnah, in which he explicitly supports the empowerment of women and their participation in a wide range of pre-independence nationalist movements:

> No nation can rise to the height of glory unless your women are side by side with you, we are victims of evil customs. It is a crime against humanity that our women are shut up within the four walls of the houses as prisoners. There is no sanction anywhere for the deplorable condition in which our women have to live. You should take your women along

> with you as comrades in every sphere of life. (as quoted in Mumtaz and Shaheed, 1987:183)

The Charter asserts that WAF is "committed to protecting and promoting the rights of women by countering all forms of oppression" by being a consciousness raising group as well as a lobby cum pressure group so as to create a heightened awareness of women's rights and mobilize support for promoting these rights, as well as "counter adverse propaganda against women."

WAF members, supported by women from various other women's groups, organized marches in early 1983 in Lahore and Karachi to protest the passage of the Law of Evidence in the *Majlis-i-Shura* (consultative assembly) and its recommendation to the President. The female demonstrators argued that the proposed Law of Evidence was not the only acceptable evidence law in Islam, and that criteria for witnesses as stated in the Qur'an are possession of sight, memory, and the ability to communicate; as long as witnesses have these, testimony should be equally weighed regardless of gender. After police beat some of the female demonstrators with *lathis* (batons) in Lahore on February 12, 1983, politically diverse groups denounced the assault on the women.

Heated disputes also erupted over the highly discriminatory way in which punishments were meted out to women who could be proven guilty through medical examinations, or from becoming pregnant following a rape, while men were often acquitted due to lack of evidence. The argument forwarded by women's groups was that besides making a woman suffer twice, the use of an illegitimate birth as a criterion for a woman's "self-confession" was discriminatory as it could not be used for men.[7] Yet it is nearly impossible to prove a man's guilt without his verbal confession, for what four *salah* (pious) Muslim men would stand by and let a woman be raped?

At WAF's second National Convention in Karachi in July 1983, its membership reiterated the organization's aims and objectives: that most importantly it was to be a consciousness-raising group remaining non-political, non-governmental and non-aligned. They also protested against the government's failure to place adequate resources at the disposal of various development programs which focus on women. In the Fall of 1983, the WAF and other women's groups organized demonstrations throughout the country to protest both the Qanoon-e-Shahadat and the public flogging of women. The following year, in 1984, the now separate WAF groups mounted a campaign against the promulgation of the proposed Qisas and Diyat Ordinance (Retaliation and Blood Money). This was successful at the time as the Zia government never enacted it (although the Nawaz Sharif government raised it again as an issue in 1991).

While APWA had always acted as an interest group promoting the uplifting of women, its emphasis had changed in the 1970s when it began to promote women's integration in the development process and expanded work opportunities for poorer women. In the 1980s, its public image underwent an additional transformation when it supported many of WAF's activities and many of their demands for women's rights. In September 1983, Begum Ra'ana publicly opposed certain aspects of the government's Islamization program and criticized some clauses of the Ansari Commission's report as being "repugnant to the Holy Qur'an and Islam, which gives women equal rights with men in all public matters."[8] At the end of the United Nations' Decade for Women in 1985, she assessed its impact on Pakistan and stated that:

> . . .we the women of Pakistan find that in spite of the progress we have made, we are still dispossessed of equal rights and equal opportunities. . . .I categorically state Islam affords complete equality of men and women. That instead of being wrongly associated with total suppression, severe physical punishments and denial of human rights, in Islam every principle is to be tempered with understanding, justice, a sense of brotherhood and forgiveness. I, therefore, assert that it is necessary to repeal certain laws and to enact new legislation which will give women their due rights and a challenging stake in the destiny of Pakistan.[9]

APWA took a strong stand and passed resolutions against "discriminatory laws which falsely claim to be based on Islam" and publicly noted "with anxiety" that crimes and violence against women had been on the increase and that the government must implement a crash program to raise female literacy levels. For example, at its Triennial Conference in Lahore in 1982, APWA supported the group's demand that the government establish a Commission on the Status of Women; after which the government did so. That a woman of Begum Ra'ana's stature so strongly supported the women's activist groups gave them and their demands greater credibility in the eyes of many Pakistanis.

By the end of martial law in December 1985, the women's movement had established a firm foundation of opposition to potentially discriminatory laws. It went on to challenge the Shariat Bill and the Ninth Amendment in 1986. Allied with twenty-eight organizations representing lawyers, trade unions, students, cultural and literary bodies, leaders of the women's movement issued a joint statement in August 1986 opposing the Shariat Bill on the grounds that it negated principles of justice, democracy and fundamental rights of citizens, and that it would give rise to sectarianism and divide the country. In November 1986, at WAF's third National Convention in Islamabad, its members established a Legal Aid Cell for indigent women and to help women who had been discriminated against.[10] In early January of 1987, ten women's organizations in Lahore passed a resolution protesting against the Ninth Amendment, considering it "extremely injurious" to the rights and status of women in Pakistan.[11] WAF members also actively opposed the gendered segregation of universities.

WAF and other supporting organizations were not small, fanatical groups on the fringe of society, but rather consisted of urban women -- mostly elites -- from influential families. Indeed, political parties started placing new emphasis on their women's wings, perhaps inadvertently encouraging the emergence of Benazir Bhutto and Syeda Abida Hussain as important national political figures.

Meanwhile, women's status was being lessened by proposed legislation; incidents of violence against women were on the increase throughout the country. While rape in the past had mostly been confined to vendettas between the men of different families, anonymous rapes were becoming more common. WAF played an active role by issuing statements condemning incidents of violence against women and bringing them to the attention of the public. Women's groups countered that it was no coincidence that as women were increasingly being denied legal safeguards by the state, they were also increasingly becoming targets of violence. By organizing processions and issuing press releases, they argued that the police had become unable to control the mounting crimes against women, as evidenced by four cases of rape occurring in Karachi in January 1987 alone (Irshad, 1987). Protest riots broke out in Pakistan's major cities: female demonstrators were charged by police in Karachi, while others set their veils ablaze in Lahore.

At the same time, a controversial delegation led by Salma Ahmed (former Secretary of the Women's Division) was addressing the United Nations' Commission on the Status of Women in New York. It was controversial in that two female members of the National Assembly had refused to join the delegation, protesting that "women had no status to speak of in the country." But the official delegation assured the United Nations that the government of Pakistan was working towards promoting the full participation of women in all spheres of life. *Viewpoint*'s January 14th edition includes an account of what was occurring in Pakistan while Mrs. Ahmad praised the government's efforts at the U.N.:

> . . . .Meanwhile, the women of Lahore advanced toward the barricades again, and faced the three-deep line of riot police. Young men attempting solidarity were pushed back by raised lathis.

Women protesting in front of the Sindh Assembly were also attacked by police with lathis, prompting additional public outcry.

At the time of Zia ul-Haq's death in August 1988, a number of outstanding draft laws which the women's movement had protested against had never been promulgated. Greatly increased access to education, the workplace, and the reins of political power enabled more women to be active in the public sphere.

Significant change in popular opinion regarding women had occurred in the country by then, prompted by many things, not the least of which was the person of Benazir Bhutto as the symbolic and actual leader of the opposition to the military government for a decade. While in 1983 women's organized protests enjoyed little public support, the victorious Pakistan People's Party had included the empowerment of women as a key theme in its manifesto released in November 1988 for the national elections. In December 1988, an important shift occurred in the paradigms of power when Benazir Bhutto and her Pakistan People's Party (PPP) formed a government. The head of state was no longer the antagonist, his cabinet a bastion of support for repressive laws vis-a-vis women. Instead, the new head of state, Benazir Bhutto, became an important symbol: a political leader as well as a woman fulfilling her familial roles. The women's movement had to respond to the challenge to transform itself again and confront the important task of lobbying a more sympathetic government. Their first priority was to get the government either to amend or repeal existing laws which are discriminatory towards women, most of which were promulgated under the former government's Islamization program. The Ministry for Women's Development had compiled a list of such laws, but activists contended that because of the Eighth Amendment restrictions on repealing laws passed under the martial law government, it was difficult for the government to garner two-thirds support in the National Assembly to push through such repeals. Additionally, women's groups tried to lobby to get the government to introduce new laws which would further empower women, continuing in the spirit of the PPP's November 1988 Manifesto.

However, within a few months of the PPP coming to power, women's groups realized that they were still fighting an uphill battle. While the platform on which the party had won favored women's empowerment, most individual members of the provincial and national assemblies remained entrenched in patriarchal views of women's place in society. The new listeners to convince were no longer the national political leaders but rather the local political elites within the system, the ones upon whom the PPP was dependent for political support and survival.

With the displacement of that government in 1990, the women's movement found itself once again in opposition to a government that was set on scape-goating women's modesty issues (hence its support and eventual passage of the Shariat Bill in the spring of 1991) to deflect public attention away from more serious economic and infrastructural matters. Finding itself unable to secure a national public voice, the women's movement shifted its concerns to three goals: to secure women's political representation in the parliament; to work to raise women's consciousness, particularly in the realm of family planning, and to counter suppression by issuing unified statements on events as they occur in an effort to raise public awareness.

The women's movement is also spawning a new generation of female activists, young women who have grown up in an environment (the 1980s) when women -- members of WAF, APWA, and other organizations -- have been active in creating a new movement. An example of this new activism can be seen in the demonstration by girls in 1989 against the government of Punjab's decision to limit medical college admissions to gender quotas (which are substantially lower for females than for males) -- and to disallow merit altogether as a basis for admission. While there is a long heritage of male university students taking out processions and demonstrating, this is a new phenomenon for female students.

The women's movement continues to make important contributions in the arena of public and private discourse. Virtually every newspaper today has a section devoted to women's issues emphasizing women's legal rights or employment-related matters, often written by a member of WAF or similar women's group. As public alienation grows in the light of political unrest, kidnapping, allegations of torture cells run by political parties, there seems to be a refreshing awareness on the part of a growing number of people that for Pakistan to progress, women must be incorporated into the changes. That the women's movement continues to make important connections between what is beneficial for Pakistan in general and Pakistani women in particular is one of the most significant contributions it can make at this time of social turmoil and change.

This chapter is based on research conducted for a larger study by the author, "The Consequences of State Policy for Women in Pakistan," in Myron Weiner and Ali Banuazizi (eds.), *The Politics of Social Transformation in Afghanistan, Iran and Pakistan*, Syracuse University Press, 1993.

Notes

1. Suttee, a former Hindu practice whereby a widow immolated herself on the funeral pyre of her husband.

2. Gail Minault (1983) has documented important events and issues which occurred in the promotion of Muslim female education in pre-Partition India.

3. For further discussion on the precedent established by women active in the Khilafat movement, refer to Gail Minault, 1980: 202.

4. For more detailed discussion and analysis of this, refer to Mumtaz and Shaheed, 1987: 60.

5. This was six years before the General Assembly approved the Convention and opened it up to signature, ratification and accession, which the Zia government then refused to attest.

6. As quoted in *The Muslim*, February 17, 1983.

7. It is interesting that this kind of evidence was explicitly omitted from a similar law enforced in the Islamic Republic of Iran.

8. *Dawn*, September 5, 1983. The Ansari Commission was assembled in 1982 with the purpose of informing the President as to which aspects of existing laws and social mores were repugnant to Islam.

9. All Pakistan Women's Association, "The U.N. Woman's Development Decade -- Its Relevance to Pakistan" (Karachi: Victoria Printing Works) 1985: 4.

10. Najma Sadeque "WAF Marches On!" *The Star*, November 27, 1986.

11. *Viewpoint*, January 15, 1987, p. 15.

References

Carroll, Lucy. "Nizam-i-Islam: Process and Conflicts in Pakistan's Programme of Islamization, with Special Reference to the Position of Women," *Journal of Commonwealth and Comparative Politics*, 20 (1982): 57-95.

Chhachhi, Amrita. "The State, Religious Fundamentalism and Women: Trends in South Asia," working paper, Subseries on Women, History and Development: Themes and Issues, No. 8, Institute of Social Studies, The Hague, September 1988.

Irshad, Sairah. "A License to Rape?," *The Herald Magazine*, 18, 2, Karachi, February 1987, pp. 93-96.

Jayawardena, Kumari. *Feminism and Nationalism in the Third World*, London, 1986.

Lateef, Shahida. *Muslim Women in India: Political and Private Realities: 1890s-1980s*, London, 1990.

Metcalf, Barbara Daly. *Perfecting Women: Maulana Ashraf Ali Thanvi's Bihishti Zewar: A Partial Translation with Commentary*, Berkeley, 1990.

Minault, Gail. "Political Change: Muslim Women in Conflict with Parda: Their Role in the Indian Nationalist Movement," in *Asian Women in Transition*, edited by Sylvia Chipp and Justin Green, College Park, 1980, pp. 194-203.

Minault, Gail, Shaikh Abdullah, and Begum Abdullah Sharif, "Education for Girls at Aligarh," in *Modernization and Social Change Among Muslims in India*, edited by Imtiaz Ahmad, Delhi, 1983, pp. 207-236.

Mirza, Sarfaraz Hussain. *Muslim Women's Role in the Pakistan Movement*, Lahore, 1969.

Mumtaz, Khawar, and Farida Shaheed. *Women of Pakistan: Two Steps Forward, One Step Back?*, London and Karachi, 1987.

Pakistan Commission on the Status of Women. "Report of the Commission on the Status of Women in Pakistan," Islamabad, 1986.

United Nations Development Project, 1990.

Weiss, Anita M. "Benazir Bhutto and the Future of Women in Pakistan," *Asian Survey* 30, No. 5 (May 1990): 433-445.

-------------- "Implications of the Islamization Program for Women," in *Islamic Reassertion in Pakistan: The Application of Islamic Laws in a Modern State*, edited by Anita Weiss, Syracuse, 1986, pp. 97-110.

Women's Action Forum. "Law of Evidence -- WAF (National) Position Paper," Women's Action Forum, Lahore Chapter, 1983.

Women's Action Forum. "Law of *Qisas* and *Diyat* as Proposed by the Council of Islamic Ideology -- Position Paper of WAF (National)," Women's Action Forum, Lahore Chapter, February 1984.

Women's Division, Government of Pakistan. *Women in Pakistan: A Statistical Profile*, Islamabad, July 1985.

World Bank. *World Development Report, 1988*, Washington, D.C., 1988.

6

The Mohajirs in Sindh: A Critical Essay

Afak Haydar

Disclaimer: This is an essay written as the observations of the author rather than an article based on empirical personal research and/or the observations of others.

The author was born, raised, and educated in what was then the United Provinces (UP), British India. He immigrated to Pakistan in the summer of 1953, after completing his graduate degree in political science from Lucknow University.

He may have had prejudices against non-Muslims, particularly Hindus -- it was impossible to be raised in the communally charged environment of the United Provinces in the 1930s and the 1940s and not be influenced by the prejudices, at least subconsciously. He may also have had prejudices against the British. It was impossible to grow up in India in the 1930s and the 1940s and not learn to dislike the British imperial masters. He may also have had, at the subconscious level, some sectarian (Shia-Sunni) prejudice. This too was common in the UP of the 1930s and the 1940s. But, he had no exposure to prejudices based on ethnic or linguistic bases. The prejudices on religious or sectarian bases, if any, may have been at the subconscious level; the environment in which the author grew up was *consciously* against these prejudices.

The author immigrated to Pakistan in 1953 and started his college teaching career in Sindh at the young age of 20, and spent a total of about ten years in Sindh (1953-1960; 1961-1963 and 1968-69). He now lives happily in the United States. But, it pains him now, as it did during his years in Sindh to see the Sindhis and the *Mohajirs* drift further and further apart from each other rather than come closer to each other.

Hijrat in Islam

It appears that mankind is migratory by nature. Physical surroundings, need for more food and better shelter, ambition for greater success, the urge for newer discoveries, and need for physical and emotional security are some of the reasons that have forced mankind to migrate from place to place.

Islam accepts this natural behavior. The first *Hijrat* (migration) in Islam took place during the fifth year of the Prophet's announcement of his prophethood. Members of his own tribe, the Quraish, became very inhospitable not only to the Prophet but also and, particularly to his followers. They ostracized him and those who had accepted the new faith. Najashi, the king of Habasha (modern Ethiopia) was considered to be a tolerant, generous and kind monarch. The Prophet asked some of his followers to migrate to Habasha. This was the first migration in modern Islam.[1]

In 622 A.D., the Prophet migrated to Yathrib, renamed Madina-tun-Nabi (the city of the Prophet), now called Madina. Many people of Yathrib had accepted Islam, and they invited the Prophet and the Muslims of Mecca to immigrate to Yathrib. A large number of Muslims accepted the invitation and moved to Yathrib before the Prophet moved in 622 A.D. Many went with him; many others including his immediate family followed him.[2]

The poet-philosopher of Pakistan, Dr. Sir Mohammed Iqbal, has given an interesting, metaphysical interpretation to hijrat in Islam in general and to the migration of Prophet Mohammed from Mecca to Madina in particular.

In his *Rumooz-e-Bekhudi*, in the chapter titled "Chun Millat-e-Mohammedia Moassis Bar Tawheed O Risalat Ast, Nihayat-e-Makani Nedard," (Since the Nation of Mohammed is Based on *Tawheed* and *Risalat*, It is Not Limited by Place)[3], Iqbal insists that the spirit of Islam is not limited by place. Islam, as a way of life, as a philosophy, as an attitude on life, is universal, unrestricted by boundaries, by homelands.

To support his interpretation of Islam he provides an unusual interpretation to the Hijrat of Prophet Mohammed from his ancestral home Mecca to a new city, Madina.

Iqbal says that the philosophy of Islam is universal; it is based on *kalima*[4] (word, and not a place). He declares that the safety of the person of the Prophet was guaranteed by the Almighty -- the Prophet had a very commanding personality and his enemies were always scared of him. Iqbal says that the people have misunderstood the reason, the meaning, and the significance of Mohammed's migration. It was not to save his person; it was to teach his followers that place is not relevant at all; belief is.

The Muslim nation rests on a belief:

Hijrat Aa-een-e-Hayat-e-Muslim Ast
In Ze Asbab-e-Thabat-e-Muslim Ast

Hijrat is the fundamental law of the
life of Muslims;
It is one of the reasons of permanence
of the Muslims. [5]

At another place, in his *Payam-e-Mashriq*, in the brief poem titled "Al-mulk-o-Lillah" (To God belongs the universe), he makes a reference to an event in early Muslim history.[6] Tariq Ibn Ziyad, one of the conquerors of Spain, is reported to have burnt his boats on reaching the shores of Spain. Iqbal narrates the event in this manner:

Tariq chun bar kanara-e-
Undlus safeena sookht
Guftand kar-e-too ba nigah-e-
khirad khata'st
Dooreem az sawad-e-watan baz
chun raseem?
Tark-e-sabab ze rooey shariat
kuja rawa'st Khandeed o dast-e-kheesh ba
shamsheer burd o guft
Har mulk mulk-e-ma'st ki mulk-
e-Khudaey mas't

When Tariq burnt his boats on the shores of Undlus (Spain), they said that your (action) is wrong in the eyes of reason. We are far away from our home; how will we get back to home, does *shariat* permit the abandonment of means of help? (Tariq) smiled, put his hand on his sword, and said: Every land is our land since it is our God's land.[7]

Iqbal lauds the statement by Tariq "*Har mulk mulk-e-ma'st ki mulk-e-khudaey-e-ma'st.*" Every land is our land since it is our God's land, meaning that Muslims are not bound to a place.

Hijrat in South Asia

In 1825 many Muslims in India accepted the fatwa (religious edict) of Syed Ahmed of Rae Bareli, UP, India (1786-1831), that India was a *dar-ul-harb* and that Muslims needed either to struggle (perform *jihad*) against those who had made the life difficult for Muslims of India, or, needed to emigrate to a *dar-ul-Islam*. Afghanistan was identified as the chosen dar-ul-Islam. Ahmed was betrayed by some of his people and was killed near Balakot in modern northern Pakistan (hence, Syed Ahmed Shaheed, meaning the martyr).[8]

As a result of the partition of British India into Bharat (India) and Pakistan in 1947, and the Hindu-Sikh-Muslim riots that preceded and followed the partition, millions of Muslims left India and immigrated to Pakistan, East Pakistan (now Bangladesh) and West Pakistan. Millions of Hindus and Sikhs migrated from Pakistan to India.

It will not be wrong to say that much, perhaps all, of the migration was spontaneous, without a well-prepared (or, even an ill-prepared) plan. However, there was a logical pattern to this spontaneous migration. Linguistic, ethnic, and cultural commonality as well as geographic proximity played a vital role in establishing the migration pattern.

Most Muslims from West Bengal (because of linguistic and ethnic homogeneity as well as geographic proximity), and from Bihar, Orrisa, and Eastern United Provinces migrated to East Pakistan.

West Bengali Muslims who migrated to East Pakistan must have had little difficulty in assimilating in the local community; they just blended into the community because they spoke Bengali. Muslims who migrated from Bihar and adjacent areas in India to East Pakistan could not blend into the Bengali community. Although they were fellow Muslims, they dressed differently, they ate different foods, and most importantly, they spoke a different language -- Urdu.

They tried to maintain their Urdu-speaking mohajir identity during 1947-1970. Since the establishment of Bangladesh, many (most?) of them are forced to live as refugees in their adopted homeland. Even after two decades of independence of Bangladesh, they are the subject not only of domestic strife in Bangladesh, of bi-national tension between Bangladesh and Pakistan, but also of international tension and concern.

Most Muslims from East Punjab in India migrated to West Punjab in Pakistan. This migration of millions of Muslims was preceded, accompanied, and later followed by large scale genocide of men, women, and children, by rape of women, by abduction of women and children, by destruction and looting of personal property, and by the disintegration of family life and by dislocation of the culture.

Most East Punjabi Muslims migrants, like their West Bengali brethren in East Pakistan, were able to assimilate relatively easily into the host community because of ethnic homogeneity. Very few non-Punjabi immigrants moved to West Punjab; those who came accepted the Punjabi culture and assimilated into the host community, without major difficulties because they spoke Punjabi.[9]

The Government of Pakistan facilitated their assimilation by giving preferential treatment to the settlement of their claims for property left behind in India. Certain areas, mostly in East Punjab and the adjoining princely states, were designated as "agreed areas." Claimants from these areas were given, in satisfaction of their evacuee property claims, agricultural land and houses left behind by Hindu and Sikh migrants to India. Their claims were settled relatively easily, in contrast to claims of persons from non-agreed areas.[10]

Muslims who migrated to the province of Sindh in Pakistan constitute the subject of this essay. They came from all parts of India, mostly from the Urdu-speaking areas of the subcontinent: Bihar, the Central Province, Hyderabad Deccan and other princely states, Orrisa, Rajputana, and the United Provinces. A majority of them settled in urban areas of Sindh, mostly in Karachi and Hyderabad.

There is very little published research on the subject of mohajirs in Sindh. It is generally agreed that as they came to Sindh in the wake of the partition, they were welcomed by the local population with traditional Muslim hospitality. It must be stated that in Pakistan the Pathans and the Sindhis are known for their hospitality even to total strangers.

Some of them came by sea, but most came by the overland route by road or by trains. Most of them, particularly those who came by the land routes, reached Pakistan with little or no worldly possessions. The caravans and trains coming to Pakistan were usually the target of looting and murder by rioters enroute.

This author migrated to Pakistan in 1953 and started teaching at a college in Hyderabad, Sindh. Until the early 1950s, one heard in Sindh from the locals as well as from the mohajirs about the extremely friendly welcome given by the people of Sindh to the immigrants; it was suggested that the locals welcomed the immigrants as the *Ansars* had welcomed the Prophet and his family and friends in Madina in 622 CE (Christian Era).[11]

During 1974-75, this author recorded oral history interviews with several prominent political leaders of Sindh including the late Pir Illahi Bakhsh, former chief Minister of Sindh, and the late Kazi Mohammed Akber, former Minister in the Sindh cabinet and later Pakistan's Ambassador to Portugal.

Kazi Akber recalled his working at the Hyderabad railway station and providing the incoming refugees with food and shelter donated by the local people. The local Sindhi population had welcomed the mohajirs and people seemed to be willing to share their possessions with the immigrants. During his political career, Kazi Akber spent several years as chairman of the Hyderabad municipality, where the mohajirs have had a majority since the early days of Pakistan.

On being asked to give his views about the reasons for the discord that seemed to have developed by 1975 between the mohajirs and the Sindhis, Kazi

Akber suggested three reasons: (1) A political role played by some bureaucrats, (2) a feeling of frustration among the Sindhis caused by the inefficient operation of the one-unit system, and (3) an "unfair" role played by some public officials, political leaders as well as others, mohajirs as well as Sindhis.

Political Role of the Bureaucrats

The reader may recall that General (later, Field Marshall) Mohammed Ayub Khan, then Commander-in-Chief of the Pakistan Army, arranged for then President Iskander Mirza to overthrow the constitutionally established government of Prime Minister Firoz Khan Noon on October 8, 1958. A few days later, he removed Iskander Mirza and installed himself as the Chief Martial Law Administrator to head a martial law regime.

At the time of the military coup Ayub Khan had declared that his ultimate goal was to establish democracy in Pakistan, but the kind of democracy that the people of Pakistan could understand and work. In 1959 he established the Basic Democracies system: a pyramidal hierarchy of legislative assemblies at the village, tehsil, district, divisional, provincial and eventually the national levels, all but those at the village level elected indirectly by the next lower assembly.[12]

Ayub Khan promulgated a constitution in 1962 and held a presidential election in 1965.[13] Miss Fatima Jinnah, sister of the founder of Pakistan, the Quaid-e-Azam, Mohammed Ali Jinnah, contested the indirect election against Ayub Khan as a candidate of the Combined Opposition Parties. Ayub Khan won the election.[14]

According to Kazi Akber, Ayub Khan believed that the Basic Democracies (BD) voters in rural Sindh could be controlled through the bureaucrats and could be manipulated into voting for Ayub Khan. By contrast, he believed that the urban BD voters were mostly in favor of Miss Jinnah. He was afraid of losing his grip on the country. (It may be recalled that most urban centers in Sindh have had a mohajir majority.) This was politically unacceptable to Ayub Khan. He thought that his position was becoming weak in the country.

Whether by design or by chance, Masroor Hasan Khan, a mohajir, became Commissioner of Hyderabad division in the mid-sixties. Kazi Akber said that Masroor Hasan Khan believed that until some new issue was created for the urban BD representatives (mostly mohajir), they would not vote for Ayub Khan. He wanted to control the urban BD members as a key to controlling the urban areas.

At first he thought of controlling the urban areas through control of the University of Sindh. There was a clash between him and Hasan Ali Abdul Rehman (a Sindhi), the Vice Chancellor the operating head of the university. This clash between two persons resulted in a clash between the Urdu-speaking and the Sindhi-speaking (euphemism for mohajir and Sindhi) students.

From listening to the recorded interview, it appears to this author that Kazi Akber believed that the Vice Chancellor was not favorably inclined towards the mohajirs. He may have been anti-mohajir. He certainly showed little concern for the feelings of the mohajir students. For example, he invited G.M. Syed to speak at a university sponsored event. This, to Kazi Akber, was not a prudent act; it must have hurt the feelings of the mohajir students and it must have intensified the tensions between the Sindhi and the mohajir students.

Kazi Akber conceded that the mohajir students faced certain difficulties at the University of Sindh. For example, it was not easy for them to obtain admission to academic programs. The mohajir and the Sindhi students were divided into two camps, one supporting the Commissioner, the other supporting the Vice Chancellor, one pro-Mohajir, the other pro-Sindhi.

The situation became worse when some students (Sindhi students?) decided to march (or, ride buses) in a procession from the university campus to the city, a distance of a few miles. The Commissioner's house and office are located in the city; the campus is located a few miles away.

The Commissioner ordered the procession to be stopped by police force. The student buses were stopped, the students were beaten and some were injured. Kazi Akber said that he did not know the extent of their injuries. Some are known to have jumped into a nearby canal. This created an unpleasant atmosphere, and it started the Sindhi-mohajir rift.

The real cause was a clash of personalities and, in retrospect today, the unacceptable behavior of two persons who held important public offices in the principal urban center in Sindh outside of Karachi. Kazi Akber felt very strongly that the placement of a person who may otherwise be very qualified but may be the wrong person at a certain place at a certain time can bring about disastrous consequences. He believed that Masroor Hasan Khan was otherwise a very qualified person, but the following statement from Kazi Akber shows his dissatisfaction with the views of Masroor Hasan Khan as Commissioner of Hyderabad division at that time:

> He had this element in him. Several times he said this to me in discussions: "We have to fight for our rights; we *have to*. This is not a question of only language; it is a question of economic survival." He told me in so many words "we have to create our own place."

Kazi Akber had similar views about two otherwise very prominent Sindhi educationists: Hasan Ali Abdul Rehman, at one time Vice Chancellor of the University of Sindh, and his successor, Professor Syed Ghulam Mustafa Shah. This author has the feeling that Kazi Akber felt that both persons failed to respect the sentiments of the mohajirs in the university.

Consequences of Inefficient Operation of the One-Unit Scheme

According to Kazi Akber, a second important factor that contributed to the development of the rift between the Sindhis and the mohajirs was a feeling of frustration and alienation among the Sindhis because of an inefficient operation of the one-unit scheme.[15]

The reader will recall that East Pakistan accounted for a majority of the population of Pakistan, yet provided a small percentage of the political, military, and civil service leadership of the country. In October 1954, the political leadership (Governor General Ghulam Mohammed) of Pakistan decided to merge the four provinces of the Western wing of the country into a single unit to be given parity with East Pakistan. This newly created province was to be called West Pakistan and the scheme was generally referred to as the one-unit scheme.[16]

The leadership of Sindh was not favorably inclined towards the one-unit plan. The then chief minister, Pirzada Abdul Sattar was opposed to the plan. He was removed from chief ministership by the Governor General and was replaced by Mohammed Ayub Khuhro, who was at that time legally debarred from holding a public office. Khuhro called a session of the Sindh Legislative Assembly to meet in Hyderabad and not at the Assembly chambers in Karachi. Was he afraid that the urban masses might demonstrate against the one-unit resolution?

This author recalls vividly how the Principal of the Government College in Hyderabad pleaded successfully with the chief minister (a former student of the Principal) not to hold the session in the large assembly hall of the college. The session was held in the District Durbar Hall, and it was brief. The one-unit resolution was adopted by the Sindh Legislative Assembly without much debate. There was no declared opposition. The Sindh government had ensured that all those members of the Assembly that were opposed to the one-unit resolution were unable to attend the session: they were physically abducted by "unknown" persons or were arrested and detained on false, fabricated charges.

In short, the one-unit scheme was implemented by the Governor General, Ghulam Mohammed and his colleagues at the center despite opposition from the people and the leadership of Sindh, and perhaps all the small provinces.

Lahore, the capital of the Punjab became the capital of the new province, called West Pakistan. The provincial government operated in a highly centralized (and inefficient) manner. It is generally believed that Sindhis do not like to travel long distances. Now they had to go several hundred miles to Lahore to get routine things done that were until recently handled in Karachi. They knew few people in Lahore, still fewer in the provincial departmental offices.

This author has heard not only from Kazi Akber but another friend who was at that time Principal of a large private college in Sindh that each of them had to go to Lahore during the first year of the one-unit at least three times to get the regularly scheduled, recurring government grant-in-aid for their colleges released by the Department of Education. This author worked in three colleges during 1954-1960 and had occasion to watch the inefficient operation of the centralized bureaucratic system.

People in all three smaller provinces (Boluchistan, the North West Frontier, and Sindh) felt alienated and frustrated. According to Kazi Akber, this frustration vented itself in anti-non-Sindhi sentiments. It gave birth to the Sindhi-non-Sindhi rift in Sindh.

Role of Some Political Leaders of Sindh

According to Kazi Akber, the third factor that contributed to the growth of the Sindhi-non-Sindhi rift was the role played by certain political leaders of the area. Kazi Akber mentioned three persons by name: Nawab Muzaffar Ali Khan, Nawab Zahid Ali, and Syed Mubarak Ali Shah. Here is how Kazi Akber looked at the role of each of these three persons.

Kazi Akber stated that he had been an active member in Sindh politics at the provincial level and he was also active in the local politics of Hyderabad. He was a member and/or chairman of the local municipality for fifteen years. A majority of the population of Hyderabad was then (as is perhaps now) mohajir. In his recorded interview, he maintained that he was very close to his constituents; he respected them, they respected him. Nobody ever thought in terms of Sindhi-mohajir conflict.

This did not suit the political aspirations of some people, for example, Nawab Muzaffar Ali was a Mohajir settled in Sindh. According to Kazi Akber, Nawab Muzaffar Ali was encouraged by Masroor Hasan Khan to establish the Mohajir-Punjabi-Pathan Mahaz, a pressure group/political party to counter the Muslim League and Kazi Akber's influence among the people of the province in general, and in Hyderabad in particular. Kazi Akber maintained that Masroor Hasan Khan also encouraged Chaudhri Ashraf to form the Punjabi Settlers Association, and Vali Bhai to form the Rajputana States Federation. Masroor Hasan Khan had his own reasons. He wanted to control these groups and their Basic Democracy (BD) voters "so that he could offer that as a gift to Ayub Khan: Here! I have been able to mobilize these non-Sindhi votes of the Basic Democrats for you."

According to Kazi Akber, Syed Mubarak Ali Shah, a prominent mohajir leader of Hyderabad who had at one time worked as an advisor to the Government of Sindh was also instrumental in creating a "situation of confrontation" between the Sindhis and the mohajirs in Hyderabad, and, therefore, in the entire province. He too was encouraged in his efforts by Masroor Hasan Khan. Another person who contributed to this development of a gulf between the two groups of people was Nawab Zahid Ali, another non-Sindhi leader of Hyderabad.

According to Kazi Akber. these were some of the people on the side of the mohajirs. On the other side, among the Sindhi political leaders G. M. Syed has been responsible for creating and widening the gap between the Sindhis and the mohajirs. Kazi Akber said that G.M. Syed was one of the strongest supporters of the Pakistan movement in Sindh. But, since his defeat in 1946 he has been very "unforgiving." His frustrations for having been rendered into a "nobody" may have left him bitter.[17]

The Contribution of Mohajirs to the Development of Post-Partition Sindh

It is true that the Muslims constituted a majority in the province of Sindh in British India. However, the Hindus, and perhaps some Parsis in Karachi, occupied a majority of the positions of leadership in business, education, local administration, and the professions. Most attorneys were Hindus; most businesses were owned (and, certainly staffed) by the Hindus; most doctors were Hindus; most teachers at the secondary or the collegiate level were Hindus; and, a disproportionately large number of civil servants were Hindu. We do not have data to indicate the number and the percentage of Muslim businessmen, civil servants, doctors, lawyers, teachers or other professionals in Sindh in pre-partition India.

There were only three non-professional post-secondary institutions in pre-partition Sindh. All were operated by Hindu groups: the D.J. Sindh College in Karachi, the D.G. National College in Hyderabad and the C. & S. College in Shikarpur. The senior management personnel and most members of the faculty at these institutions were Hindus. Most of them left for India in 1946-47 and this resulted in the closure of the colleges. The Government of Sindh took over the colleges and reopened them, as faculty became available.

It is true that most mohajirs who migrated to Sindh came from rural areas in India; most of them were unskilled even illiterate. It is also true that most headed for Karachi or Hyderabad, the two largest urban centers of Sindh. Most unskilled or semi-skilled persons sought and obtained some manual, work: in construction; in a factory, as rickshaw pullers, etc. Some started small businesses to provide the goods and services needed by the increasing population of the cities.

It must be remembered that the mohajirs left India under indescribably unfortunate and unusually trying circumstances. Most of them had to leave behind their homes, their property, their relatives, their friends, their memories. Many of them had to endure unbelievable atrocities: brutal murders of their close relatives, the rape of their women, the kidnapping of their children, the burning of their homes, the destruction of their property, and their personal humiliation. Many members of the "partition" generation have said to this author that they accepted all this as Allah's will and as their contribution to the creation of Pakistan. They were very happy when they reached the land of the pure -- Pakistan, and happier when they were able to get a job.

The two major urban centers of Sindh, Karachi and Hyderabad, attracted a large number of professionally trained persons: lawyers, doctors, teachers, etc. It was, therefore, relatively easy to find qualified instructors to staff the colleges in Karachi. They were happy to get a job and the community was happy to be able to keep the institutions and services operating.

According to information available, the colleges in Hyderabad and Shikarpur were reopened in June 1948.[18] Five out of the twenty-five members of the faculty who reopened the college in Hyderabad were Sindhi, twenty were recruited from amongst the mohajirs. The ratio between the Sindhi and the mohajir instructors at the college in Shikarpur could not be ascertained.

It is evident from the number of mohajir instructors hired to reopen the college in Hyderabad that Sindh did not have an adequate number of qualified Sindhi personnel to staff the colleges, or most other professions. Even in late 1953, when this author moved to Sindh, while the number of instructors at the Government College had almost doubled, the number of Sindhi instructors was very small, five out of fifty-one.

This author recalls how he was persuaded against his will by Professor Syed Ghulam Mustafa Shah[19] to accept a teaching position at the Government College in Hyderabad, in 1953. Professor Shah had left the college earlier that year and the college had no instructor of political science for several months; the only other political scientist had been awarded a scholarship for studies in Spain. In November 1953, when he joined the faculty of the college, this author was the most junior member of the faculty which numbered fifty-one. All members of the faculty except five were mohajirs.

Personal Experiences in Sindh

This part of the essay records the personal experiences and observations of the author in the mohajir-Sindhi relationship over a period of eleven years in the Sindh.

He has sweet and pleasant memories of almost seven years of his stay in Sindh, four in Hyderabad, a predominantly mohajir city, and the balance in Shikarpur and Larkana, the heart of upper Sindh. The author cannot recall a single incident of discrimination against him because of his being a mohajir during his stay in Hyderabad or Shikarpur. Most people were nice, kind, and generous, or at least "neutral." There may have been an incident or two in the last years of his stay in Larkana and Sukkur that could be attributed to the Sindhi-mohajir dichotomy.

His closest contacts were with his students and his colleagues, mohajirs and Sindhis. During his stay in Sindh, he developed lifelong associations and friendships, many with Sindhi families. Although there is no legal adoption in Islam, the author's family has "adopted" a son of a prominent Sindhi family and treats, and is treated by, them as family. Many close friends are Sindhis.

During his last year at Larkana and during his stay in Sukkur, the author noticed traces of discrimination, of souring of relationship between the Sindhis and the mohajirs. While his personal relationships stayed healthy, he recalls the issue of being a Sindhi or a mohajir being raised by people at places and events that should not have been viewed as Sindhi or mohajir issues or events. On more than one occasion the author heard some of his Sindhi colleagues complain that the position of seniority (and, therefore authority) that the mohajirs occupied in the college or in the civil administration would have been occupied by the Sindhis if there had been no "others" in Sindh. A proper evaluation of these remarks requires us to remember that because of the opening of colleges in several cities and the University of Sindh in Hyderabad, higher education had become available to and was attained by the Sindhis. This meant that a cadre of qualified Sindhis was now available to fill professional positions in Sindh, something that was not true in the early years of Pakistan. They wanted to fill these positions but faced vigorous competition from the mohajirs, many of whom occupied even higher positions because of seniority.

This was the period of "one-unit." Inter-regional postings of government employees were common, particularly at the senior level. College professors belonged to this category. People from other regions of West Pakistan (the Punjab, the North West Frontier, and Boluchistan) could, and did acquire positions in institutions in Sindh.

The author feels that the relations between the Sindhis and the mohajirs during the 1953-1960 period were more pleasant, more friendly, more amicable than during the later years. These relations were probably more pleasant during 1947-1953. The author must add a word of caution: since he has had no prejudices based on ethnic grounds, he is a very poor judge of ethnic relationships. As an untrained person, he can and he did notice a deterioration of relationships.

The Souring of Relations

As stated earlier, this author believes that Sindhi-mohajir relations were friendly and amicable until the early 1960's but the relations began to deteriorate in the mid-1960's and the primary reason for the souring of the relations was frustration. While discussing the causes for the deterioration of relations between the Sindhis and the mohajirs, Kazi Akber also placed the deterioration in the mid-1960s. This is also the period when Altaf Husain says he started to think of the fifth nationality: the mohajirs.[20]

The relations were friendly in the initial period because of a number of factors:

First, the Sindhis demonstrated a special accommodation for the mohajirs: Sindhis are by cultural orientation a hospitable people; Islam has a historical episode of migration (hijrat) and the mohajirs came as *refugees* to Sindh under unfortunate circumstances.

Second, the mohajirs had helped establish Pakistan. The people of Sindh (as well as of Boluchistan, East Bengal, the Punjab, and the North West Frontier) owed it to the mohajirs to be hospitable to them. It was the right thing to do.

Third, they developed a symbiotic interdependence with each other: the mohajirs needed a place to live and make a living in their new homeland; the Sindhis needed trained Muslim professionals to fill the vacuum created by the departure of the Hindu professionals. But for the mohajirs the Sindhis would have had no school teachers, doctors, lawyers, nor economic infrastructure personnel to carry on the normal functions of life today and in the future. They were glad to have the mohajirs.

The relations began to deteriorate in the mid-1960s. Perhaps Kazi Akber is right, that the deterioration was brought about by three factors: the unfortunate political role of some senior bureaucrats who had limited vision; the inefficient operation of the one-unit; and, the "unfair" role of some political leaders. However, it is the view of this author that these factors may have helped the deterioration of relationship, the real cause was frustration on the part of both the Sindhis and the mohajirs.

This author believes that the frustration may have been caused by the breakdown of the symbiotic interdependence between the Sindhis and the mohajirs. The mohajirs may have come to believe that they had a right to claim at least an equal partnership if not sole proprietorship in the affairs of Sindh: business, economic, educational, cultural, and political. The Sindhis may have realized that Sindh was, after all, theirs. Most of its affairs had come to be controlled by all "others" and very little by Sindhis. These "others" included the mohajirs, who may have had some claim to stay in Sindh because they had nowhere else to call home. They were in Sindh to stay for good. But, thanks to the one-unit the Boluchis, the Pathans, and the Punjabis also controlled Sindh, although they had their own territories.

This frustration gave birth to the *Jeeye Sindh* sentiments. The days when they needed "others" to help them tend to their (Sindhi) affairs were over; they now had developed the manpower infrastructure that was needed to run their affairs. They had come of age.

The mohajirs also developed a sense of frustration because, as Altaf Husain points out in his book, the system acknowledged the existence of the Boluchis, the Pakhtuns, the Punjabis, and the Sindhis as separate units, as separate nationalities. The mohajirs were not recognized as anything. Everyone else could claim to be the "son of the soil" (son of some segment of the soil);[21] the mohajirs could not say "This land is my land" for any region, not even Sindh, where they had raised a new generation since coming to Pakistan as mohajirs in 1947.

These frustrations among both the Sindhis and the mohajirs gave rise to a feeling of distrust, of alienation, of hostility among and between the two communities. This hostility eventually demonstrated itself as riots between the Sindhis and the mohajirs, sometimes in the form of language riots, sometimes as just riots. It created and strengthened the Jeeye Sindh movement; it created and strengthened the *Mohajir Qaumi Movement* (MQM).[22] These frustrations tore apart the two ethnic groups of people who "are residents of the same land; who eat the grain raised from the same land, . . . who drink the water that flows through the same land, . . . whose dead bodies are buried in the same land, . . . and who spend their hard earned money in the same region and do not send the wealth raised here to some other region."

Conclusion

The mohajirs who came to Sindh lacked cultural homogeneity with the people of Sindh. They came from different parts of Muslim minority provinces in India. This was unlike the mohajirs from East Punjab in India who went to West Punjab in Pakistan or the Bengalis who went from West Bengal to East Pakistan. The Punjabis and the Bengalis were able to assimilate in the host society without much difficulty. The mohajirs in Sindh were welcomed by the Sindhis for a variety of reasons: Sindhi hospitality; symbiotic interdependence, and the unfortunate circumstances under which the refugees came. But, because of lack of cultural homogeneity, they could not easily be assimilated into the host society.

In the mid-1960s the two communities began to drift apart. According to the late Kazi Mohammed Akber, the gulf was created by the actions of some persons: some bureaucrats who wanted to please President Mohammed Ayub Khan; some self-seeking political leaders, Sindhi and mohajir, because of the poor operation of the one-unit scheme.

This author believes that the gulf was created because of frustrations on both sides: frustrations among the Sindhis who viewed the preeminence of the non-Sindhis including the mohajirs (and the Boluchis, the Pathans, and the Punjabis) in Sindhi affairs at the cost of the Sindhis as a threat to their hegemony, and frustrations among the mohajirs for the inability of the Pakistani society to recognize the status and role of the mohajirs. The Sindhis feared that they were becoming second class citizens in their own land; the mohajirs believed that after having sacrificed everything they had to help create Pakistan, and after having raised a generation in Sindh, they were still aliens in their new homeland.

The Jeeye Sindh movement and the Mohajir Qaumi Movement (MQM) with all their positive and negative ramifications, are the products of this frustration. The MQM may be dead as a political force. Are the issues raised by the MQM also dead? Not by a long shot. What is the future?

Unless the Sindhis and the mohajirs decide to allow the development of a new cultural identity for the residents of Sindh, an identity that is indigenous to modern Sindh and does not dwell on past hatred, it appears that peace will be difficult to return to the land of Shah Latif.

Notes

1. Abi Jafar Mohammed Bin Jareer Tabari, *Tareekh-ul-Umam-wal-Mulook* (History of Nations and Kings), (in Arabic), Vol. I (*Seerat-un-Nabi*), translated in Urdu by Syed Mohammed Ibrahim, *Tareekh Tabari* (*Seerat-un-Nabi*) Karachi (Pakistan): Nafees Academy, (n.d.), p. 95.

Also see Shah Moinuddin Ahmed, *Tareekh-e-Islam* (History of Islam), (in Urdu), Karachi: Dar-ul-Isha'at, (1985), pp. 33-35.

2. Tabari, p. 132 ff.

3. Dr. Sir Mohammed Iqbal, *Kulliyyat-e-Iqbal: Farsi* (Complete Works of Iqbal: Special Edition) (in Farsi), Lahore, Iqbal Academy, 1990, pp. 123-125. Interested readers are encouraged to read this and other related works of Dr. Iqbal. Also see, Abdul Mughni, *Iqbal Ka Nazariya-e-Khudi* (Iqbal's Concept of Self), (in Urdu), New Delhi: Maktaba-e-Jami'a, 1990, pp. 263-4.

4. The Arabic word *kalima* literally means "word, what has been said." In Muslim theology and belief, the word kalima is used to connote the acceptance and utterance of one or all of the statements of faith, including the *kalimatush-shahadah*: the statement to bear testimony that there is no deity except God (Allah) and that Mohammed is His (last) Prophet.

5. Iqbal, p. 124.

6. Tabari, Vol. V, p. 450.

7. Iqbal, p. 280.

8. R.C. Majumdar, "Discontent, Disturbances and Armed Resistance" in R. C. Majumdar, (General Editor), *The History and Culture of the Indian People: British Paramountcy and Indian Renaissance*, 1963, Bombay: Bharatiya Vidya Bhavan, p. 884 ff. See, Anjum Zahid, *Taqseem Ki Bunyad* (The Basis for Partition), (in Urdu), 1986, Darussalam, Tanzania. Anjum Publications, pp. 50-51. For a definition of the terms dar-ul-harb and dar-al-Islam, see Zakaria

Bashier, *Hijra: Story and Significance*, Leicester. Islamic Foundation, 1983, pp. 90-94.

9. For an excellent discussion of the large scale migration of Muslims from the East Punjab to the West Punjab and of Hindus and Sikhs from the West Punjab to the East Punjab; of the relative cash values of the properties, both personal property (moveable property) and real estate (immoveable property), rural, or urban, agricultural, residential, or commercial, left behind by the migrating families; of the handling of the resettlement of the immigrants by the Governments of India and Pakistan and the two provincial governments, see Satya M. Rai, *Partition of the Punjab: A Study of Its Effects on the Politics and Administration of the Punjab (I): 1947-1956.* 1965, New York: Asia Publishing House. For transfer of population, see Satya M. Rai, section I: "Transfer of Population" in chapter IV: "Transfer of Population and Evacuee Organization (pp. 72-87); for a discussion of evacuees and evacuee property see section II. "Review of the Work Done in Connection With Evacuation" (pp. 87-89). For "Indo-Pak Negotiations on Evacuee Property and the Punjab Problem," see section III, in chapter V: "Effects on Administration" (pp. 112-120).

10. For an excellent and probably the most authentic review of the holocaust and the rehabilitation efforts of the Governments of India and Pakistan (particularly the Government of Pakistan), see Chaudhri Mohammed Ali, *The Emergence of Pakistan.* 1967, New York, NY: Columbia University Press, particularly chapter 13 titled "The Great Holocaust and the Rehabilitation of Refugees." The chapter lists the "agreed areas," p. 270. It may be recalled that Chaudhri Mohammed Ali was a prominent bureaucrat and later a political leader of Pakistan. He started as the Secretary General of the Government of Pakistan in 1947; was appointed Finance Minister in 1951, and served as Prime Minister in 1956-57.

11. The word *ansar* (plural of *nasir*) in Arabic means friends. This was the term used to denote the hosts in Yathrib (Madina) when Prophet Mohammed, his family, friends, and followers migrated to Yathrib in 622 CE.

For a public acknowledgment of the debt owed by the mohajirs to the Sindhis for having given the mohajirs refuge in Sindh, see Khalid Athar, *Safar-e-Zindagi: MQM Ki Kahani, Altaf Husain Ki Zabani* (in Urdu), (Life's Journey: The story of the MQM: In the Words of Altaf Husain), Lahore, 1990, p. 115. The publishers state that the book is based on several long interviews granted by Altaf Husain to the writer, Khalid Athar.

12. For a fuller discussion see Afak Haydar, *Basic Democracies in Pakistan*, Hyderabad, Sindh: Popular Printers, 1963.

13. Government of Pakistan, Manager of Publications, *The Constitution of the Islamic Republic of Pakistan*, 1962. Karachi, Government of Pakistan Press.

14. Beside numerous other excellent works on this subject, see Rafiullah Shehab, *Fifty Years of Pakistan,* 1990. Lahore, Maqbool Academy, pp. 141-2. Also see Tariq Ali, *Military Rule or People's Power,* 1970. New York: William Morrow and Company.

15. Shehab, pp. 104-106.

16. For the genesis of the one-unit see a "Memorandum" written by General Mohammed Ayub Khan, then Commander-in-Chief of the Pakistan Army on October 4, 1954, published as Appendix A to Hasan Askari Rizvi, *The Military and Politics in Pakistan: 1947 to 1986.* 1988, New Delhi.

17. See Zaffar Abbas, "G. M. Syed: Saint or Sinner," *Herald*, (Vol. 23; Number 2, February 1992), 1992, Karachi. Pakistan Herald Publications, pp. 22-38.

18. Letter from Professor Nasir Zaidi, Principal, Government College, Hyderabad, dated March 18, 1993. Professor Zaidi's elder brother, Professor Shaid Zaidi was one the faculty members who reopened the college in 1948.

19. This author met Professor Syed Ghulam Mustafa Shah, then Principal of Sindh Muslim College, Karachi, at a dinner in July 1953. Professor Shah asked him to see Mr. O.H. Ansari, then Director, Public Instruction, Government of Sindh to receive his assignment as a lecturer at Government College, Hyderabad. This is the position Professor Shah had resigned to accept the principalship in Karachi. The author did not want to start working so soon after leaving graduate school and he did not go to see Mr. Ansari. A few months later, he met Professor Shah again at the same host's house. Professor Shah assumed that the author was working at the college in Hyderabad and inquired about the welfare of Dr. Adrian Duarte, Principal of the college. Since the author was not working at the college in Hyderabad, he said he did not know who Dr. Duarte was. Professor Shah was very upset with the author's failure to accept a job that needed to be done and for which no other qualified person was available. The author met with Mr. Ansari the very next day and accepted a teaching position at the college in Hyderabad. It may be recalled that Professor Shah has served education in Sindh and in Pakistan in a variety of assignments: as professor of political science at the D.G. National Government College, Hyderabad; as Principal, Sindh Muslim College, Karachi; as Vice Chancellor, University of Sind; and, most recently as Minister of Education, Government of Pakistan in the Benazir Bhutto cabinet.

20. Athar, p. 22.

21. Athar, p. 23 ff.

22. For an understanding of the enormous political power wielded by the Mohajir Qaumi Movement (MQM) and its leader, Altaf Husain, from the inception of the MQM in 1984 to its unbelievable fall in summer 1992, among other sources, see Khalid Ather's rendition of Altaf Husain's story, *Safar-e-Zindagi: MQM Ki Kahani, Altaf Husain Ki Zabani.* In this book Altaf

Husain explains his frustrations as a student at the University of Karachi. His realization that despite their past generations' sacrifices for the establishment of Pakistan and despite their being born and raised in Sindh, the mohajirs had no place to call their own. His disillusionment that they were aliens in their own homeland prompted him to organize the All Pakistan Mohajir Student Organization in March, 1984. He fought for the establishment of the Mohajir Qaumi Movement as a legitimate political party. His success with the MQM was achieved not only among the Mohajirs in Karachi and other urban centers in Sindh, but he also had the support of political leaders in all parts of the country. He became a hero for the mohajirs.

The monthly news magazine *Herald*, published by the Dawn Group, carried several extensive and illuminating articles in its issues of June 1992, July 1992, and October 1992. These and other articles published in other news magazines in Pakistan describe the split within the MQM; the Pakistan Army's operations in Sindh; the discovery of torture cells operated by the MQM to keep dissidents and opponents in line; and, the eventual "fall" of the MQM from not only power but also from grace.

7

The Impact and Legacy of the Afghan Refugees in Pakistan

Marvin G. Weinbaum

Over 14 years of war in Afghanistan, Pakistan carried the major responsibility for absorbing the conflict's refugees. With much difficulty and more than a little international assistance, Pakistan managed to cope with the influx of displaced Afghans. Their presence was both a source of pride and a the basis for domestic controversy. Pakistanis shared a sense of concern about the threat posed by refugees to their country's political stability and security. Even more visible were their worries about the socio-economic impact of the refugees on the country. Popular concern was expressed for the long-term consequences should the war carry on indefinitely: that the refugees would set roots so firm in Pakistan that it would be difficult for them ever to return home. In time, the size of the Afghan community was believed bound to factor more directly in the politics of Pakistan.

Restiveness about the presence of the refugees notwithstanding, a reservoir of good feeling remained through the years, a sympathy for Muslims fighting for their freedom in a "holy war" against communists. Few in the broad public in Pakistan argued for the authorities in Islamabad to expel the Afghans to a war zone. Nor were Pakistan's governments anxious to take the heat of international reaction or, more important, to face the almost certain resistance of the heavily armed refugee community to a forced repatriation. If the sense of obligation to protect and assist the Afghans weakened over time, it occurred only gradually.

By the time of the collapse of the Kabul regime and the installation of a government by the Afghan resistance parties in May 1992, the repatriation process was well underway. Barring renewed large-scale fighting in a protracted Afghan civil war, the probability was that most of the refugees sheltered in Pakistan would eventually return to their homeland. What remains unclear, however, is the pace and pattern of their return, and Pakistan's role in the refugees' rehabilitation and Afghanistan's reconstruction. Nor is it possible to calculate as yet the losses to local economies in Pakistan with the departure of the refugees and the foreign relief aid that went with them. Other legacies for Pakistan seem more certain and lasting, most of all the diffusion of arms throughout Pakistan that made traditional societal violence more lethal. And should postwar Afghanistan fail to integrate at least partially its many ethnic and ideological elements, long-standing fears of a rekindled Pashtun nationalism, with its potential for the territorial dismemberment of Pakistan, cannot be dismissed.

The Welcome

The hospitality or at least toleration shown by Pakistan toward the Afghans was, by all measures, quite extraordinary. Over the course of the war, the number of Afghan refugees settled in Pakistan exceeded 3.2 million. Taking responsibility for the Afghans fleeing to Pakistan -- both for security and to take up arms -- followed Muslim and tribal traditions that require giving protection to those asking for it. Even while hoping for the early repatriation of the refugees, most Pakistanis appreciated that Afghans would probably be unable to return until they could do so in peace and honor, to an independent country, and then not without some assistance. In general, most Pakistanis took pride in having borne the political and economic burdens in the true spirit of Islamic brotherhood. Probably most important, the Pushtuns are ethnic cousins of Pakistan's Pathans, with whom they share linguistic and cultural ties as well as religious ones.

Afghan migration into Pakistan was not entirely a new phenomenon or one necessarily related to the fighting. Even before the Soviet invasion, it is estimated that normally about 75,000 Afghans crossed the border yearly.[1] When Afghans were faced with an unpopular, repressive regime and the invasion of their country by Soviet troops, Pakistan was a convenient and logical place of refuge. Indeed, it would have been nearly impossible, given the porous border, to have blocked their entry into Pakistan.

The flow of political refugees across the border had actually begun on a small scale even before Moscow's armed intervention. Having failed in a 1974 insurgency against the Afghan Republic's president, Mohammed Daoud, Muslim fundamentalist participants escaped to Pakistan. They were welcomed by Pakistan's prime minister, Zulfikar Ali Bhutto, who had given support to the rebellion in the hopes of discouraging Daoud's expected pressing of the Pushtunistan issue.[2] But the massive exodus to Pakistan began soon following the communist coup of April 1978, and the flow followed the intensity of the conflict inside Afghanistan. Now a more diverse group of refugees, Afghans were fleeing from the armed struggle that had begun in the countryside by the summer of 1978 after the communists had tried to impose their ideologically inspired reform program. Conformity was also imposed on the cities, and large numbers of government officials and intellectuals departed.

A steadily increasing flow of refugees to Pakistan occurred from the end of November 1979, just before the Soviet invasion, when there were approximately 315,000 registered refugees, to the end of March 1981 when the number had jumped to 1.8 million.[3] In the summer of 1984 the number had reached 2.86 million. No figures were very accurate, however, given the difficulty in registering refugees once they had crossed the border and the limited personnel available to the Pakistan refugee administration to enumerate the population. Some arrivals failed to register with Pakistani authorities, but according to UN sources there were more cases of over-enumeration resulting from bogus or multiple registration by those claiming dependents eligible for rations. Just as it served the Afghans' interest to exaggerate their numbers, Pakistani authorities were motivated to raise the figures on which foreign aid was based.[4] Larger numbers also helped to dramatize the acuteness of the refugee problem.

Very clearly, Pakistan was not prepared for the massive movement of Afghans across the border. The long-term problem of settling the refugees received little thought in Islamabad, and haphazard policies prevailed, initially giving district administrators considerable discretion.[5] Prior to the post-Soviet invasion influx, there had been few official camps, and the refugees settled as best they could in the border, tribal areas. On the advice of the UN High Commission for Refugees (UNHCR) to which Pakistan had turned for help in caring for the refugees in April 1979 camps were gradually established and moved farther from the border in the two eastern provinces, North West Frontier (NWFP) and Boluchistan.[6] Attempts to coordinate relief efforts with the UNHCR and others led in 1981 to overall supervision of the refugees being transferred to a Chief Commissionerate for Afghan Refugees (CCAR), with its main office in Islamabad and sub-offices in Peshawar and Quetta. The Commissioner was charged with implementing the policy set by various cabinet ministries and President Zia, administering services through civil servants at the provincial level.

The refugee camps, more than 350 in Pakistan, typically encompassed about 10,000 inhabitants and were divided into refugee villages, each serving about 1,200 to 1,300 families. One of the largest, however, had a population of 120,000 and covered five square miles. Every settlement was assigned several officials who helped administer the available services, maintained order, and occasionally helped settle disputes among the refugees. In all, by the time the bulk of refugees had arrived in the mid-1980s, somewhere between 10,000 and 12,000 people, mostly local Pakistanis, were involved in the governmental and nongovernmental administrative infrastructure.[7]

Until January 1979 the Islamabad government allocated its own resources to care for the refugees, paying a subsistence allowance for the hundreds of thousands. At this time, about $12 per capita was the official monthly allowance for the refugees. The designated subsidy was lowered by more than half when the UNHCR, World Food Program, and others joined the relief effort as commodity aid (e.g., wheat, edible oil, powdered milk, sugar) was supposed to supplement the cash payments. The assistance also provided limited vocational training as well as a primary and middle school in each tent village. Official government figures listed three high schools, 125 middle schools, and 571 primary schools with 2,877 teachers, two-thirds of whom were from among the refugees. Refugees could also receive free medical services at health units provided by the government and private voluntary agencies. In all, Pakistan claimed that there were 186 Basic Health Units and 66 satellite units staffed by 295 doctors and 2,000 paramedical personnel.[8] Pakistan transported and distributed the basic foodstuffs supplied by relief agencies. Dependency on outsiders was made inevitable by Pakistan's regulations preventing Afghans from cultivating the land. (In Iran, with more than two million refugees, little or no financial support was given to individual Afghans, and only small number of aid agencies were permitted to operate. Few refugees were settled in camps and most were forced to fend for themselves. Consequentially, Afghans had both greater independence and suffered more hardships than in Pakistan.)

By mid-1980s, the Government of Pakistan was officially responsible for 45 percent of the cost of maintaining the refugees, the UNHCR 25 percent, the World Food Program 25 percent, and others, including Saudi Arabia and Kuwait as well as the Red Cross, the additional 5 percent.[9] Pakistan assumed the costs of the internal transport of refugee aid, a figure estimated at $70 million yearly in the mid-1980s, along with its responsibility for the administration and security of commodities.[10] In all, Pakistan's share was supposedly in excess of $1 million daily and has been called a considerable drain on the national budget. The figure is in fact misleading; it did not take into consideration other monies that were brought into the Pakistan's NWFP and Boluchistan by virtue of the Afghans' presence and the stimulus of the refugees on local economies. The size of the contribution may itself have been grossly inflated. By most reports, the rupee cash allowance, which made up much of Pakistan's publicized expenditure for refugees, seldom in fact reached refugee families.[11]

Arriving refugees from Afghanistan were expected to become affiliated with one of the Afghan political groups in order to be certified as refugees. To qualify for rations from the Pakistan government, they had also to settle in a government-designated camp area. In effect, the procedures served as an endorsement by the Pakistan government of the mujahidin groups and, more accurately, allowed a bias in favor of those that could best organize the camps. By carrying out relief work of various kinds, these parties could cultivate support among the refugees. Especially in the early years, Pakistan's fundamentalist party Jama'at-i-Islami also had good access to the camps. The party's presence facilitated the operations of strongly Islamist groups among the Afghans.

Hezb-i-Islami was particularly favored by the Pakistani refugee administration. Many camp officials provided easier registration and earlier assistance if individuals identified with Hekmatyar's party. Licenses for trucks owned by Afghan refugees were facilitated for those who joined the Hezb-i-Islami. UN monitored funds were regularly diverted to the Hezb-i-Islami, enabling it to gain more than its fair share of rations, tents, and other relief aid.[12] To please the Hezb-i-Islami and the other Islamist parties, and also to assure that any Afghan nationalist ideas were kept to a minimum, the Pakistanis gave the Islamists a stronger voice in the educational programs in the camps and, later, in the cross-border transfer of educational materials and the establishment of schools inside Afghanistan.

Overall control in the each of the camps was delegated to a Pakistani official whose legitimacy came not only from his government appointment but also from the approval of the dominant political group in the camp along with the camp's elders. The Pakistani camp managers dealt, then, with a camp leadership that was often not part of the traditional elite. The Afghan camp heads, or maliks, were often called "ration maliks" for their ability to get people on the list and to offer other favors. Expected to get along with the authorities, the maliks were more the choice of Pakistani officials than the refugees.[13] Under Pakistani administration, *jirgas* (assemblies) were also formed to deal with problems facing the refugees. Although often politicized by those Afghan parties favored by the authorities, these councils usually operated along traditional lines.

A critical component in the relief operation were the private voluntary organizations, or PVOs, that were given permission by Pakistan to work among the refugees. Very early in the war, Pakistan authorities sought to minimize the arrival of refugees in the NWFP and Boluchistan. No official policy in Islamabad on the activities of relief organizations was in effect; to the extent that they were regulated, provincial governments regulated them. In June 1980, however, the Zia government issued policies on the PVOs that sharply restricted most of their activities, especially in the border tribal areas. Despite this, the Islamabad government allowed officials from the International Rescue Committee to complete plans to set up a medical program in the camps.

Initially, at least, most of the PVO officials and UN experts sent to administer the aid programs displayed little understanding of the social structure and organization as well as the needs of the Afghans.[14] Allowing foreigners more first-hand experience in the tribal areas where most of the camps had been located also carried drawbacks: it could allow the Kabul government and the Soviets to claim that foreign advisors were training Afghan guerrillas, thus giving the communists a possible pretext for expanding the war into Pakistan.[15] Pakistani officials did authorize a number of countries' humanitarian aid organizations, such as those from Sweden and Austria, to open offices in Peshawar. The Islamabad government was more cautious, as was the U.S. government, about the involvement of private U.S. groups, fearing that their presence would draw charges that they were CIA front operations.[16] For several years, then, nearly all U.S. assistance was channeled through the UN.

The resentment that could be detected among Pakistani authorities against the PVOs, that is, against the foreign relief personnel, was particularly evident in the early years when they had difficulty receiving clearances for travel and were beset with bureaucratic delays and "obfuscation."[17] Religious parties and Arab associations in Pakistan tried to convince the Pakistan government that Western volunteer organizations were engaged in missionary activities or that they were communists. Foreigners faced long delays in obtaining official permission from Pakistani authorities to work for PVOs, and many did so illegally on tourist visas. In general, fuller cooperation came from officials in the NWFP government than in the capital. Islamabad was especially slow to give clearance to foreigners employed by PVOs engaged in cross-border relief programs. There is evidence of bribery and extortion in the form of "transit fees" being imposed on foreign aid workers by Pakistani border police as well as certain mujahidin groups. The Pakistan army, police and refugee administration, often in connivance with members of Afghan resistance parties, operated scams to sell relief supplies, weapons, and favors.[18]

The prime figure in suppressing PVO activities between 1980 and mid-1983 was the Pakistani appointed as commissioner for the refugees, Sheikh Abdullah Khan. A deeply committed Muslim, he made little effort to disguise his suspicion of the Western relief groups, and he managed to discourage several. It was through Abdullah's efforts that the Afghan hard-line Islamic parties gained ready access to the refugee camps; he was especially partial toward the resistance's *Hezb-i-Islami* (Islamic Party). Only after considerable foreign pressures on Islamabad was Abdullah finally removed. Subsequent commissioners were far less ideological and were not viewed as obstacles to foreign relief work.

As the burden of administering to the refugees grew and international interest in the needs of Afghan civilians both in the camps and across the border also increased, Pakistani authorities permitted larger numbers of relief organizations to set up shop in Peshawar. In 1983, 17 PVOs were registered. The only identifiable U.S. group among those operating in 1983 was the International Rescue Committee. By the end of the decade, 75 foreign organizations, 43 of them from Europe and 14 from North America, maintained offices in Pakistan, many with operations both among the refugees and involved in cross-border activities. Approximately 6,000 local people were employed in both the nongovernmental relief organizations and UN-related projects.[19] In 1990, 22 of these private voluntary organizations were receiving financial support from UNHCR for assistance programs.[20]

Afghan resistance parties in Peshawar, despite their suspicions, placed many of their own followers in the employ of the PVOs on whose activities they were expected to report. The relief organizations accepted this infiltration as a necessary price to pay for carrying out their mission. There existed a loose quota in hiring, although followers of Hesb-i-Islami were best represented, a token of the influence of the resistance party and the fact that they were often the most qualified employees. Because at least some PVOs, working as subcontractors to international or foreign country projects, were obliged to work directly with the Afghan Interim Government (AIG), formed in 1989, they also came under the watchful eye of Pakistan's military intelligence. Many PVOs felt obliged to hire Pakistani administrators to help them cut red tape in dealing with the Islamabad government.

Demands were frequently heard that more PVOs should be under direct Afghan control and that these organizations begin to replace Western-led groups. Western expatriate managers and directors usually expressed sympathy with the need to hire Afghans or turn activities over to Afghan organizations, but insisted that there were simply not enough qualified Afghans available. In any case, Pakistani authorities were not helpful. The several Afghan PVOs that managed to form found it difficult to obtain the "no objection certificates" from the government necessary to hire a staff. The Pakistanis, in fact, preferred the Western organizations that brought their own funds and that were more successful than Afghan PVOs in remaining independent of particular mujahidin groups.

Even though the presence of PVOs also meant that the local administration was obliged to share control over the refugees, many in the Pakistani bureaucracy were also appreciative of the efforts of foreign groups and, in general, did not interfere in their activities, whether in Pakistan or cross-border. Humanitarian aid in commodities and services inside Afghanistan begun in 1985 by USAID -- distributed through local resistance commanders and their *shuras* (councils) -- required transport through Pakistan with government approval. In cooperation with Pakistani authorities, USAID in 1988 established the Afghan Construction and Logistic Unit that in addition to the transport of goods also improved and constructed necessary roads and bridges. The unit, employing 200 Afghan drivers, maintained a facility on the outskirts of Peshawar. U.S. Air Force planes also landed goods in Pakistan donated by American private organizations for use across the border.[21] Yet the Islamabad government was at times inconsistent and self-defeating by applying restrictions on the PVOs engaged in cross border relief efforts. Some of these restrictions, including those on the transfer of wheat, edible oil, sugar, and other commodities to Afghanistan and on the number of border cross points, were justified by concerns that the transfers to Afghanistan had raised prices in nearby Pakistani markets and spurred smuggling of essential commodities. At other times, policies that made the work of these PVOs programs more difficult appeared to result from normal bureaucratic confusion in ad hoc policies, or was a reflection of the frustrations over the failure of PVOs to induce more refugees to return.

Anxious to have the refugees return home at the earliest possible time, the Pakistan government was prepared to facilitate the international relief groups and PVOs in activities that might hasten repatriation. Islamabad was particularly supportive of demining operations -- essential if refugees were to find it safe to return -- and allowed them to be run out of military camps in Pakistan. By the end of the 1980s, however, humanitarian aid offered by Western relief groups was more often viewed in Pakistan as offering an incentive for refugees to delay or refuse to leave.

Refugees as an Issue

Pakistani authorities tried for many years to give the impression that there were no serious domestic political, social, or economic problems associated with the settlement of refugees. They were proud to point out that the Afghan refugees were normally free to move about throughout Pakistan; no where were there restricting check-points or fences around villages. But Pakistanis were quick to acknowledge the impact of the refugees on their economy and society. A well-armed population, the refugees were also believed to have made the country politically more volatile. There were frequent references to the "Kalashnikov culture," an intensification of violence in the society. And with Pakistan already beset with serious cleavages between secular westernizers and Islamic radicals, political conservatives and left-oriented populists, there was added the implications of Afghan refugees, some 80 percent of them ethnic Pushtuns, on the regional politics of Pakistan, specifically the continued political and economic dominance by the county's Punjabis.

Overall, the refugees came to represent about 20 percent of the population in the two most affected provinces, the North West Frontier and Boluchistan. In some areas, however, the ratio of refugees to local population was one-to-one, and in a few areas they outnumbered the local population. The refugees thus upset a balance of population among tribes and sects in certain tribal areas. The influx of Afghans into Boluchistan tipped the ethnic balance in favor of the ethnic Pathans over the Boluch. Sectarian tensions were also heightened as the balance in the Kurram Agency of the NWFP was altered with the influx of thousands of Sunni Afghans into the homelands of a traditional majority of Shi'as. At the same time, Persian-speaking Hazaras arriving from central Afghanistan, mostly Shi'as, affected the ratio between this group and Sunnis.[22] The decision to settle the overwhelming number of Afghans in the two provinces and border areas served both mujahidin interests and those of the Islamabad government. Afghans were not anxious to settle down in camps distant from war zone or far from the population centers of Peshawar and Quetta where they were among their ethno-linguistic cousins and closer to the center of international relief groups. (Almost four-fifths of the camps were located in NWFP, and roughly 61 -- almost 20 percent of the refugee population -- around Peshawar city and district.) For a time, the Pakistani authorities thought it wise to move refugee camps farther from the border, mainly in order to relieve the pressure on resources and improve the law and order situation. They succeeded in 1987 in establishing refugee villages in the Mianwali District in the Punjab, bordering the NWFP. But ethno-linguistic differences and the extreme heat made these camps highly unpopular among the Afghans.[23] More important, many Pakistanis argued that large refugee settlements should be kept out of the country's largest province. It was seen as unwise symbolically to transfer the refugee settlements into the heartland of the Pakistanis, among the Punjabis with their history of antagonism toward Pathans. National acceptance of the Afghans as refugees was strengthened by placing them at a safe distance from the dominant, sensitive Punjabi population.

Evidence of widespread ill feeling toward the Afghan refugees was scarce during the first few years following their arrival. At most, a few petty law suits occurred, mostly over land appropriated for refugee camps.[24] Pakistanis from South Waziristan and other tribal areas were among the first to complain about the privileges accorded the refugees that, they claimed, enabled the Afghans to live better than they did. Namely, they criticized the wide array of services available in the camps as compared with far less accessibility to education, housing, and health-related services available to border-area Pakistanis. Locals especially resented cash payments provided the refugees. The food commodities supplied the Afghans assured that there was no starvation in the camps and few cases of severe malnutrition. Locals believed that domestic expenditures on the refugees meant that assistance was at the expense of development programs for their impoverished areas. Disputes also erupted over control and use of grazing fields and water resources, the consumption of forest wood, and the employment competition in agriculture and construction.[25] The refugees brought with them as many as three million head of livestock, which has had a detrimental effort on the environment because of grazing on the scarce pasture land and fragile soil. Serious deforestation in Pakistan's Chitral, Dir, and Hazara border could be easily traced to refugees seeking firewood for cooking and heating.

The competition of refugees in trade and the crafts and their alleged displacement of local Pakistanis made resentments inevitable in the cities. An adult male wage earner could be found in the great majority of refugee families. Desperate for work, the poorer Afghans were hired by Pakistani traders and builders. They were often transported long distances and paid very modest salaries. Because the Afghans in the labor force usually worked for less (in part made possible because of their camp welfare programs), they depressed wages and put thousands of Pakistani workers, those at the bottom of the pay scale, out of work. Better-off Afghans, sometimes with Pakistani partners, opened restaurants, hotels, and retail shops, usually displaying more enterprise than their local competition. The competition for jobs even extended to doctors where there was an oversupply. Refugees who had brought trucks and buses with them quickly took up transport activities. Since Afghan trucks generally have a greater load capacity to transport goods than Pakistani ones, it gave them a particular advantage on longer haul transportation. Also, the Afghans were able to compete in providing the public with private bus service in Peshawar and Islamabad.[26] Importantly, Afghan entrepreneurs employed their brethren Afghan refugees rather than local low class "Windki." Most were accused, moreover, of not paying taxes.[27]

Many refugees are said to have secured "unjust and illegal benefits" from the relief program as a result of connections and corrupt practices, and through manipulation of the relief system with and without the knowledge of Pakistani officials at the district level and below. Some refugees were accused of settling on private property, refusing to move or give compensation to the landowner. Although non-Pakistanis were prohibited from purchasing immovable property, many better-off refugees in fact managed to get around the restrictions through legal means and purchase real estate. As a result prices, in particular house rents, were inflated, adding to the resentments of middle- and lower-class Pakistani residents of Peshawar and Quetta. In general, Afghans were accused of pushing up the prices of goods.[28] Shortages of wheat and rice in Pakistani markets were blamed on the smuggling of these commodities into Afghanistan. Despite Pakistan's bumper wheat crop in 1989, for example, the country was forced to import 1.8 million tons of wheat, a result, it was widely believed, of grains being smuggled to higher priced markets in Afghanistan as well as India. At the same time, other refugees were making a living selling carpets and other goods smuggled from Afghanistan. When Pakistani authorities early in 1990 managed to close the major smuggling route across the Pakistan-Afghanistan border, anger was aroused not only among the Afghans but among Pakistani tribal traders who were themselves selling illegally imported goods from the Soviet Union, Japan, and the West.

The refugees stood accused of contributing to the serious breakdown in law and order in host provinces and throughout Pakistan. There was greater lawlessness in the schools and on the roads. Afghans were held responsible for an increase in armed robberies. At least some attacks were aimed at Peshawar-based foreign relief agencies, in a number of instances by people incited by their leaders into believing that the groups were engaged in Christian missionary activities. The illegal sale and spread of weapons throughout Pakistan was also linked to the Afghans. By some estimates, about a quarter of the arms from the United States, Saudi Arabia, and China were thought to have been diverted for use by Pakistani secessionists, bandits, and others.[29] More than ever, with more small arms in circulation, Pakistanis were using weapons to settle differences. Violent ethnic conflicts in the metropolitan areas of the Sindh were blamed on the refugees, if only indirectly.[30]

Refugees were accused of involvement in international drug trafficking. To be sure, Afghans had long been active in the heroin trade which escalated during the war. Incentives increased for Pakistani farmers in the border areas to grow more poppies and, together with resistance-controlled areas of Afghanistan, the region became one of the world's major suppliers to the West. Opium, refined into heroin in laboratories along the border, was typically brought into Pakistan by trucks and mules on their return trips from bringing CIA-purchased arms into Afghanistan.[31] Heroin addiction for the first time also became a serious problem within Pakistan. (Prior to the war, very little heroin had been refined in Pakistan.) By the end of the 1980s, Pakistan was known to have well more than a million drug addicts.[32] Income from the production and purification of heroin and hashish understandably had a major, distorting impact on Pakistan's economy. The illegitimate money, moving in covert channels, could not enter the formal sectors of the economy. Instead it flowed into a gray market that influenced the country's internal commerce in the form of conspicuous consumption and speculative investment, particularly in real estate in all of Pakistan's major cities.[33]

The presence of the Afghans, it was charged, had attracted foreign saboteurs and infiltrators who were seen as posing a threat to Pakistan's security. The Soviets and the Kabul government, directly and indirectly responsible for sabotage efforts and cross-border penetrations of Pakistani airspace and territory, sought to exploit local feelings. It was widely believed that Kabul government agents infiltrated the camps with the intention of creating antagonisms and fomenting riots among the Afghans and with Pakistanis. With all of this, the popular perception among Pakistanis was that the government had not cracked down hard enough on the refugees in their illegal activities.

The refugees have their explanations and their own complaints. A widespread view exists that refugees have not been treated equally under the laws; if there is a dispute with a local Pakistani, the Afghan is held to blame. In general, the refugees have seen themselves as scapegoats for many of Pakistan's social problems, exploited when it becomes convenient. Refugees are forced to accept lower wages: an Afghan hired as a construction worker will earn 15 rupees to 20 for a Pakistani.[34] Afghan leaders have insisted that drug offenses were neither inspired nor condoned by the refugee community. The offenses alleged are portrayed as only minor incidents involving truck drivers motived by greed.[35]

Refugee leaders regularly complained about CCAR's provincial administration of relief efforts. There is widespread belief in the camps that officials in charge of ration distribution have been able to appropriate much of the aid for themselves. Cash subsidies and provisions intended for the refugees have often been delayed, and fees have been exacted for the registration of refugees. Normally, the system of contracting allows for bribes or skimming off of 10 percent. But when Pakistani officials have gone beyond these culturally allowable bounds, demanding 20 or 30 percent, complaints increased and pressures mounted for a crackdown. The authorities were forced to admit to lapses by ill-trained and hastily recruited officials and from time to time were obliged to punish employees with transfers, demotions, and even dismissals.[36] As early as 1981, 225 persons assigned to administrative duties had had punitive action taken against them.[37] More typically, the Pakistan government denied leaks in the humanitarian aid pipeline and refuted allegations of corruption among high CCAR officials.

The health clinics and schools, although appreciated by the refugees, seldom had enough doctors and nurses, and teachers and books were in short supply. In many cases, the level of education was below standard, the curriculum poorly designed, and the teachers unqualified. The Pakistanis also often attempted to control the curriculum, at least to the extent of discouraging the teaching of materials stressing Afghan nationalism. They also vetoed some teaching programs, such as those that taught vocational skills applicable in the local economy, for fear that those less dependent on charity might have more incentive to remain in Pakistan. Thus, the ministries in Islamabad held up releasing funds for a World Bank-sponsored income-generating project for refugees.[38] Government officials tried to limit the refugees to self-contained projects such as truck farming or to involvement with camp-related infrastructural construction, where they would be less able to put down economic roots. Carpet-weaving projects sponsored by the government did take hold among certain ethnic groups but not among the Pushtuns who have no tradition in the carpet trade.

Despite these services, most unavailable in rural Afghanistan and certain to raise popular expectations in the future, the camps have hardly been desirable places to live on a long-term basis. Women, in particular, were obliged to remain cooped up in the camps and missed the freedom of movement that they had once had in Afghanistan; they were anxious to return to more productive lives.[39] Afghan urban, middle class women suffered in particular from ultra-conservative attitudes in Pakistan society that sought to limit or deny them education or career opportunities. Tradition-minded Afghans lamented the deterioration in the Afghan social structure and the emergence of new social groups and individuals disrespectful of previous authority figures. Pakistani authorities were not entirely apologetic about physical and social conditions. The lives of the refugees were, after all, not supposed to be so comfortable that most would not want to return once the fighting had ceased in Afghanistan.

Many Afghans also expressed the existence of a climate of fear in Peshawar for those who might express themselves in a fashion critical of Pakistan. They claimed that they could not speak freely. These Afghans, mainly outside the favored parties, were bitter about the local authorities' inability to halt assassinations and apparent lack of interest in pursuing the killers of well-known Afghan personalities among the refugee community. The PVOs often expressed similar concerns about the need for better protection by Pakistani authorities for their foreign and Afghan personnel.

The inability of the Afghan resistance parties in Peshawar to mount an effective united front against the Kabul government no doubt contributed to the erosion of public sympathy in Pakistan. But in the changing opinion climate, refugees were never constricted in the freedom of movement within Pakistan and, indeed, many were permitted, even encouraged, to pursue vocations outside the camps in order to supplement their relief payments. To be sure, had the Pakistani authorities attempted to restrict the movement of the refugees, forcing them to remain or return to camps, the possibility of armed clashes might have occurred. And whatever frictions emerged between the refugees and local Pakistanis, government officials normally tried to minimize their importance. (Pakistani police also frequently avoided intervention in clashes between rival groups of refugees.) Still, given the increased animosities and opportunities for friction between the refugees and their hosts in the NWFP and Boluchistan, there have been remarkably few incidents of violence between the two communities in the cities or countryside.

After the Soviet Army and Kabul Communists

The government of Pakistan had always conceived of the refugee problem as a temporary one. As a consequence, no long-term plans for the integration or assimilation of the Afghans in the socio-economic fabric of Pakistani society was considered.[40] It also meant that many policies adopted toward the refugees, not entirely popular in Pakistan, were made more tolerable because they could be viewed as only applicable for a time. The distortions that the refugees brought to Pakistan's development priorities and plans would sooner or later be corrected.

It had not come to pass as many predicted that the influx of refugees would intensify national feelings and in seeking greater political autonomy on Pakistani soil, create a de facto Pushtunistan. Many had believed that since it was relatively easy to obtain a National Identity Card or demonstrate a domicile, sooner or later, the Afghan refugee population would be drawn into Pakistani political campaigns and elections.[41] The exiled Afghans might enter coalitions with other political groups or, worst of all, evolve into a state within a state, able to defy the central government.[42] What had been for so long the avoidance of major confrontation between Afghan exiles and the local population, many believed, could not be sustained indefinitely.

A case can be made that Afghan Pushtuns had failed to strengthen regionalist feelings and a nationalist movement as a result of a history and customs that differed to some extent from their Pakistani ethnic cousins. Moreover, the refugees were not numerous enough to assure a major impact on the NWFP with its upwards of 15 million citizens. But should large numbers of refugees become indefinitely residents of Pakistan, either by choice or as a result of a protracted struggle in Afghanistan among the victorious mujahidin, the refugees' economic stake in national politics could come to resemble that of the local population, with significant implications for ethnic politics. In Boluchistan, where the addition of the refugees had probably already tipped the balance to a Pushtun majority, tensions ran higher, and a domestic political fallout might be more immediate.[43]

Until the collapse of the Kabul government, the Pakistan government could not be sure that it might not be forced to reconcile its adherence to the principle of voluntary repatriation with domestic demands that the refugees leave. The concern in Islamabad had been that if the war with the Najibullah regime had dragged on indefinitely, international humanitarian aid would be reduced substantially or ended. To avoid severely aggravating the hardship among the refugees, Pakistan would have had to bear more of the burden. Initially, there seemed little to be worried about. In the expectation of an early repatriation of the refugees following completion of the Soviet withdrawal in February 1989, the UN had announced its "Operation Salam" to raise money to implement programs for the reconstruction and rehabilitation inside Afghanistan. Offices were established in Islamabad, Peshawar, and Quetta as well as in Kabul. But with the war's prolongation -- with increased fighting an additional 70,000 refugees entered and were registered in Pakistan in early 1989 -- pledges of international support for "Salam" fell far short of the anticipated $1.16 billion target.

The Soviet Union promised $600 million for the fund. By early 1992 Moscow's commitments had become meaningless. The mujahidin insistence on billions of dollars in war reparations for Afghanistan from the Soviet Union remained a formal demand until the country's breakup in late 1991. Whatever the good intentions of the leaders in Moscow to work in a common effort for reconstruction after the devastation caused by the war, it seems unlikely that an economically prostrate Russia and others that might inherit the obligations of the former Soviet Union will have much to offer financially. Leaders insisted, in any case, that member states of the Commonwealth could not be held responsible for past mistakes.

Most of the international community hesitated to make large commitments until the conditions for return seemed more favorable. Such potential donor countries as Japan made it clear that their contributions would be delayed until the fighting and divisions among the resistance groups ended. By 1991 the entire UN program had been sharply scaled down and many of its projects canceled; its budget was cut by $31 million. Operation Salam lacked almost $95 million and 61,000 tons of wheat in a projected 1992 budget for returning refugees.[44]

Cross-border operations were also affected by continuing corruption and conflict among the resistance elements. A U.S. program worth $30 million in food aid to the mujahidin had in early 1990 been suspended because of evidence that wheat deliveries were siphoned off by ISI officials for private gain.[45] Peshawar-based ACBAR, which represented 58 foreign and Afghan non-governmental relief organizations, was forced in mid-1991 to suspend activities in the provinces after intense mujahidin infighting and the looting of ACBAR's offices. The work of PVOs was further handicapped when the Pakistani government in early September 1991, following several kidnapping, announced that expatriate aid personnel other than those from the UN would be prevented from crossing into Afghanistan.

Assistance to Afghan refugees in Pakistan was also curtailed. About $400 million in UN and bilateral aid had been spent in 1988; the amount expended in 1990 was one-third less.[46] By the end of 1989 there had been a 25 percent cut in assistance provided the UNHCR. Correspondingly, during the following year most PVOs (whose combined annual budgets had been $107 million) cut back their programs at least 25 to 30 percent as a result of a drying up of private donations and UN and national funds that had been put into their programs.[47] Wheat supplies in 1991 were reported to have been reduced by 25 percent.[48] By some accounts relief supplies furnished to the UNHCR had been diverted to others in need, including Kurdish refugees. Also, as a consequence of the Persian Gulf war, twelve Islamic relief associations grouped as the Islamic Coordination Council and heavily supported by Saudi Arabia and Kuwait saw a reduction of funds and closing of relief centers. Finally, by late 1991 UNHCR financial assistance for the refugees, which had been over $200 million annually, was cut substantially.[49] The reductions affected not only refugee aid in Pakistan but UNHCR-funded projects for reconstruction and rehabilitation inside Afghanistan.

The shortfall in wheat and other commodities as a result of declining deliveries from foreign donors such as the EEC and Japan through the World Food Program had forced Islamabad to draw from its own stocks -- with hope of replenishment later. Rations had been reduced from 500 grams per refugee to 400 grams. Malnutrition, which had never been a problem in the refugee camps, was at least threatened. Reduced food aid to the refugees was said to have prompted thousands of people to flee the camps and, in exchange for modest loans, to enter bonded labor contracts with unscrupulous Pakistani traders.[50] Many more refugees shifted from the camps to the cities, forcing down wage labor rates still further.[51] Dependence on scarce forest wood for fuel increased as the supply of kerosene oil was reduced in half. Yet the hardships in a slowdown in the delivery of relief support was also seen as serving Pakistan's interest in encouraging refugees to seek early repatriation.

Through 1991, the resistance parties in Pakistan had sought to discourage, even prevent, repatriation, declaring it a betrayal of the jihad. However, Pakistan cooperated in devising with the UNHCR and the UN-backed Operation Salam in mid-1990 a three-month pilot project designed to return voluntarily roughly 250,000 Afghans. A year later only about 60,000 Afghans had in fact been repatriated -- most to those border provinces in Afghanistan already secure from Kabul government control.[52] When the UNHCR suggested in November 1991 that Pakistan consider granting citizenship to Afghan refugees who would not or could not return, the Islamabad government flatly rejected the idea of legal integration.[53]

In the Pakistanis' tendency to stress the distortions created by the refugees to local economies, the on balance positive economic stimulus of the Afghans to the border provinces has often been depreciated, if at all acknowledged. At least some of the infrastructure created by their presence is permanent, including water systems, and will remain for local populations. The effect of repatriation can be expected in fact to vary greatly with locality. Of the thousands of Afghans employed by the relief organizations, some can be transferred to Afghanistan. Many others, particularly Pakistanis working in the refugee bureaucracy, will be left unemployed; the impact of lost incomes could have massive effects, especially on the NWFP. The closing of the Peshawar-based AIG ministries at the end of 1991 put upwards of 20,000 Afghans out of work, with obvious impact on the local economy.

To repair the damage left by the refugees, including damage to the environment, Pakistan can be expected to turn to its traditional aid donors for assistance, describing its problem as one of rehabilitation as a result of having welcomed the refugees. But in view of the halt in overall U.S. economic assistance to Pakistan in 1991 and the donor fatigue evident among traditional Western donors, the prospects are not promising.

Refugees and Repatriation

A worst case scenario for Pakistan would have occurred if the war against the former communist regime had continued indefinitely and international aid groups had tired of their relief role. The onus of financing the refugees and their rehabilitation could have fallen heavily on Pakistan. In the end, despite Pakistan's displeasure with the international community's eagerness to abandon their long-held obligations, the country was spared from watching the relief organizations wash their hands entirely of the refugees, as might have happened if Islamic forces had not prevailed when they did -- in late April 1992.

Authorities had been concerned that the local economy could not in the future support the disproportionately young, poorly educated refugee population that would soon grow into a restless mass prone to crime and violence and unable to find jobs. The situation would certainly have become desperate if many of the Pakistanis working abroad were forced to return to the domestic work force, a development partly realized with the jobs lost in Iraq in 1990. The Punjabi-led military had been fearful of one day having to face an uprising among the refugees resisting national authority. Officials were uneasy about the large stock of weapons in the hands of resident Afghans.

Pakistan was also relieved from having to face the difficult decision whether to cut off support in an effort to force the refugees back into Afghanistan. Violence might have followed had there been a negotiated solution acceptable to the government and public but resisted by the mujahidin and their political allies. Islamabad would, in all likelihood, have tried to step up pressure for the resistance leadership to approve an agreement while also beginning the process of repatriation of the refugees. Certainly, economic pressure would have been applied long before any military-supported measures. Any form of armed confrontation with the mujahidin held out the wider possibility of undermining the Pakistani state.

Even with the defeat of the Kabul regime, the largest number of Afghans are not expected to leave until the inter-factional warfare that erupted in summer 1992 ends. (Indeed, the heavy fighting and high food prices have created thousands of new refugees from Kabul, many of them taking refuge in Pakistan.) Even then, the Afghans most reluctant to leave will be those who have succeeded in Pakistan's urban economy; many of them may stay indefinitely. Large numbers of refugees hesitate to commit their families to a return until reconstruction can provide them with something like the services (e.g., water, health, electricity and jobs) that have been generally available in Pakistan. Some will reject the idea of returning immediately for ideological reasons, unsure of the social and political restrictions to be encountered under an Islamic government.

The first to take their chances in returning are those refugees who have had difficulty finding work in Pakistan. Most now anticipate a cut-off of services in the camps in the near future. Aside from problems of food and shelter in Afghanistan, they have reason to be concerned about mines; more than 10 million are scattered around the country.[54] The largely uncharted mines were certain to pose an obstacle to farming and grazing. Despite this, by July, 1992, more than 25,000 were crossing the border weekly and, over all, more than 800,000 had been repatriated. To encourage them, on turning in their ration books at the border crossing, each family received from the UN the equivalent of $135 in cash and about 650 pounds of wheat. A shortage of funds no doubt precluded faster repatriation.[55] The exodus then slowed, however, with the eruption of heavy factional fighting in Kabul and elsewhere and, indeed, there began in August a reverse flow that led the Pakistan government to close the borders to returning refugees.

The eventual transfer of most private aid groups from Peshawar to Kabul and elsewhere in Afghanistan is expected to increase the willingness of many refugees to return. Although the PVOs have been advised by the UN to delay their transfer to Kabul as their presence would pose a burden on the new government, most relief organizations have petitioned the mujahidin-led government in Kabul to permit them to shift their offices. The departure of aid workers from Pakistan will likely accelerate as the Pakistan government has begun to refuse to extend aid workers visas and has removed the certification of some groups. The exodus of private agencies is almost certain to bring in time new hardship to those refugees as yet not able or willing to return to Afghanistan.

Pakistani authorities do not expect to see all their refugee-related problems eliminated once the camps are closed. On one hand, with fewer refugees much of the smuggling of guns and consumer goods will probably drop off. On the other, many repatriated Afghan farmers will depend on drug money in an effort to survive when they return to devastated farms and villages. An effective program of drug control on both sides of the frontier cannot occur until alternative, marketable crops have been introduced. During the war, the drug trade routes between the tribal areas of Pakistan and Afghanistan helped to financed resistance groups. With the withdrawal of U.S. and other country's military assistance, armed Afghan groups may well become more deeply involved in poppy cultivation. Informal sector financing becomes an attractive substitute source of money if the warring factions in Afghanistan, many with connections to the international drug trade, become desperate for resources.

Much of the planning of the Pakistanis for returning refugees is premised on the proposition that fundamental changes have occurred in Afghan society. The experiences of the refugees in Pakistan, living under military and civilian governments, will undoubtedly affect Afghans' expectations and preferences. They will no doubt be far more demanding of an Afghan government for services. Refugees are unlikely to forget quickly the educational and medical assistance they received for the first time in Pakistan. They may also be less tolerant of the traditionally ineffective Afghan central authorities. At the same time, however, many of those who are claimants for power in Kabul may not feel especially accountable to popular opinions, especially where they believe that their principal task in ruling is to carry out God's will.

The attitude among the returning Afghans toward Pakistan is ambivalent. There remains gratitude for hospitality and brotherly assistance in a sacred war. Even so, there is a strong residue of resentment for Pakistan's manipulation of Afghan refugees and resistance politics. Many Afghans share the view that Pakistan is likely to be mainly interested in shaping the postwar balance of power and in heading off any revival of a strong Pushtun nationalism. The lasting legacy of the refugees in Pakistan may rest on future developments in relations between the two countries, above all, on the willingness of governments in Islamabad to forego the kind of patronizing role that came so naturally when the Afghans found shelter in Pakistan.

Notes

1. Farr, Grant M. "The Effect of the Refugees on Pakistan," in Craig Baxter (ed.), *Zia's Pakistan; Politics and Stability in a Frontline State* (Boulder CO: Westview, 1985), p. 94.

2. Amin, Tahir. "Afghan Resistance: Past, Present and Future," *Asian Survey*, 24, 4 (April 1984): p. 378.

3. Malik, Hafeez. "The Afghan Crisis and its Impact on Pakistan," *Journal of South Asian and Middle Eastern Studies*, Vol. 5, No. 3 (Spring 1982): p. 43. Also see the discussion by Mohammed Ayoob, "Dateline Pakistan: A Passage to Anarchy," *Foreign Policy*, No. 59 (Summer 1985): p. 164.

4. Farr, p. 95.

5. Akbar, S. Ahmed, "Afghan Refugees, Aid, and Anthropologists," *Internationales Asienforum*, Vol. 12, No. 1 (1981): p. 83.

6. Farr, p. 161.

7. Girardet, Edward. *Afghanistan: The Soviet War*, New York: St. Martin's Press, 1985, p. 205, reports a figure of 7,000 in the administrative infrastructure mid-decade.

8. A Pakistan government advertisement, *The New York Times*, September 21, 1987, p. 19.

9. Rizvi, Askari. "Afghan Refugees in Pakistan: Influx, Humanitarian Assistance and Implications," *Pakistan Horizon*, Vol. 36, No. 1: p. 49.

10. Dupree, Nancy. "Demographic Reporting on Afghan Refugees in Pakistan," *Modern Asian Studies*, Vol. 25, No. 2 (1988): p. 244.

11. Dupree, Louis. *Modern Asian Studies*, 243. Also, Robert Wirsing, "Pakistan and the War in Afghanistan," in *Asian Affairs*, Vol. 14, No. 2 (Summer 1987): p. 74.

12. Fullerton, John. "A Rift Among Rebels," *Far Eastern Economic Review*, October 29, 1982, p. 20.

13. Carter, A. Lynn and Kerry Connor, "A Preliminary Investigation of Contemporary Afghan Councils," unpublished report to the Agency Coordinating Body for Afghan Relief (ACBAR), Peshawar, April 1989, pp. 18-19.

14. Ahmed, pp. 86-87.

15. Hamman, Henry. "The Afghan Refugee Crisis," unpublished paper, 1980, pp. 47-48.

16. Magnus, Ralph H. "Afghanistan: Humanitarian Response to the Inhuman Strategy," in Grant M. Farr, and John G. Merriam (eds.), *Afghan Resistance: The Politics of Survival*, (Boulder CO: Westview Press, 1987), pp. 204-205.

17. Hamman, pp. 47-48.

18. Girardet, Edward. "Corrupt Officials Reap Spoils of Afghan War," *Christian Science Monitor*, September 7, 1988.

19. Bennett, Jon. Executive Director of ACBAR, at an address at the Afghanistan Relief Committee Conference of Afghanistan Humanitarian Support Organizations, held February 8-10, 1991 in New York City, reported in *Afghanistan Forum*, March 1991, p. 23. Also see Louis and Nancy Dupree, "Afghan Refugees in Pakistan," *World Refugee Survey: 1987 in Review*. U.S. Committee for Refugees, March 15, 1988, p. 18; Dawn (Karachi) May 13, 1989.

20. *Frontier Post* (Peshawar), February 17, 1990.

21. *Pakistan Times*, (Islamabad), May 27, 1990.
Humanitarian aid inside Afghanistan was originally funded by USAID's office of Foreign Disaster Assistance and later by the office of the AID representative for Afghanistan. International Rescue Committee (IRC) was the prime grantee, and made sub-contracts with other PVOs, most European organizations. In 1988, the assistance effort became known as Rural Assistance Program. Other cross-border programs, such as the University of Nebraska at Omaha's educational assistance, were separately funded. From information provided by Louis Wiesner, a former foreign service officer who worked with IRC.

22. Matinuddin, Kamal. "Afghanistan Refugees: The Geostrategic Context," in Ewan Anderson and Nancy Hatch Dupree (eds.), *The Cultural Basis of Afghan Nationalism*, London and New York: Pinter Publishers, 1990, p. 223.

23. Dupree, Louis and Nancy. Pp. 17-18. The authors also note that a refugee village was established outside of Karachi for 18,500 unregistered non-Pushtun refugees, most of whom had their quarters in the city destroyed by authorities during a search for smugglers and drug dealers.

24. Janata, Alfred. "Afghanistan: The Ethnic Dimension," in Anderson and Dupree, p. 68.

25. Rizvi, p. 51, p. 53.

26. *Frontier Post*, November 11, 1991.

27. Janata, p. 68. Also see Hafeez Malik, *Journal of Middle East and South Asian Studies*, Vol. 5, No. 3 (Spring 1982): pp. 45-56. Officials in the NWFP, in a brief effort during 1984 to reduce the number of Afghans entering the job market in the cities imposed half-hearted measures to confine the refugees to their camps. *The New York Times*, November 25, 1984. Concern about the disparity in treatment of refugees and Pakistanis in the refugee-affected

areas led to a program under a cooperative arrangement in 1990 between the government of Pakistan, the UNHCR, and World Bank. The program was designed to create employment opportunities for Pakistani citizens as well as Afghan refugees. *Frontier Post*, February 17, 1990.

28. Khan, Azmat H. "The Afghanistan Problem: Its Impact and Pakistan," *Central Asian Studies* (Peshawar), No. 24 (Summer 1989): p. 142.

29. "Silent Voices #1," a report by the Refugee Council in association with the British Agencies Afghan Groups, reprinted in *Afghanistan Forum*, May 1991, p. 14.

30. Kazi, Aftab A. "Ethnic Nationalism and Super-powers in South Asia: Sindhis and Boluchis, in the *Journal of Asian and African Affairs*, Vol. 1, No. 1 (July 1989): p. 7.

31. Weiner, p. 151. The author reports that by 1989 total production and transshipment of heroin was as much as the rest of the world combined.

32. *The New York Times*, July 30 1989.

33. Burki, Shahid Javed. *Muslim* (Islamabad), February 14, 1989.

34. UNHCR report, February 1986, cited in Hafizullah Emadi, "Resettlement Pattern: The Afghan Refugees in Pakistan," *Cultural Survival Quarterly*, Vol. 12, No. 4 (1988): p. 22.

35. A summary of proceeding from the International Symposium "The Crisis of Migration from Afghanistan: Domestic and Foreign Implications," co-sponsored by the Refugee Studies Program. Oxford University, March 29-April 2, 1987, p. 12. Arab volunteers were probably responsible for many of the crimes blamed on Afghan refugees, including the smuggling of military equipment. Salamat Ali, *Far Eastern Economic Review*, May 23, 1991, pp. 23-24. There were also reports that Pakistani officials were ignoring charges that the Arab volunteers were keeping Afghan women as slaves as well as buying Soviet POWs from mujahidin and killing them. *The Friday Times* (Lahore), March 19-25, 1992 and *Rising Nepal* (Kathmandu), in an Associated Press report from Peshawar, March 14, 1992.

36. Azar, Said. "Refugees in Pakistan: The Pakistani View," in Anderson and Dupree, p. 112.

37. *Muslim*, October 19, 1981.

38. *Muslim*, June 14, 1989.

39. Dupree in Saikal, p. 36.

40. Azar, p. 109.

41. Rizvi, p. 57.

42. See Malik, p. 46.

43. Farr notes (p. 175) that the Zia regime, realizing the explosiveness of the ethnic tensions in Boluchistan, tried to buy off the traditional Boluch leaders with promises of development projects.

44. Foreign Broadcast Information Service (FBIS), South Asia and the Middle East, November, 29, 1991, p. 42 from a statement by the UN's representative Benon Sevan, reported by AFP, November 27, 1991.

45. *The New York Times*, February 2, 1990. Direct U.S. humanitarian aid for the Afghans, including the refugees, amounted to about $70 million, not counting that aid contributed to international agencies. *Ibid.*, April 26, 1992.

46. Address by Jon Bennett, Executive Director of ACBAR on February 10, 1991 reported in Afghanistan Forum, March 1991, p. 23.

47. Bennett, p. 16.

48. BBC Foreign Service reported in *Afghan Jihad*, Vol. 4, No. 4 (July-September 1991): p. 312.

49. *Frontier Post*, November 2, 1991. There were some new commitments of assistance during the period. The Saudi Ambassador to Pakistan pledged $7.5 million for education programs in both Pakistan and Afghanistan. The existing schools had been closed for a lack of funds. AFGHANews, November 15, 1991.

50. Kelsey, Tim. In *The Independent* (Islamabad), August 14, 1991.

51. *Frontier Post*, November 2, 1991.

52. Zehra, Nasim. "Afghan Refugee Repatriation: A Pakistani Perspective" in Suroosh Irfani and Fazul-ur-Rahman (eds.), *Afghanistan: Looking to the Future* (Islamabad: Institute of Strategic Studies, 1992), p. 49.

53. *Frontier Post*, November 2, 1991.

54. Burke, Justin. In the *Christian Science Monitor*, May 14, 1992. The UN estimates that 200,000 people were killed during the war by mines and 400,000 maimed during the 14-year war. At most only 22,000 mines had been removed during two years of de-mining operations.

55. The UN had hoped for $180 million in June for Afghan repatriation and reconstruction activities but received only $29 million, mainly owing to the competing demands for refugee funds in Yugoslavia, Cambodia, and the horn of Africa. *The New York Times*, July 1, 1992.

8

The Geopolitics of the Asian Subcontinent: Pakistan's Security Environment

Lawrence Ziring

The Cold War only indirectly impacted on the subcontinent. In spite of the hostilities on the Korean peninsula, as well as Indochina and the Middle East, South Asia seemed somewhat removed from the range of superpower maneuvering -- that is, up until the Soviet invasion of Afghanistan. For a brief period in the 1950s, the United States used an airfield outside Peshawar for reconnaissance overflights of the Soviet Union, while the Soviets enjoyed port call options at Indian naval facilities, -- but neither superpower actually committed forces to either country. The primary Cold War antagonists nonetheless entered into treaty arrangements with the indigenous principals. Either alliances or understandings were forged that were supposed to provide for equilibrium and hence assure the security and territorial integrity of the subcontinent's major actors. The United States did so with Pakistan in 1954 and 1956, reaffirming its commitment in 1959, while the Soviet Union entered into a treaty of friendship and cooperation with India in 1971. Each South Asian state became a recipient of substantial military transfers, but in matters of foreign policy and no less so in national security areas, both New Delhi and Islamabad responded to their own perceptions of national need.

Neither Pakistan nor India allowed themselves to be significantly influenced by their associations with the superpowers. Moreover, Pakistan maintained diplomatic arrangements with Moscow, and enjoyed an excellent relationship with the People's Republic of China -- much before it became fashionable in the West. In fact, it was Pakistan that literally cleared a path for Washington to begin its long process of rapprochement with Beijing. India also continued to do business with Washington, despite its close ties to Moscow, and the Americans were sustained in the belief that India was the world's largest democracy and that its arrangements with the Soviets were expedient not ideological.[1]

New Delhi, however, displayed deep irritation with the United States from the earliest days following the country's independence. New Delhi was distressed by American military actions on the Korean peninsula. The Indian government informed Washington the Chinese would send their forces across the Yalu river if the United States pressed its offensive to the Chinese border, and it was significantly distressed that the Americans refused to heed their warning of an expanded conflict. India also was among Washington's harshest critics in the Indochinese fighting and it condemned American intervention in the Vietnamese civil war. Indian government officials vehemently and consistently disapproved of American military transfers to Pakistan, provided ostensibly to ward off communist threats, but which they argued would only be used against India. They also objected to the American intrusion in the region, and were highly critical of U.S. naval and air operations from the Indian Ocean island of Diego Garcia. The American presence in the Indian Ocean, according to prominent Indian spokesmen, increased rather than reduced the likelihood of conflict in the subcontinent.

When India intervened in Pakistan's civil war in 1971, it was the U.S. that condemned New Delhi, and this time it was New Delhi's turn to ignore the complaint. Washington's despatch of a nuclear aircraft carrier battle group to the Bay of Bengal illustrated the magnitude of the strained relations, but that exercise did not deflect Indian authorities from pursuing their campaign in East Pakistan, which included successful attacks on West Pakistani military installations, command centers, and infrastructure. Nor could Washington prevent India from overrunning Pakistan's eastern province, forcing the surrender of the Pakistani garrison, or midwifing the creation of the independent state of Bangladesh.

Despite Moscow's complicity in the dismemberment of Pakistan, Islamabad's criticism of the Soviet Union was subdued and during the subsequent administration of Zulfikar Ali Bhutto serious efforts were made at normalizing relations with the communist superpower. Only after Moscow's invasion of Afghanistan in 1979, was Islamabad forced to take a stronger stand against the Soviet state. Moreover, the strain in Pakistan-Soviet relations caused by the Kremlin's decision to forcibly intervene in Afghanistan was managed by the general who had deposed and ultimately had Bhutto executed.[2]

General Mohammed Zia ul-Haq entered into substantial defense agreements with Ronald Reagan that reaffirmed American commitment in support of Pakistan's national security. American military assistance to Islamabad, although largely in abeyance up until that time, resumed in earnest when Soviet troops were deployed along the Pakistan border. The magnitude of that American support stiffened Pakistani resolve and the country was touted as America's "frontline state" in the containment of a more aggressive Soviet imperialism. Indeed it was during this episode that Ronald Reagan referred to the Soviet Union as the "Evil Empire." Pakistanis, however, had reason to be skeptical of Washington's long-term commitments. That commitment was not only questioned, it was literally overwhelmed by the controversy between Washington and Islamabad over Pakistan's nuclear program. Indeed the nuclear issue could not be contained after the Soviet army withdrew from Afghanistan. Moreover, Zia's death in the explosion of his military aircraft in 1988, coming as it did after the UN-mediated Soviet withdrawal, altered American relations with Islamabad dramatically. The Americans were delighted with Benazir Bhutto's subsequent electoral victory as well as the return of the government to civilian control.

Although the war in Afghanistan continued after the Soviet withdrawal, and although a Marxist regime remained in control of Kabul for several years thereafter, the U.S. judged the Afghan problem short-term and not nearly as serious as Pakistan's atomic enterprise. Benazir's success in captivating Washington, however, temporarily obscured difficulties in the relationship. In fact the strains in American-Pakistani relations were not apparent until August 1990, following Benazir's forced removal by President Ghulam Ishaq Khan on grounds that her government was ineffective and corrupt. Washington's decision to discontinue all aid to Islamabad was said to be based upon the Pressler Amendment to the U.S. trade act which prevented the transfer of assistance to countries not certified by the President as being free of nuclear weapons programs. But an unstated explanation for the aid cut-off was clearly Washington's dissatisfaction over the Bhutto ouster, and the belief that the Pakistani military was too strong a political force in the country. Washington seemed resigned to a nuclear Pakistan. In the aftermath of the Cold War, however, in the absence of a Soviet threat to South Asia, it preferred a government in Islamabad not only controlled by civilians, but one with which it had reason to believe it had some rapport.[3]

Changing Security Perceptions

The subcontinent faded as a focal point of superpower maneuvering after the U.S.-Soviet detente reached new levels of understanding in 1991. The Soviets reduced their military support to India. Fewer Soviet naval vessels operated in the Indian Ocean, and Moscow expressed a desire to improve relations with all the countries of the region. The pressure on the Pakistani frontier with Afghanistan was virtually eliminated after the Soviet troop withdrawal, and Moscow ceased its vitriolic attacks on Pakistani officials following Zia's death. The United States, too, seemed to prefer a lower profile in the region, and diplomatic efforts were more aimed at normalizing relations with India than acknowledging a new relationship with Pakistan. Indeed, legislation that would have forced India to conform to the Pressler amendment was deemed harmful by important members of the Congress, and India did not suffer the same fate as Pakistan. In spite of a vote in the House of Representatives that approved a cut-off of technical and military aid to India, New Delhi's supporters in the Congress strongly opposed applying the same standards to India that had been imposed on Pakistan.

India-Pakistan rivalry intensified rather than diminished in the aftermath of the Cold War. The Kashmir dispute flared anew and the ferocity of the encounter between Indian troops and Kashmiri liberation organizations was attributed to the support provided the latter by Islamabad. Pakistan argued that the uprising was spontaneous, but perhaps keyed by the *intifada* on the West Bank as well as the heightened call for self-determination among many of the former republics of the Soviet Union. Although offering moral and diplomatic support to the Kashmiris, Islamabad insisted it was neither infiltrating irregulars into the region nor providing the resistance with weapons or training. Of course India believed none of this. But whatever the reason or the complicity of the parties, the strife in Kashmir demonstrated the volatility in the region and that the parties were prepared to pursue their individual interests irrespective of the mayhem it caused.[4]

India-Pakistan hostility, however, was not the only problem plaguing the subcontinent. Ethnic and religious elements within Sri Lanka remained unreconciled, and violence and counter-violence became permanent features of life and death in the island nation. Indian army intervention in the 1980s failed to put an end to the bloodletting or the destruction of property. Tribal warfare in Bangladesh's Chittagong Hill Tracts spilled over into India with Burma causing problems for all three countries. Bangladesh was involved in a long-term dispute with India over the use of the Ganges/Brahmaputra river system, while Bengali migrants to Assam aroused passionate attacks that the settlers could not adequately defend themselves against. Civil unrest in Burma assumed new dimensions in 1991-92, and the Rangoon government in part diverted popular attention from itself through the victimization of its Muslim minority. Burmese Muslims sought refuge in Bangladesh, and the marshaling of Rangoon's forces on the Bangladesh frontier was not only disturbing to Dhaka, it also caused Pakistan's foreign ministry to register its concern for the Muslim refugees crowding into Bangladeshi camps.

Nepal sought to resist Indian encroachment on its trade and commerce, but New Delhi continued to toy with that country's sovereignty. Efforts at a peaceful resolution of their joint border problem, and Indian fears that China would gain inroads into Nepal further exacerbated conditions between New Delhi and Beijing. Nepal and Bhutan could not ignore India's earlier occupation and annexation of neighboring Sikkim, or that only China among the world's nations seemed to notice. Indeed, none of these "other" South Asian dilemmas drew much attention from the outside world.

Nevertheless, to strategists observing the larger region, one segment of the subcontinent, no matter how remote, could not be divorced from the larger whole, nor indeed from the extended area around it. With the passing of the Cold War, the geopolitics of the subcontinent demanded a new frame of reference, one which defined an Asian rather than a global context; one more driven by internal questions and decidedly less influenced by the once vaunted superpowers. Above all, more attention needed to be given subnational and ethnic questions, and there was considerable need for regional understandings and cooperation. The creation of the South Asian Association of Regional Cooperation (SAARC) in the 1980s was prompted by the smaller states of the subcontinent which hoped its formation would offset the preponderance of Indian power and influence and permit them greater self-expression.[5] SAARC in the 1990s, however, remained a promise, hardly a reality.

The Geopolitical Background

The lowering of the Union Jack on the subcontinent in August 1947 ended an era and began another. Independence brought the partition of British India and the formation of two independent, sovereign states. India was a known entity and a charter member of the United Nations, while Pakistan was totally new and an uncertain addition to the list of emerging states. India, after China, was the largest of the third world nations; Pakistan was second only to Indonesia in housing the largest Muslim population. Each country also aspired to leadership roles beyond their immediate surroundings. India made gestures at leading the third world, while Pakistan saw itself in the vanguard of independent Muslim states. Neither, however, was able to transcend the parochial, restricted setting of the subcontinent and their representation of international movements was seldom successful.

Most important, India and Pakistan were enemies at independence and they remained so during the length of the Cold War. The two countries made war on one another on the eve of their emergence in 1947, again in 1965, and engaged in a climactic struggle in 1971 which caused the dismemberment of Pakistan and the creation of still another new sovereign entity, the Bengali state of Bangladesh.[6] Bangladesh, however, was not the root cause of Indo-Pakistani hostility.

The territorial dispute that keyed their mutual antagonism was the Muslim-majority state of Kashmir, in the north central extremity of the subcontinent. The war that erupted at independence was fought for control of this region and neither army was able to decisively defeat the other. The Kashmir area was divided by the occupying armies of both nations, the Indians holding the verdant, Muslim-dominant Vale and more southernly region of Jammu, while the Pakistanis controlled the western territory which they called Azad (Free) Kashmir. The United Nations tried to mediate a settlement satisfactory to both parties. Somewhat in despair, it ultimately called for a plebiscite which New Delhi ignored, thus ensuring the conflict would be protracted. In 1957, India announced Kashmir had become a state within the Indian union. Only Pakistan seriously challenged the action, and its refusal to acknowledge the *fait accompli* led inexorably to the Indo-Pakistani war of 1965 wherein an over-confident Pakistani government expected to chase the Indian army from the disputed territory. The failure to achieve that objective, however, only provided more fuel for the passionate populations on both sides of their international border.

The United States earlier tried to mediate the dispute but it, too, failed to move the parties, and when the 1965 war broke out, Washington, although tied to Pakistan through a series of treaties, preferred to ignore the contest. The United States embargoed arms to both countries, but the impact of the action was felt only in Pakistan.[7] The Soviet Union, on the other hand, as early as 1955 had declared its support for the Indian claim to Kashmir. Moreover, in 1965 the Soviets began a major arms transfer to India. That arms transfer reached its highest level in the 1970s and 80s.

Thus it was left to China to befriend Pakistan in its hour of need. Although initially friendly to India, China had shifted its position to favor Islamabad when New Delhi refused to negotiate a border settlement along the Tibetan frontier. Indeed, in 1962, China invaded India's northeastern territories and Beijing's army quickly routed the Indian forces in the mountainous region. Although China withdrew its forces from much of the conquered territory, it drew its own line of control between the two opposed armies. Moreover, the Chinese attack frightened the Americans, who immediately despatched weapons to the Indian army, over the protests of the Pakistani government.[8] When the border skirmish drew to a close, India and China had become mortal enemies, but Soviet arms merchants, rather than Americans were welcomed in New Delhi. India's actions were not only a response to the Sino-Soviet schism, but also a criticism of Washington's assertion of continuing ties to Pakistan.

With the Soviet Union and the United States little more than observers during the 1965 Indo-Pakistani war, Beijing publicly warned New Delhi that it would again send its forces across the Tibetan border into India if New Delhi did not cease and desist in its actions against Pakistan in Kashmir--and against Pakistan's vital Punjab province. The acceptance of a UN-arranged cease-fire by New Delhi and Islamabad put an end to the threat of a wider war in the area, but it was not the international body that engineered a settlement between the warring parties.

The Soviets were the clear beneficiaries of the 1965 conflict, and it was the Kremlin that brokered an agreement between the Pakistani president and the Indian prime minister in Tashkent in 1966. Nevertheless, even this action could not put an end to the quarrel between the two largest subcontinental states. Nor did it prevent the Indo-Pakistani War of 1971, or, in fact, allow Moscow to continue its role as "honest" broker. In that latter conflict Moscow assisted India by casting a veto in the UN Security Council and thus nullified international efforts at terminating the intrusion before the Pakistani army suffered total defeat. Moreover, the United States disapproved of India's role in severing Pakistan's Bengal province from greater Pakistan, but Moscow was eager to recognize the new independent state of Bangladesh, and the United States eventually did so as well.[9]

The physical breakup of Pakistan left a rump Pakistan in the western region of the subcontinent and Zulfikar Ali Bhutto was called upon to "pick up the pieces" of a demoralized nation and bankrupt government. With the Pakistani army humiliated by its defeat, with 93,000 Pakistani soldiers prisoners of war in India, with Bangladesh an accomplished fact, Bhutto moved quickly to reorganize the armed forces so as to ensure its loyalty to his command. Within weeks of his consolidation of power, Bhutto forced into retirement generals he described as "bonapartist." Strengthened by popular support as well as a chastened army, Bhutto acknowledged India's military supremacy in the subcontinent. He was then able to do what Ayub Khan could not do at Tashkent, he met with Indian Prime Minister Indira Gandhi and agreed to arrangements that were aimed at reducing the antagonism between the two countries, but which could not be accomplished without yielding to Indian hegemonic claims.

Although Bhutto supporters argue to the contrary, the evidence reveals Bhutto yielded on the Kashmir issue. Without disparaging the Muslim quest for a dominant voice in Kashmiri affairs, he nonetheless canceled Pakistan's claim to the territory. In calling for the mutual recognition of each country's territorial integrity, Bhutto also legitimated the earlier Indian action making Kashmir a part of the Indian Union. The Simla Summit, therefore, was the first serious round of diplomacy entered into between the heretofore mortal foes. Before Bhutto's sudden removal from the Prime Minister's office in 1977, indeed before his incarceration and death on the gallows, Pakistan and India were to restore diplomatic relations, an action that had its roots in Simla.[10]

In the eleven years that followed Bhutto's ouster, Pakistan was governed by one dominant personality, General Mohammed Zia ul-Haq. Zia had to contend with the Soviet invasion of Afghanistan. Not less significant, he had to prevent India from pressing against Pakistan's eastern frontier at the same time that the Soviet Union seemed to be threatening the country's western border. The 1977 ouster of Bhutto coincided with Indira Gandhi's electoral defeat that same year. General Zia found Indira's immediate successor, Moraji Desai, a more pliable personality and more ready to reduce the tension between New Delhi and Islamabad. Desai also offered to normalize relations with the United States, still strained by the Bangladesh affair. For a brief period relations between India, Pakistan and the United States appeared to improve.

Indira's return in 1980 caused a setback in these efforts. Moreover, New Delhi, under her leadership, postured support for the Marxist government in Kabul and hence for the Soviet cause, even if this was not the intention. Tensions between India and Pakistan continued to mount, and they became even more intense with a growing Sikh problem within India. Pakistan appeared to be sympathetic to the more radical Sikhs who voiced secessionist demands. Moreover, Pakistan was perceived as aiding and abetting the Sikhs, in part as retribution for Indian interference in Pakistan's civil war and its befriending of the Bengalis. New Delhi not only accused Islamabad of providing safe haven for militant Sikhs, but also said they were providing training and weapons in Pakistan, and that the purpose of the exercise was nothing less than the destruction of the Indian Union.

Indira's authorized assault on Sikh dissidents holed up in the Golden Temple in Amritsar in 1984, and the ferocity of that encounter highlighted New Delhi's concern that the Sikh problem, if allowed to spread and deepen, would prove the undoing of the Indian polity. Pakistan was implicated in this action too. Moreover, Prime Minister Gandhi's assassination at the hands of her Sikh bodyguards later in 1984, further exacerbated relations between New Delhi and Islamabad. The emergence of Rajiv Gandhi as Prime Minister of India did not relieve the situation. On the one side, Rajiv sought to make peace with Sikh moderates, while on the other, he appeared to threaten Pakistan. Neither tactic worked. Sikh moderates were killed by their more fanatical brethren and the fratricide in the Punjab continued unabated. On the other hand, Pakistan resisted all Indian pressures, and because of the war in Afghanistan, was bolstered in its military defenses by U.S.weapons transfers.

In 1986 India and Pakistan massed troops on opposite sides of their shared frontier and a new, more destructive conflict was forecast. Only the surprise decision by General Zia ul-Haq to fly to India to meet with his Indian counterpart in February 1987 averted a major conflict. In what was described as "cricket diplomacy" (the stated purpose of Zia's India trip was to view a cricket match) the two leaders agreed to pull back their respective forces and open a more concerted dialogue at the foreign minister's level-- their objective was the avoidance of a war neither country wanted, nor could afford.

Although a showdown was avoided several times between 1986 and 1988, small-scale fighting broke out on the line dividing Indian from Pakistani-held Kashmir. Clashes over the Siachen Glacier, seized by India, caused almost daily casualties. Diplomacy again tried to meet the test but it only proved capable of isolating, not ending, the conflict.

After Zia's death in the explosion of his military air transport in August 1988, the political climate underwent significant change inside Pakistan. Benazir Bhutto's political organization, the Pakistan People's Party (PPP), managed a significant showing in the November 1988 national election and Benazir was called upon to form a new civilian government. The young woman, the first to head a Muslim government, on the surface at least, seemed to find rapport with her Indian counterpart, the equally youthful Rajiv Gandhi. Their meeting together seemed to promise a reduction in the hostility between their two countries. Moreover, New Delhi signalled its readiness to deal with a Pakistan government no longer managed by men in uniform. But Benazir's nineteen months in office were crowned with no more success in reconciling Pakistani-Indian relations than her predecessors. Moreover, during that brief tenure the situation in Indian Kashmir again flared into conflict.

Somewhat provoked by domestic conditions within Kashmir, in part prompted by Pakistani members of the clandestine services, and in some measure imitative of the intifada in the West Bank territory under Israeli occupation, young Kashmiris renewed their agitation against New Delhi. Calling for self-determination, determined bands of youthful demonstrators assaulted Indian installations within the state. They also called upon the Islamabad government for assistance. Pakistan endeavored to popularize the cause of the Kashmiris by bringing the matter before international fora within as well as outside the Islamic world. The United Nations, the scene of the original complaint, was again made the setting for the most concerted diplomatic effort--with Islamabad leading the way. But as in the past, so this time too, the world seemed little interested in the plight of the Kashmiris. Moreover, problems elsewhere, especially in the Middle East in 1990, prevented the Kashmir question from being given serious international attention.

The United States and the Soviet Union were nevertheless disturbed by developments in the region. In May 1990 war between India and Pakistan again appeared imminent. President Bush sent a special emissary to Islamabad with the purpose of defusing the conflict.[11] India was an acknowledged nuclear power, having detonated an atomic device in 1974. Since that time Pakistan had feverishly, more often clandestinely, sought to emulate India, believing but never stating publicly that its survival was dependent upon its capacity to develop nuclear weapons.

Zulfikar Ali Bhutto had called for the construction of an "Islamic bomb" in the mid-70s and Pakistan, like India, had declined becoming a signatory to the nuclear non-proliferation treaty. After Bhutto, General Zia continued the Pakistani program, in fact in 1981 had even accelerated it. The U.S. government, which had hardly displayed any interest in India's nuclear development, and moreover had continued to supply New Delhi with nuclear fuel even after the explosion in the Rajasthan desert, was overtly distressed with the Pakistani program. Pakistan cited the double standard and reminded

Washington that Islamabad not India had security treaty ties with the United States. Islamabad also argued that its nuclear program was solely concerned with the peaceful uses of the atom, that Pakistan wanted energy independence, and that this was the only purpose of its program. Bhutto's original call for a bomb, however, continued to sound menacing in Washington circles.

By the spring of 1990, given the tension between India and Pakistan, and India's capacity to produce atomic weapons as well as Pakistan's determination to do so, United States intelligence concluded a nuclear exchange on the subcontinent was a real possibility, and that such an exchange might well be sparked by the Kashmir problem. The American mission to Pakistan and a parallel Soviet mission to India during that period were momentarily successful in that the two antagonists agreed to reopen their suspended diplomatic dialogue. But if a decision on Kashmir was anticipated, all opportunities seemed to evaporate when the interest of the world community was drawn away from that trouble spot to another in the Middle East. Iraq's invasion of Kuwait on August 2, 1990 provided the necessary cover for India to contain the Kashmiri uprising unimpeded by international opinion let alone counteraction.

The Dissolution of the Soviet Union

Operation Desert Shield was mounted to deter an anticipated Iraqi advance into Saudi Arabia, but quickly escalated into an international effort to liberate Kuwait from Iraqi occupation. The success of Desert Shield produced Operation Desert Storm and the latter proved to be the offensive phase of the program that forced Baghdad to relinquish control of the small oil kingdom. The success of that endeavor also relieved the pressure on Saudi Arabia. The Soviet Union provided the necessary diplomatic support for both the military buildup and ultimately its use in the Gulf war. Indeed, Moscow's decision to support the UN resolutions against its Iraqi ally was a telltale sign that all was not well within the once solid Kremlin. The coup attempt by reputed Kremlin hardliners, only months following the successful campaign against Iraq, precipitated the dramatic events of September-December 1991. Although he resisted the conspirators, Gorbachev was swept from power and with him went the last vestiges of the Marxist-Leninist state. The Soviet Union shattered along republic lines of its own creation and even Gorbachev's proposed Union of Sovereign States failed to gain the approval of those insisting on a far looser arrangement.

Boris Yeltsin led the movement to separate into national states and the world looked on in stunned amazement as fifteen new nations, insistent on their national prerogatives, assumed their positions in a variety of international organizations. Although some states hesitated in granting recognition to the new entities, others leaped at the opportunity to make communion with them.

Pakistan was especially moved by the independence of the Central Asian states. Pakistanis spoke of cultural and historic ties to the Muslims of the once "soft underbelly" of the Soviet Union and both public and privately sponsored missions were despatched to the region.

From New Delhi's vantage point Pakistani links with Central Asian Muslims were threatening. India had lost its most important patron in the collapse of the Soviet Union, and in the zero-sum rivalries of the subcontinent its principal nemesis stood to gain what it had lost. Given the unreconciled differences between India and Pakistan, Pakistan's diplomatic thrust into Central Asia was perceived a serious effort in the creation of a pan-Islamic bloc that might also include liberated Afghanistan, revolutionary Iran, and a metamorphosed Turkey. For New Delhi, the termination of the Cold War required little more than a ratchet adjustment. The passing of the USSR, however, necessitated a total overhaul of the country's foreign and national security policies.

In the absence of the countervailing power represented by the Soviet Union, New Delhi needed to address its national security needs in ways not heretofore contemplated. China, still a nemesis, required delicate handling, while the United States, long a perceived troublemaker, now loomed important in providing the necessary insulation against reconfigured threats from a potentially hostile Islamic grouping as well as a China harboring deep-seated differences with New Delhi. Indian efforts to woo the Americans while signalling flexibility to China, also were aimed at neutralizing and isolating Pakistan. At the same time, Indian actions were geared to reinforce American fears of a resurgent, aggressive Islamic world, as well as Chinese concerns that a pan-Islamic movement that linked Central Asia, could well spill across the western borders of China, a region inhabited by Turkic Muslim peoples. For this and other reasons, some overlapping, some divergent, both Beijing and Washington registered interest in improving their relations with India.

The dialectical struggle had been defined by Karl Marx in terms that emphasized class warfare. Indeed the ideological division between communist and non-communist societies lay at the center of the Cold War. So long as it was sustained, the Soviet Union itself was sustainable. Moscow assumed the role of leader of the "have nots," the exploited and deprived, and for almost seventy-five years it claimed to represent those peoples most harmed by the industrial revolution.[12] A more humane representation of industrialization lay at the heart of Marxist philosophy; it also gave credibility to political experiments promising a more equitable and just world. The intertwining of doctrine with political and economic performance was epitomized in the Leninist state that emerged from the ashes of World War I. The assumption that industrialization was the last stage in humankind's mastery of the planet demanded a counterforce to those commanding the economic and political heights. Moreover, imperialism, neo colonialism, was perceived the final obstacle before the metamorphosing of the human experience into something more profound, more noble, and above all more beneficial to the forgotten masses of this world. The Leninists, the legatees of the Russian Empire, placed themselves in the vanguard of this Utopian movement, ignoring their lack of experience or preparation for tackling such an assignment. Indeed, the Russian empire was poorly suited to represent Marxist prophecy.

History reveals the Bolsheviks were ill-equipped for the role they tried to play. No less significant, they not only failed to grasp the importance of scientific and technological change, they endeavored to obscure the fundamentals of the social experience that divides humanity into distinct and separate groupings.[13] The passing of the industrial age and the dawn of the technetronic era made obsolete an economic order rooted in the nineteenth century. New configurations of power and influence prompted by worldwide networking of financial and commercial activity, and made possible by undreamed of advances in communication and the delivery of information, not only altered workways, but also forecast a different political order.

The new world order so ambiguously addressed by leaders and peoples across the planet in the wake of the dissolution of the Soviet Union supposedly advances the cause and purposes of the more prosperous, and hence more modern, of the world's political units and combinations. But lest it again be ignored, it is the human element in the change process that demands understanding and accommodation. The world has been made small by human inventiveness and creativity, but the shrinking of the planet, the closing of physical distance between peoples, does more to exaggerate their differences than catalyze their harmonious interaction. The dialectic of the twenty-first century will not be found in clashing ideas, or class struggle, but in juxtaposed cultures that remain distinct and instinctive. The world speaks to us less in electronic impulses and more in the character of ancient ritual and belief. Moreover, the new technologies not only do not replace traditional identities, they provide them with the tools to better project their peculiarities.

It is imperative that this dialectic of cultural expression be understood, not neglected; unleashed, not suppressed. It is within this framework of a new world that we discern an older one, the former projecting an order that continues to exaggerate the importance of scientific adaptation while attributing to the latter the anarchy that stems from socio-political exclusiveness. What can not be misunderstood is the melding of the one with the other. There cannot be a new order until the old order's ancient yearnings are satisfactorily and peacefully addressed. Such reconciliation is not in the immediate offing and hence the new challenges are really the old ones, long ignored or obscured by other manifestations of power and influence.[14]

South Asia in the New World Order

No purpose is served by viewing South Asia in a vacuum. One cannot separate the subcontinent from the rest of Asia, let alone the world. India is alive with revitalized Hindu fundamentalism.[15] Pakistan speaks to the world in terms of Islamic destiny. Sri Lanka represents a Buddhist outpost determined to shape its future in accordance with elaborate rituals. But it is more than religious experience that defines their juxtapositions, let alone their expressions.

Southern Asia houses populations of shared as well as opposed experiences. The intermingling of peoples can be traced over millennia, but notions of community are more specific than general, more limited than universal. The people of Southern Asia have displayed little cooperative instinct. Their achievements are often measured more in philosophical and spiritual distinctiveness than in collective, mutually beneficial actions. The Moghuls imposed their will over the larger region, like the British later, not because they were culturally or racially superior, but because the local inhabitants seemed to respond more positively to governors beyond their immediate experience. Those governors, it should be noted, once established within the subcontinent, added still another strain to the congeries, but nevertheless took on the same characteristics as the indigenous population. When they no longer represented a third force, they too proved unacceptable to the extended population. Add to this scenario the winds of change which brought nationalism to the subcontinent in the nineteenth century, and one begins to understand the emergence of the principal forces that were to receive the transfer of power from the British in 1947.[16]

It also assists in understanding the makeup of the states of the region, their projections, as well as their concerns. India's Congress Party, not Pakistan's Muslim League, opposed the British Cabinet Mission plan of 1946 that was aimed at sustaining a unified India. The failure of that plan meant the subcontinent would be divided along religious lines, and, indeed, partition unleashed communal violence of immense proportions. It also precipitated a vast shifting of populations, as well as a number of unresolved territorial and demographic issues. At its base, independent India was a Hindu dominant state with a sizeable Muslim minority that needed constant overseeing. It is interesting to note that Pakistan never made the appeals to India's Muslims that it has to Muslims elsewhere. Moreover, Pakistan's sentimental attachment to the relatively unknown Muslims of Central Asia is in no way replicated by Pakistani associations with their confreres in India. In another way, Pakistani concern with the plight of the Kashmiri Muslims is difficult to evaluate against the backdrop of the civil war which prompted the creation of Bangladesh.

The point that needs to be made here is that India, for all its secular claims and international representations, is an isolated land, isolated by the unique character of its overriding culture. Pakistan, from the Indian point of view, was untimely ripped from the womb of Mother India. More significant, it was seen more as an extension of a revived Islamic world, a Trojan Horse, with the potential power to undermine and eventually dominate the whole of the subcontinent. Representations of "Akhand Bharat," United India, are generally ascribed to Hindu militants, but the notion of a single, unified subcontinent is also in the thoughts if not the policies of those who have guided India from 1947 to date. Why the Congress leaders rejected the British Cabinet Mission proposal cannot be examined here. Suffice it to say, the Congress leadership believed Pakistan would still not materialize, or if it did, -- that it would not survive partition.[17] India's dominant political organization committed a grievous error and their miscalculation is at the heart of the raging controversy between India and Pakistan today.

In point of fact, the Indians created the very conditions they wished to avoid. Pakistan the state was inchoate but there was nothing ambiguous about the Muslim connection with Islamic tradition. Moreover, Pakistan's emergence as an independent state came at a moment when independent Muslim states were gaining or about to achieve their freedom all the way from Morocco on the Atlantic to Indonesia in the South Pacific. India thus had cause to conclude that it was "an island surrounded by a Muslim sea," but it also was an island much of its own making.[18]

Under Nehru, India sought to reach out to the so-called non-aligned world, ever mindful that Pakistan had committed itself to the United States and its western alliances. The purpose of the Indian policy was to separate Pakistan from other third world nations, and especially from the Muslim states not associated with the West, and indeed with grievances toward the United States. In this way, too, the self-proclaimed guides of the third world further divided it, and Indian leaders sought advantages from the division that would ensure Pakistan's isolation. Hence no Muslim nation came to Pakistan's defense in its wars with India. And in the 1971 war, India demonstrated how isolated Pakistan was when it befriended the Muslims of East Bengal in their creation of Bangladesh but never hinted that a greater Bengali state that would include Indian Bengal was a desirable goal.[19] New Delhi was determined to neutralize Pakistan and the condition known as the Cold War aided and abetted that objective.

But the Cold War is history and India must live in the present. Non-alignment is no longer a suitable policy and the principal question challenging Indian policymakers is how to strengthen ties with Washington without yielding any of its initiatives. United States direct investment in India in 1991 totalled $533 million.[20] Moreover, Washington gave India $300,000 in 1991 for the purpose of training Indian military students in the United States. More important, U.S. military sales to India have increased and American companies have been encouraged to do business with New Delhi. General Electric provides India with the engines for its Light Combat Aircraft (LCA). It also supplies the gas turbines for India's new naval frigates. Other American corporations such as Honeywell and Northrop envisage opportunities for their industries, given the domestic scaling down of American military procurement. It is anticipated that India will receive state of the art rocket radar systems and very low frequency communications technology, the latter for use in its submarines.

Gone are the days when New Delhi described the U.S. as the principal purveyor of violence. Regular high-level seminars hosted by the U.S. National Defense University and India's Institute for Defence Studies and Analysis have been held since the death of Pakistan's Mohammed Zia ul-Haq and the tumbling of the Berlin Wall. The fact that such high-level meetings between senior military officers of both nations began at a time when the Soviet-Indian treaty was still operative, illustrated the significance given to joint defense planning and security cooperation in South Asia and the Indian Ocean. Need it be noted that India provided U.S. military aircraft with refueling stations during the Gulf war. Nor does the U.S. have to be reminded that India is the regional superpower, or that its 1.3 million-man army is the world's fourth largest, that it possesses slightly less than a thousand combat aircraft, and that its navy includes two aircraft carriers. Clearly, from Washington's vantage point, India assumes a larger role in pacifying the Indian Ocean region, as conversely, the American naval presence is reduced and American strategies are altered to cope with very specific operational needs, e.g. the American intervention in Somalia in December 1992.

The new harmony of interests with India is contrasted with the dissonance in U.S.-Pakistan relations. Pakistan seems more determined than ever to see a resolution to the Kashmir problem but without Washington's unequivocal support there is little chance of achieving much satisfaction. Pakistan was exercised by President Bush's call for a new world order, and many Pakistanis saw it as a blatant attempt to impose a restrictive *Pax Americana* on the third world, and particularly on the Muslim nations. Washington is sometimes described by Pakistanis as the 21st century's sole imperium, its objective to divide and conquer, with Islam its prime target. The passage from Bush to Bill Clinton seems more likely to intensify this argument but the new president is nonetheless an unknown quantity in the U.S.-Pakistan equation.

The ferocity of the American assault on Iraq, the pressure on Libya, indeed the use of the United Nations to effect selective American policy in the Middle East, and the feverish efforts at preventing Muslim countries from achieving nuclear status are cause for complaint and anger throughout Pakistan. Moreover, President Clinton's reputation as a friend of Israel reinforces long-held negative views concerning the machinations of the United States. Seeking a sign that would suggest even-handedness, Pakistanis rhetorically ask why the United States refuses to use its influence in the United Nations to force India to allow the Kashmiris to decide their own future. And, given the critical dimensions of the Babri Masjid affair, they continue to wonder where Washington is when Muslims are subjected to persecution by militant Hindus.

The Burton amendment calling for a plebiscite in Kashmir attempted to get the U.S. involved but it was challenged on the floor of the House. In defeating the measure Representative Stephen Solarz put forth the argument that "forty years of history clearly establish Kashmir as part of India." Solarz introduced a substitute amendment in 1991 which called for the "differences over Kashmir to be resolved within the framework of the 1972 Simla Declaration." Solarz's amendment was in fact adopted, and the U.S. Congress went on record to withdraw American government support for a UN-conducted plebiscite in Kashmir. Solarz's defeat in the 1992 New York primary election removed the influential representative from the legislative body but his absence only hinted at the possibility of new congressional directions.

Senator Larry Pressler's visit to India and Pakistan in January 1992 was further acknowledgement that bridging U.S.-Pakistani differences would require more than platitudes or implied threats. Pressler publicly declared that unlike Islamabad's nuclear weapons program, India was solely concerned with the peaceful uses of nuclear power. Pressler's statements impacted on Pakistanis in a variety of ways; it proved most embarrassing for the Islamabad government which had projected improved relations with Washington following the visit to the United States of General Asif Nawaz. Neither President Ghulam Ishaq Khan nor Prime Minister Nawaz Sharif dared risk an audience with the outspoken senator.

Moreover, Pressler did not confine his comments to nuclear issues. He also focused on the Central Asian republics which he feared would threaten India if they were linked to the Muslim states of the former northern tier. Writing in *The Muslim*, Shireen Mazari scoffed at the charge and noted that it stemmed from the West's dire fear of Islamic fundamentalism. If the Americans wish to understand the ideological threat to the region, she said, they would do better to center their attention on Hindu fundamentalism. It was Indian stubbornness and Indian intransigence that stymied diplomacy and prevented solutions to South Asian dilemmas. She concluded with the thought that Pakistani officials had agreed to meet with their Indian counterparts, and were more than willing to entertain a larger conference that would include the U.S., China, and Russia, but that it could not enter into a Camp David-like discussion with India, as Pressler had suggested. Camp David, she concluded, represented Muslim capitulation to U.S.-Zionist designs and there would be no more such displays of servility.

Despite a passionate debate within Pakistan, the Islamabad government is determined to maintain an association with the United States.[21] But any new understanding would have to recognize the new realities that Pakistan had attained nuclear status. Pakistan's Defense Minister, Syed Ghous Ali Shah, declared in March 1992 that Pakistan had acquired nuclear capability, but only to maintain the balance of power in the region. The Defense Minister reiterated that it remained Pakistan's policy to use such capability for peaceful purposes, but he also noted it was the Kashmir issue that compelled his country to seek nuclear safeguards. Pakistan, he said, had offered India *quid pro quo* on signing the Non Proliferation Treaty (NPT), but that India had rejected the compromise. Pakistan had called for the region to be declared a nuclear-free zone but India had rejected that proposal as well. Nawaz Sharif's call for a five-nation conference to establish a nuclear-free zone in South Asia, a conference that would bring together the United States, Russia, China, as well as India and Pakistan, was also declined by New Delhi.[22]

Emphasizing a more candid and direct diplomacy, Islamabad replaced its ambassador to Washington, Najmuddin Shaikh, a comparatively colorless figure, with Begum Syeda Abida Hussain, the country's most effective woman politician. In her first public statement she observed that the "central obstacle to the kind of close, cooperative relationship that would again benefit both our nations," was the nuclear issue. Her government, she said, was committed to the principle of nuclear non-proliferation, and she acknowledged that misunderstandings on this matter had brought Pakistan's relations with the United States to a crossroads. The ambassador noted there was no reason to fear her country's intentions, and she cited the steps taken to democratize the political process in Pakistan and the reforms that emphasized an expanded free enterprise economic structure, including the denationalizing of state enterprises. She invited American investment in her country and also pledged Islamabad's assistance in generating unrestricted trade.

On a more solemn note Abida Hussain cautioned that, although the ideological confrontation between the superpowers had been terminated, small states continue to be threatened and armed conflicts "fester in various regions of the world." Pakistan, she said, would be more assured if all nations, large and small, abided by the principles of the United Nations and agreed to settle their disputes peaceably. She then turned to India and the Kashmir dispute which she described as a claim for self-determination, reinforced by a number of UN resolutions. The UN Security Council and the UN Commission for India and Pakistan have both insisted on the right of the Kashmiri people to decide their own destiny. Only India, she declared, was responsible for the lawlessness in the state as well as the grave violations of human rights. Ultimately, it is the international community's responsibility to insist that the UN resolutions be complied with. Pakistan, she reiterated, did nothing to provoke this most recent Kashmiri uprising and indeed Islamabad has called for the stationing of impartial international observers in the mountain state. It is India, she argues, which has rejected all recommendations for a peaceful solution.

To demonstrate its good faith and desire for a peaceful settlement, in March 1992, Pakistani troops prevented movement of Pakistani militants into Kashmir. This diplomatic signal followed Pakistan's earlier announcement that it had suspended all arms shipments to the Afghan mujahidin in order to clear the way for a UN mediated settlement of that long conflict. Indeed, in the new frankness of Pakistani foreign policy, the foreign office let it be known that Pakistan's nuclear program was a posture aimed at convincing India it was time to settle their differences at the conference table. In the larger scheme of unfolding events, Pakistan's future could only be enhanced in an ambiance of political stability, reinforced by adequate security measures from within as well as outside the subcontinent.

Future Prospects

The creation of confidence-building measures has never been more urgent in South Asia and the surrounding area.[23] And never has it been more difficult. India is a regional state of significant diversity whereas Pakistan is an extra-territorial expression confined to South Asia but with its roots in distant lands extending to Central and Southwestern Asia. Both countries are manifestations of colonial dispensations fabricated in Europe and influenced by European notions of nationhood. Both are also inchoate entities, alive with contradictions and moved by visions that transcend the immediate circumstances of their origin. India is only a segment of what its leaders envisaged in the years of the freedom movement; Pakistan was something of an afterthought, an expression bordering on despair that found solace and purpose in a revitalized and idealized Islamic community. India is rooted in the exclusive, historic traditions of the subcontinent, Pakistan is an amorphous actor whose ultimate fulfillment may well be found in extended confederation.

The problems experienced in living together, in sharing the same geographic region, are deep and complex, but have been made even more intractable by the events of the last half century. Division, not unity, characterizes the extended region; fear, not mutual satisfaction, motivates behavior. No liberation war announced the independence of the two major states of South Asia. There was little to celebrate at the time and there is even less factual memory today of what was accomplished in attaining independence. The communal wars that raged over the country at partition took their toll of the innocent and there is only the agony of separation to remind Indians and Pakistanis about their origins.

Clearly, the decision to continue the struggle between the communities was assumed and perpetuated by the formal governments of the two dominions who sensed a need to clarify as well as justify the internecine bloodletting. Mayhem and anarchy were refashioned so as to represent a nobler cause and purpose. The war in 1965 and the more significant conflict in 1971, however, were more tactical exercises than pitched battles. The more deadly military performances are observed in India's assault on the Nagas, the crushing of the Naxalites, or the invasion of the Sikh Golden Temple. For counterpoint in Pakistan there is the brutalization of the Bengalis, the stifling of the Boluch or the neutralizing of the Sindhudesh nationalists. Although each subcontinental power accuses the other of meddling in their domestic affairs, only the Indian intervention in East Bengal was a clear-cut and incontrovertible campaign to disassemble a neighboring sovereign state.

The lesson of Bangladesh, however, can not be ignored. India, whatever the reason, albeit the justification, acted to permanently alter the correlation of forces in the region. New Delhi emerged from the 1971 war the hegemonic power in South Asia. The detonation of its nuclear device in 1974 provided the exclamation point to that claim. But the action also galvanized the Pakistani army, which was not only determined to overcome its humiliation, but to mount a counterforce that New Delhi could not ignore. Pakistan's nuclear weapons program was the immediate response.[24] And although the Afghan-Soviet war raised new problems for the frontline state, that protracted but limited encounter instead of jeopardizing, actually accelerated Pakistan's nuclear arms program. Moreover, the Reagan Doctrine supporting wars of liberation against entrenched yet beleaguered Marxist governments in the third world provided additional cover for Pakistan's nuclear quest, and beyond that, the United States also assisted in the modernization of the Pakistani armed forces. Although it was not stated American intention, Pakistan not only overcame the dismemberment of 1971 with an assist from the United States, it grew in sufficient strength and determination to cast doubt on India's hegemonic capacity.

India's political disarray is more apparent in the wake of the assassination of Rajiv Gandhi, the last member of the Nehru clan. India's vaunted military prowess somewhat obscures gross political and administrative deficiencies, but it is no substitute for a vibrant, dynamic socio-economic polity. The country has awakened a bit late in acknowledging the failure of its overregulated state-driven economy. Moreover, the weakness of Indian governments in the face of growing popular demands, indeed their ineffectiveness in coping with soaring population growth, portends a difficult future for peoples and leaders alike.[25] The spreading specter of Hindu fundamentalism is directly related to the disintegration of the Congress Party, and especially to the general malaise that grips the nation. Faced with a crisis of leadership, the Indian lumpen proletariat will follow their demagogic mentors, who even if they do not promise an end to their frustrations, signal a masochistic release from the vagaries of daily existence.

The United States, the only definitive external actor remaining in the South Asian realm, must examine its involvement long term and with all the necessary wisdom borne of several decades of experience in the region. Reconciling the desirable with the possible is essential in circumstances that are beyond anyone's power to manage. Washington must learn to address the many problems plaguing South Asia from a studied but selective and aloof vantage point. The United States must comprehend the meaning of the new geopolitics. American interests are not jeopardized by strategic disengagement. There is nothing Washington can do to deny the Afghans their blood feuds. The Soviets were defeated by the very tribal orders they sought to transform. The major actors must adjust to a portion of the world that looks backward not ahead. They must also recognize that their erstwhile involvement did nothing to advance the cause of progress in the region. The only thing that has changed in the period since World War II is the nature and level of violence.

The United States need not fear the projected networking of northern tier and central Asian states. There is sufficient rivalry between and among the several actors to guarantee a long period of maneuvering. There is no central cause or theme or personality to rally the Muslims of rimland Asia. Islamic fundamentalism is not nearly the threat it is perceived to be in the outer world. Islam is not a militant faith, nor does it encourage mindless bloodletting. The West, and particularly Americans, must grasp the needs of the Muslim community, in all its diversity, to achieve a stature denied it in the epoch now behind us. The geopolitics of the future is not so much concerned with space and location as it is with humanity, and the variety of social orders that it identifies with. Providing credence, conferring respectability on long deprived social groups is the essence of the new geopolitics. Moreover, the United States is positioned to address this phenomenon but it must first learn to avoid taking sides, or converting friends and former allies in the Cold War to enemies now that it has passed.

There is no longer a pressing need to provide sophisticated weapons to peoples engaged in controversies that are never really understood by the outside world. It is enough to recognize that there are rival moral claims and they do not yield to simple solutions. Moreover, the time has passed when ideological position was sufficient to confirm support for one party or another. It is doubtful Americans can today articulate exactly what camp they wish to represent. The emotional baggage we all carry must be handled more deftly than in the past, and with far more acumen and understanding than was judged necessary in the "heat" of the Cold War.

Only Indians and Pakistanis are capable of resolving the Kashmir issue. Only they can address their individual societies and the many divisions that they represent. Only they can decide whether the possession of weapons of mass destruction is beneficial or deleterious to the health of their respective populations. Only they can grasp the true meaning of their ethos and what it suggests for their separate and combined futures.

From the outside, however, it is more than obvious that cooperation and accommodation will do more to energize and satisfy their people, bind up their nations, elevate their status, and project a more profound and meaningful future.

But if that sounds too idealistic let it be noted that the countries of South Asia, like those spread across the planet, are inhabited by people who judge forbearance to be weakness and compromise to be appeasement. It is possible to paint a grim scenario for South Asia but it would be inexcusable if in the immediate aftermath of the Cold War, we, but especially they, did not recognize the opportunity for new directions.

This study was made possible by a Faculty Research Fellowship provided by Research and Sponsored Programs, Western Michigan University.

Notes

1. See: S.M. Burke and Lawrence Ziring, *Pakistan's Foreign Policy*, Karachi: Oxford University Press, 1990; J. Vinod, *United States Foreign Policy Towards India*, New Delhi: Lancers Books, 1991.

2. Thomas T. Hammond, *Red Flag Over Afghanistan*, Boulder: Westview Press, 1984, pp. 216-221.

3. Lawrence Ziring, "Public Policy Dilemmas and Pakistan's Nationality Problem: The Legacy of Zia ul-Haq," *Asian Survey*, 28, 8, August 1988, pp. 795-812. See also: *Pakistan Under the Military*, Boulder: Westview Press, 1991.

4. *The Pakistan Times* (Overseas Weekly), October 30, 1992.

5. See: Emajuddin Ahmed, *SARC: Seeds of Harmony*, Dhaka: University Press, Ltd., 1985.

6. A number of books examine the Indo-Pakistani wars. Some which can be cited here are: Kalim Siddiqui, *Conflict, Crisis and War in Pakistan*, New York: Praeger, 1972; Mumtaz Ahmed Khan, *Pakistan's Long Autumn*, Lahore: Idra-e-Iqdam, 1979; Safdar Mahmood, *The Deliberate Debacle*, Lahore: Sh. Mohammed Ashraf, 1976; Ricard Sisson and Leo Rose, *War and Secession: Pakistan and India and the Creation of Bangladesh*, Berkeley: University of California Press, 1990.

7. Agha Shahi, *Pakistan's Security and Foreign Policy*, Lahore: Progressive Publishers, 1988, pp. 155-162.

8. The India-China controversy is examined in the following: Girilal Jain, *India Meets China in Nepal*, New Delhi: Asia Publishing House, 1959; P.C. Chakravarti, *India's China Policy*, Bloomington: Indiana University Press, 1962; Wayne A. Wilcox, *India, Pakistan and the Rise of China*, New York, Walker, 1964; Anwar H. Syed, *China and Pakistan: Diplomacy of an Entente Cordiale*, Amherst: University of Massachusetts Press, 1974; B.L. Sharma, *The Pakistan-China Axis*, New Delhi: Asia Publishing House, 1968.

9. Two interesting but different books on the subject are: Anthony Mascarenhas, *The Rape of Bangladesh*, New Delhi: Vikas, 1972; and Mohammed Ayoob and K. Subrahmanyam, *The Liberation War,* New Delhi: S. Chand, 1972.

10. Z.A. Bhutto, "If I Am Assassinated. . . ." New Delhi: Vikas, 1979, p. 223.

11. Lawrence Ziring, "Pakistan in 1990: The Fall of Benazir Bhutto" *Asian Survey*, 31, 2, February 1991, pp. 113-124.

12. Alfred G. Meyer, "Reflections of Democratization: The Collapse of Soviet Communism in Global Perspective, or Making the Bear Dance," in Lawrence Ziring, ed., *The New Europe and the World*, Kalamazoo: New Issues Press, 1993, pp. 35-60.

13. C.A. Macartney, *National States and National Minorities*, New York: Russell and Russell, 1968, pp. 450-463.

14. William A. Ritchie, "Cassandra's Echo: Exclusionary Democracy in the New Europe," in Lawrence Ziring, ed., *The New Europe and the World*, Kalamazoo, Michigan: New Issues Press, pp. 73-102.

15. *The New York Times*, December 9, 1992. See also: Bernard Lewis, "The Roots of Muslim Rage," *The Atlantic Monthly*, September 1990, pp. 47-60.

16. Ishtiaq Husain Qureshi, *The Muslim Community of the Indo-Pakistan Subcontinent*, Gravenhage: Mouton, 1962, pp. 125-148.

17. See: Sikandar Hayat, *Aspects of the Pakistan Movement*, Lahore: Progressive Publishers, 1991.

18. Personal Interview, November 23, 1981.

19. Lawrence Ziring, *Bangladesh From Mujib to Ershad: An Interpretive Study*, Karachi: Oxford University Press, 1992, pp. 216-221

20. Richard Fisher and William Bonde, *U.S.-Asia Statistical Handbook, 1992 Edition*, Washington, D.C.: The Heritage Foundation, pp. 36-37.

21. *The Pakistan Times* (Overseas Weekly), November 17, 1992.

22. *The Pakistan Times* (Overseas Weekly), October 30, 1992.

23. See: Arthur G. Rubinoff, "The Multilateral Imperative in India's Foreign Policy," *The Round Table*, 319 (1991), pp. 313-334; Raju G.C. Thomas, "Security and Democracy in South Asia," unpublished manuscript delivered at the Lawrence Livermore National Laboratory, University of California, August 1991; A. Martin Wainwright, "Indian Security and the Language of Sovereignty During the Transfer of Power," unpublished manuscript delivered at the MCISS Workshop on South Asian Security, Madison, Wisconsin, October 31, 1991.

24. Mario Carranza, "Indo-Pakistani Strategic Interactions and the End of the Cold War," unpublished manuscript delivered at the MCISS Workshop on South Asian Security, Madison, Wisconsin, October 31, 1991.

25. Mohammed Ayoob, "Indian Democracy at the Crossroads," unpublished manuscript delivered at the MCISS Workshop on South Asian Security, Madison, Wisconsin, October 31, 1991.

9

Another Try at Democracy

Robert LaPorte, Jr.

This chapter describes and analyzes Pakistan's several attempts to develop democratic institutions and governance, focusing upon the most current attempt. The author argues that several factors mitigated against democratic governance from Pakistan's beginning in August 1947 and that the current attempt, dating from 1979, is still confronting some of these factors. Although some scholars talk about "political decay" and are pessimistic about the future of democratic institutions and governance in Pakistan, this chapter maintains that there have been some positive developments during the last decade that offer hope for those who advocate that Pakistan's political system should and can be democratically based. In the strict sense of the term, a true democracy has never existed, and never will exist.[1]

As a contemporary problem confronting Pakistan today, the development of a political system based on democratic institutions and governance has a history which parallels the independence of the nation. In fact, from the beginning, several forces were arrayed against the development of a democratically based political system.

First, the system of governance inherited from the British was not a "democratic" system of government, nor did it pretend to be democratically based. The so-called viceregal system was designed to rule a subjected people and its principal functions were the maintenance of law and order and revenue collection. The institutions it developed, the military and the civil bureaucracy, were themselves not representative of the diverse, heterogeneous population of India. This was the system of government that the founding fathers of Pakistan knew best.

Second, the regional conflict that the nation found itself in as a result of the partition of British India was a factor mitigating against the development and use of democratic procedures. The settlement of millions of refugees from India, the economic readjustments that had to be made as a result of the partitioning of British India between India and Pakistan and the almost immediate outbreak of hostilities with India over Kashmir were all part of the emergency frame of mind of the leadership of the new nation. National emergencies tend to constrain democracy.

Third, the internal political situation was complicated by the geography of the new nation -- two land masses (the province of West Pakistan and the province of East Pakistan) with different populations separated by a thousand miles of "hostile Indian territory." The socio-cultural differences between the western province and East Bengal contributed to the refusal of some leadership to share in the governance of the new nation, hence impeding the movement toward democratization.

Finally, the death of the one paramount leader, Mohammed Ali Jinnah, in 1948 left a political vacuum that was never completely filled. The leadership which followed Jinnah could not agree among themselves on a constitutional framework and it was not until 1956 that a constitution was imposed upon the nation.

Even consensus on what kind of government Pakistan should have has been difficult to develop, as this chapter relates. Pakistan has had three constitutions (1956, 1962 and 1973) with a substantial change (the addition of the Eighth Amendment) to the 1973 constitution. The nation has experienced long periods of martial law with the military -- the "specialists on violence"[2] -- in charge of the nation's affairs.

Although scholars have continually debated what constitutes "democracy," the definition of democracy found in *Webster's New Twentieth Century Dictionary of the English Language* (Unabridged),[3] will serve the purposes of this chapter: democracy is:

> . . . popular government, from *demos,* the people, and *kratein,* to rule.
> 1. government by the people, either directly or through elected representatives; rule by the ruled.
> 2. a country, state, community, etc. with such government.
> 3. majority rule.
> 4. the acceptance and practice of the principle of equality of rights, opportunity, and treatment.
> 5. the common people. . . .

Other definitions include reference to periodically-held free elections. Democracy, therefore, involves form and processes (periodic, free elections based on universal suffrage), institutions (political parties and legislative assemblies) and substance (toleration of opposition and the agreement to abide by majority rule). It should be noted that democracy varies from one polity to another and democratic processes and institutions sometimes have long gestation periods.[4]

The comparative politics literature of the 1960s and 1970s went to considerable lengths in developing typologies of political systems and placing countries in various categories -- developed versus developing.[5] Currently, there is debate among scholars regarding how democratization is faring globally.[6] In Pakistan, the debate over what form of government is best suited to the people of Pakistan has been waged since independence on August 14, 1947. The development of democratic institutions in Pakistan has not been easy. Several attempts have been made to install democratic institutions and the current attempt must be seen in light of the previous efforts.

This chapter will examine and analyze Pakistan's current attempt at democracy. In doing so, the author will examine and analyze: (1) attempts at democratization in Pakistan; (2) lessons learned from each attempt -- what was learned and by whom; (3) the present attempt at democratization; (4) groups in support of the present attempt; and (5) groups in opposition to the present attempt. The chapter will conclude with some observations on Pakistan's current attempt at democratization and its prospects for the future.

The First Attempt at Democratization: The Parliamentary Period of the 1950s[7]

On August 14, 1947, the British transferred power to an independent, Islamic Republic of Pakistan. The legal basis for this new nation was the Government of India Act of 1935 and the Indian Independence Act of 1947. Mohammed Ali Jinnah became the Governor-General and the President of the Constituent Assembly of Pakistan. The national legislature for this new nation, the Constituent Assembly of Pakistan,

> . . .was born without the formal blessing of law. Its conception lay in the British Cabinet Mission Plan of May 1946 and the Viceroy's statement of June 3, 1947, which announced the agreement to partition the sub-continent. The 1946 Plan envisioned a single Constituent Assembly for undivided India. This was to be an assembly of representatives chosen by the elected members of the provincial Legislative Assemblies with the addition of delegates from the princely states.[8]

Members of the provincial legislative assemblies were not elected on the basis of universal suffrage:

> The franchise for participation in provincial elections was narrow. . . .the right to vote was based on education and property, and it is unlikely that

> anywhere more than 15 per cent of the total population was entitled to vote.[9]

Because of partition, there was a need to create a separate Constituent Assembly of Pakistan and this was accomplished by installing the sitting members from the undivided provinces (Sindh and Northwest Frontier provinces) as members and having West Punjab and East Bengal select new representatives.

This assembly, based on a very limited franchise, was assigned the responsibility of drafting a constitution for the new nation. The first Constituent Assembly did not accomplish this task because, on October 24, 1954, Governor-General Ghulam Mohammed declared a State of Emergency and by Proclamation dismissed the Constituent Assembly. He appointed a new cabinet, described as a "Ministry of Talent," as well as a new Constituent Assembly, and the first constitution (the 1956 Constitution) was promulgated. Under this Constitution, the title of the head of state was changed from Governor-General to President and Iskandar Mirza became the first president.[10]

What some may describe as the first attempt to democratize in Pakistan, in the 1950s "parliamentary period," ended when

> . . .on the morning of October 7, 1958, General Ayub Khan, the army's commander-in-chief, removed the prime minister and his cabinet, dismissed the National Assembly, abrogated the constitution, dissolved all political parties, banned all political activity, and set himself up as the dictator with the title of chief marshal law administrator. Twenty days later, the general staged another coup -- this time directed against Iskander Mirza, the president of the republic, who had originally invited Ayub Khan to take some of these draconian measures. October 27, 1958, marked the beginning of the era of one-man rule that has lasted to this day.[11]

In retrospect, the question that might be raised is: were there serious attempts made to establish democratic institutions during the first decade of independence? The answer is no. For a number of reasons, the leadership of Pakistan during this time period felt that it was not in the best interests of the new nation to democratize. The power struggle over the shape of governance in Pakistan was won by the believers in the traditional viceregal system of government inherited from the British. The limited involvement of politicians in policy making during the so-called parliamentary period, coupled with the fear of a political system dominated by Bengalis from East Pakistan influenced those in power to avoid pursuing a government "of the people, by the people and for the people."

The Ayub Period, 1958-1969: Lessons Learned from the 1950s[12]

The lesson of this first decade of independence appeared to be the following. If you permit politicians to debate the issues they will only succeed in agitating the masses. As Iskander Mirza maintained, it is better to have controlled democracy if democracy is to be introduced at all. The learner of this lesson was General (later Field Marshal) Mohammed Ayub Khan who assumed the position of President of Pakistan and promulgated his own constitution (the 1962 Constitution) complete with Basic Democracy -- a very controlled form of participation. As an active partner, the General enlisted the support of the civil bureaucracy whose elite had not relinquished power during the 1950s but had felt the pressure of the civilian politicians who occupied positions as ministers.[13]

The system of government imposed by Ayub was a form of "tutelary democracy."[14] Ayub had laid out his scheme for what Pakistan needed in terms of government in his "A Short Appreciation of Present and Future Problems of Pakistan" (Memorandum written by General Mohammed Ayub Khan, Defense Minister, October 4, 1954).[15] Control in the system was exercised by the president and the elite bureaucracy. Ministers did not have much influence over the senior civil servants who reported to them. In essence, the system of government was a continuation of the British viceregal system with the addition of the "Basic Democrats" who were elected indirectly by the people and served as an electoral college for the election of the president. The National Assembly during Ayub's rule was basically a rubber stamp operation.

Ayub's fall from power came about in March 1969. Urban-based demonstrations involving students and others against the government and culminating in a general strike caused one Western journalist to write:

> . . . .The fact remains that in four short months, an inchoate popular uprising had brought down an entrenched regime and not even the armed forces dared to intervene. . . .After a decade of army coups in the developing nations, military regimes have been forced to give way to democracy and there could be little doubt that this was what Pakistanis wanted.[16]

However, the succession in Pakistan was an orderly one, passing from one military official to another. Ayub's successor, General Agha Mohammed Yahya Khan, Commander-in-Chief of the Pakistan army, accepted Ayub's resignation. Almost immediately, Yahya abrogated the 1962 Constitution, banned all political activity, dismissed the national and provincial assemblies, issued martial law regulations and finally (April 1, 1969) retroactively proclaimed himself President of Pakistan.

General Yahya took three important steps in the attempt to respond to the political demands of the citizens of what was still a united Pakistan. He abolished the One-Unit (Governor-General Ghulam Mohammed had merged the four provinces in West Pakistan, Punjab, Sindh, NWFP and Boluchistan, into the province of West Pakistan). He declared that elections based on one person one vote would be held. Finally, because East Pakistan had a majority of the population, more National Assembly seats were allotted to that province.

In his announcement of November 28, 1969, Yahya gave his political timetable: full political activity would be permitted after January 1, 1970, and general elections would be held on October 5, 1970.[17] The elections were postponed until December 1970,[18] but when they were held, the two triumphant political parties were the Awami League (headed by Sheikh Mujibur Rahman) in East Pakistan and the People's Party of Pakistan -- PPP (headed by Zulfikar Ali Bhutto) in West Pakistan. The Awami League captured the majority of seats in the National Assembly (160 out of 300) but the PPP gained a majority of the National Assembly seats (81) in the four provinces of West Pakistan.

The newly elected National Assembly never met. Disagreement between Sheikh Mujib and Bhutto that Yahya was not able to mediate led to a stand-off and, on March 25, 1971, civil war broke out in East Pakistan after the Pakistan Army moved in force against Awami League supporters. The civil war lasted until December 17, 1971. The result was what some have termed the second partitioning of the subcontinent and the emergence of an independent Bangladesh. Zulfikar Ali Bhutto was made president of what was left of Pakistan.

The Second Attempt at Democratization: The Zulfikar Ali Bhutto Period, 1971-1977[19]

About eight months after Zulfikar Ali Bhutto was installed as President of the Islamic Republic of Pakistan following the end of the civil war in December 1971, I discussed the prospects for democracy in Pakistan with a senior Pakistani civil servant. He indicated that the democratization process that had begun with the first general elections based on universal suffrage that were held in 1970 was not the first time Pakistan attempted to introduce democracy. "In fact," he said, "you must remember that in Pakistan, democracy begins with the As, Bs and Cs but always ends up with the GHQ."[20] What appeared to me at the time as cynicism was, in reality, pragmatism because no t quite five years later (July 5, 1977), General Mohammed Zia ul-Haq, chief of the army staff, led a bloodless coup against Mr. Bhutto and began the longest tenure in office of a ruler in Pakistan's history. The newly established National Assembly of a now divided Pakistan (composed of 139 members -- the 138 elected from the provinces of West Pakistan and one non-Awami League member from East

Pakistan)[21] was convened by Bhutto on April 4, 1972. This was the first National Assembly whose members had been elected by universal suffrage. Agreement on a constitutional accord was reached on October 20, 1972, and the constitution was authenticated by Bhutto on April 12, 1973.[22]

There were lessons to be learned from the Ayub period and Zulfikar Ali Bhutto thought he had learned them. The first lesson was that if you want civilian rule, the military has to be controlled. Bhutto attempted to do this by (1) retiring or appointing senior military officers as ambassadors, and (2) introducing civilian control over the military by changing the title of Commander-in-Chief of the Pakistan Army to Chief of the Army Staff (COAS) and making the president the commander-in-chief of the armed forces. The second lesson was that the elite bureaucracy as an inside source of opposition must be controlled. This Bhutto did by having the Civil Service Reform Act of 1973 enacted which replaced the constitutional guarantees for civil servants that had existed since independence. He also purged the civil bureaucracy by retiring or removing over 4,000 civil servants and replacing them, through lateral entry procedures, with his own supporters. The third lesson was to neutralize or control potential opposition outside of government. One potential source of opposition was the business-industrial elite. Bhutto neutralized this group by nationalizing domestic banking and insurance firms and many private manufacturing concerns.[23] The combined result was a restructuring of policy and decision making so that the office of prime minister (which Bhutto occupied after the 1973 constitution was adopted) was *the* office of power and authority in the system.

Bhutto would have preferred a presidential form of government, one not too different from that of Ayub Khan, but he was persuaded to accept a modified parliamentary system. The modification was intended to protect the prime minister from frivolous changes in party loyalty of the type that had paralyzed governments in the period before Ayub Khan. Under the procedures of the new constitution, the exercise of considerable political will was required in order to remove the prime minister. A vote of no-confidence against the prime minister was made virtually impossible, at least for ten years.[24]

The new system of governance introduced by Bhutto lasted until July 5, 1977, when, after street demonstrations against the rigged elections of March 1977, General Mohammed Zia ul-Haq, Chief of the Army Staff, seized power and placed Bhutto and other non-PPP leaders under arrest, declared martial law and became the Chief Martial Law Administrator (CMLA), suspended the 1973 Constitution, banned all political activity, dismissed the national and provincial assemblies, and announced that new elections would be held in 90 days.[25] Zia subjected the Bhutto government to an "accountability process" whose result was the execution of Zulfikar Ali Bhutto on April 4, 1979.[26]

Zia had been considered by many as a non-political army officer. In fact, Bhutto appointed him as chief of the army staff in March 1976 over a dozen more senior army officers based on the advice he received regarding Zia's ". . .professionalism and lack of interest in politics."[27] What Bhutto did not realize until it was too late was that merely changing the title from commander-in-chief to chief of the army staff would not prevent the military from once again assuming power.

The Zia Period, 1977-1988: Lessons Learned from the Bhutto Period

Perhaps the primary lesson to be learned from the Zulfikar Ali Bhutto period should have been Lord Acton's political axiom that "power tends to corrupt and absolute power corrupts absolutely." Once in power, however, General Zia did not relinquish the control he assumed even though after 1985 he shared power in a limited sense. He did learn the lesson that a politician with unchecked power such as Z. A. Bhutto could create havoc and that there should be constitutional guarantees against unchecked power. Hence, the adoption of the so called Eighth Amendment[28] of November 9, 1985, which strengthened the role of the president and was the legal basis for Zia's dismissal of the national and provincial assemblies in May 1988 and Ghulam Ishaq Khan's dismissal of the national and provincial assemblies in August 1990.

Zia also thought that politicians could be kept in line if elections were held on a non-partisan or partyless[29] basis. However, once he appointed Mohammed Khan Junejo as prime minister following the February 25, 1985, partyless national and provincial assembly elections, Junejo resurrected the political parties (which had been banned by Zia)[30] in January 1986 shortly after Zia had lifted martial law on December 30, 1985.[31]

What Zia learned from the Ayub period was to never give up control of your most important base of support -- the army. General Zia occupied the position of chief of the army staff throughout his tenure as president. He gave himself extensions in that position.

Finally, what Zia appeared to learn from the Bhutto period, although it took a long time and was very frustrating at times, is that power has to be shared to some degree because people want some sense of participation. He tried to appease the demand for elections at first by establishing new local government councils (the so-called Local Bodies Scheme) in all four provinces and holding partyless elections to these councils in 1979.[32] Next, he appointed a partyless national assembly, the 350-member nominated *Majlis-i-Shura*, on December 24, 1981. Zia then held a national referendum on his Islamic policies on December 19, 1984 -- approval of which would mean his reelection for another five years.

Government officials claimed that "62 percent of the voters participated of which 97.7 percent voted in favor of continuing Islamic policies."[33] Other estimates of turnout range from a low of 5 to 10 percent to a high of 20-25 percent. Finally, he held partyless elections for the national and provincial assemblies on February 25, 1985.

The Third Attempt at Democratization: 1979 until the Present

Although most of the attention on Pakistan's present democratization attempt has focused on the November 1988 elections, the process really began in 1979. Pressure to hold elections and to lift martial law had been building domestically as well as coming from overseas.[34] For a number of reasons, the Zia government decided to replace the integrated rural development program that the Bhutto government had initiated with a program called the Local Bodies Scheme and this new limited authority local government scheme became the launching pad for Zia's version of controlled democracy.

The origins of this latest attempt at democratization may be traced to Zia's Local Bodies Scheme and the local partyless elections that were first held in 1979. Although Zia's local government scheme did not provide elected officials with much power and authority (law and order and revenue collection powers were continued to be exercised by the bureaucracy), these elections were the "only show in town" so to speak. The 1979 elections followed by the ones in 1983 introduced a number of individuals into politics for the first time. When the partyless national and provincial assembly elections were held in 1985, many of the elected local councilors were successful in being elected to either a provincial or the national assembly. Although the first test of the continuity of this present attempt at democratization did not come until the November 1988 elections, many Pakistanis had their first taste of participating as voters in elections for local councilors in 1979.

As was mentioned previously, Zia held a referendum in December 1984 which was tantamount to reelection for another five year term as president. The voters had a simple "yes" or "no" choice -- no other alternatives were offered. The referendum question was, essentially, "Do you approve of Pakistan becoming an Islamic society and state?" "Yes" votes were interpreted to mean support for Zia for a five year term as president. This referendum was followed by the February 25, 1985, partyless national and provincial assembly elections. By most accounts, it was termed a "clean" election and one indication was that several individuals close to General Zia were defeated. No members of the assemblies participated as members of political parties. Many who contested at the national and provincial levels had been elected as local councilors in the local government elections of 1979 and 1983.[35]

Zia's selection of Mohammed Khan Junejo, a Sindhi *wadera*[36] who had served as a cabinet member during the Ayub period, as prime minister was not considered a surprise appointment. He was a former Muslim Leaguer with moderate to conservative views and certainly was not known for his charisma. After accepting the prime ministership, Junejo put together a cabinet of prominent politicians who would not pose any threat to President Zia. Junejo did, however, begin almost immediately to resurrect political parties.

Junejo began to assert himself as prime minister. He took credit for the lifting of martial law on December 30, 1985.[37] Holding the portfolio for defence, Junejo sought to control military promotions.[38] He attempted to develop a political base independent of his selection by Zia as prime minister through the revival of the Muslim League of which he assumed leadership.

On May 29, 1988, President Zia dismissed Prime Minister Junejo, his cabinet and the national and provincial assemblies stating that:

> . . . .The Junejo government was slow in enacting legislation on the *shariah*,[39] it was corrupt, it had not managed the economy properly, and it had allowed the law and order situation to deteriorate.[40]

The 1973 Constitution required that new elections must be held within 90 days after the dismissal of the government but Zia procrastinated and finally announced November 17, 1988, as the election date.

Zia's impact on the political system of Pakistan is just now being assessed and evaluated[41] but there are some discernable changes introduced during this time period with which Zia's successors have to work. One is the constitutional change and the other is the attempt to address the concerns of what Burki identifies as "the middle class -- the *shurafaa* (the respectable citizens) of Pakistan."[42] The former (the Eighth Amendment) constrains the prime minister while the latter (trying to build political support by catering to the needs of a major segment of Pakistani society) has created expectations.

The changes that he made in governance are based on the Eighth Amendment he had added to the 1973 Constitution. This amendment provided for a strengthened role for the president, including powers to dismiss the National Assembly -- powers that would be exercised by Ghulam Ishaq Khan in 1990. A strengthened role for the president and a continuing role of the chief of the army staff gave governance in Pakistan a "three-legged stool" appearance -- one leg being the prime minister and the other two being the president and the chief of the army staff.

Another impact is less tangible -- addressing the social and economic needs and demands of the middle class without input through periodic elections and greater participation in governance. Two ways that he tried to meet these needs was through his Islamization "to allay the fears of Pakistan's shurafaa. . .[who felt]. . .that Bhutto had little love for Islam"[43] and how he wanted Pakistan's economy to be managed.[44]

On August 17, 1988, General Zia along with 29 others died when the Pakistan Air Force C-130 aircraft they were in crashed near Bahawalpur in Punjab. Ghulam Ishaq Khan, Chairman of the Senate and the former Minister of Finance during a greater part of Zia's rule, was sworn in as Acting President and General Mirza Aslam Beg, Vice Chief of the Army Staff, was appointed as chief of the army staff. One of the first actions taken by Ghulam Ishaq Khan was to announce that the national and provincial assembly elections promised would be held on November 17, 1988, on a *party basis*.[45]

The People's Party of Pakistan led by Benazir Bhutto (the daughter of the late Zulfikar Ali Bhutto) won a plurality of seats in the National Assembly and a majority in the Sindh Legislative Assembly. The Islami Jamhorri Ittehad (Islamic Democratic Alliance), or IJI, a nine party alliance dominated by the Pakistan Muslim League headed by Mohammed Khan Junejo won a majority of the seats in the Punjab Legislative Assembly catapulting Mian Nawaz Sharif (a political protege of General Zia's who served as chief minister of the Punjab during the 1985-1988 period) into the leadership of the IJI. This was also a "clean" election with only a few protests of rigging.

In December 1988, Acting President Ghulam Ishaq Khan appointed Benazir Bhutto as prime minister. Later in the same month, Ghulam Ishaq Khan was elected to a five year term as president.[46] The PPP had to go into coalition to form a government. Benazir successfully weathered a no-confidence measure in October 1989 but her government lasted only 20 months. On August 6, 1990, President Ghulam Ishaq Khan "dissolved the National Assembly, dismissed the Cabinet of Prime Minister Benazir Bhutto, and announced fresh election[s] to the Assembly to be held on October 24 this year."[47] Ghulam Ishaq Khan also announced the appointment of Ghulam Mustafa Jatoi, a leader of the opposition, as the caretaker prime minister.

What were the reasons which led to such a limited tenure in office for the first woman prime minister of Pakistan? A newspaper account stated that Ghulam Ishaq Khan "listed corruption, Centre-province confrontation, flouting of [the] Constitution, political horse-trading, encroachment on provincial autonomy, disrespect of [the] higher judiciary and misuse of official machinery and resources as [the] fundamental causes of this 'extreme step'."[48] Beyond the news accounts lay tensions that had developed between Prime Minister Benazir Bhutto on the one hand and President Ghulam Ishaq Khan and General Mirza Aslam Beg on the other. But these reasons do not provide a full explanation of the PPP's loss of support. Toward the end of the 20 months, even strong supporters from such groups as the Women's Action Forum (WAF) had become disenchanted with the lack of performance by the PPP government. The inability or unwillingness of the PPP government to address pressing women's issues and to push ahead on other important socio-economic issues caused a lack of enthusiasm resulting in a decline of support. The performance of the PPP in the October 1990 elections lends support to the thesis that the party under Benazir Bhutto's leadership had not been successful in maintaining her support base among critical segments of Pakistani society.

Pre-election forecasts indicated that the PPP would not do as well in the contests for seats in the National Assembly as it did in 1988 but few if any pundits forecasted the losses that the party sustained at either the national or provincial levels.

In the National Assembly, the PPP went from 93 in the 1988 election to 45 seats in the 1990 elections.[49] (The National Assembly has 198 members.) In terms of percentage of votes, the PPP went from 38.7 percent in 1988 to 36.65 percent in 1990. The major winner was the IJI which captured 105 seats in 1990 compared to 54 in 1988. IJI's percentage of the vote rose from 30.6 percent in 1988 to 37.27 percent in 1990.

At the provincial level, the PPP lost its majority in the Sindh Legislative Assembly winning only 46 out of 100 seats (the IJI won six); IJI increased its majority substantially in Punjab winning 216 out of 240 seats (PPP won only 10 seats); PPP lost ground in the North West Frontier Province (NWFP) winning only eight seats out of 80 (the IJI won 29); and in Boluchistan, the PPP/PDA won only one seat while the IJI won seven. Sherry Rehman, editor of the *Herald* described the results as follows:

> The night the results of the National Assembly election poured in to change the course of history in Pakistan, the number of people rejoicing and mourning all over the country seemed almost equal. The one overwhelming sentiment that most people shared that night, however, was a singular sense of surprise. . . .the *Herald* gave the PDA an arithmetically clear run of 99 NA [National Assembly] seats, the IJI was also given 62, with strong chances of forming a coalition government with the help of its allies. . . .Obviously, a hung parliament, as even a major Urdu daily had predicted, or as foreign, local and diplomatic intelligence had calibrated, was in the offing. Clearly, everyone was wrong.[50]

Election observers from France said that "there appeared to have been extremely sophisticated fraud."[51] And Barnett R. Rubin, who was a member of the international observer delegation organized by the National Democratic Institute for International Affairs, stated that ". . .a lot of questions have to be answered before anyone can be sure that the elections reflect the true wishes of the people of Pakistan."[52] Be that as it may, the Pakistan Muslim League (the major party in the IJI and the big winner in the elections) nominated Mian

Nawaz Sharif as prime minister over both Ghulam Mustafa Jatoi (who had been caretaker prime minister) and Mohammed Khan Junejo who is president of the Pakistan Muslim League. President Ghulam Ishaq Khan asked Nawaz Sharif to form a government and he took office on November 6, 1990. The IJI formed governments in Punjab and NWFP while Jam Sadiq Ali (an independent) formed a coalition government in Sindh.

At the national level, the government of Nawaz Sharif moved on several fronts. It has begun to privatize (i.e., denationalize) firms that had been nationalized during the Bhutto period. The first was the privatization of the Muslim Commercial Bank. The government moved to liberalize the economy. One initial step was in the area of deregulation -- currency declarations upon entering the country have been relaxed and Pakistanis are now permitted to open up foreign exchange accounts. The government also tried to streamline the bureaucracy by removing excess bureaucrats and placing them in a "pool" for reassignment. However, government jobs are valuable patronage rewards and although one leading politician maintains that the IJI government has the "political will" necessary to streamline, "this will is yet to be tested."[53]

A relatively young man (early 40s), Nawaz Sharif appointed prominent individuals in his cabinet such as Sartaj Aziz (a former minister during the Zia period) as Minister of Finance and Syed Fakhar Imam (also a minister during the Zia period as well as the first Speaker of the National Assembly and later leader of the opposition during the Junejo period) as Minister of Education. Nawaz's "kitchen" cabinet is reportedly composed of the Minister of Commerce (Malik Naeem), the Minister of Fuel and Power (Nisar Ali Chaudhry), the Interior Minister (Chaudhry Shujjat Hussain), Anwar Zahid (Special Assistant to the Prime Minister) and Shahbaz Sharif (Member of the National Assembly and the prime minister's brother). Since Nawaz Sharif is a businessman, the interests of business are well represented although some businessmen in Karachi feel that they are not consulted and that the prime minister only solicits the views of a few businessmen from Lahore. He is described as an individual who wants "things to happen" and gets impatient when they do not.

Politically, Nawaz appears to have neutralized the issue of Islamization. The Shariat bill became law but according to some observers, its symbolism is greater than its practical effect on women in Pakistan (this view, however, is not universally shared).

Nawaz has not experienced the kinds of problems that plagued Benazir Bhutto. His relations with the president (Ghulam Ishaq Khan) and the chief of the army staff (Mirza Aslam Beg) appear not to be tension filled, although the Twelfth Amendment which passed both the National Assembly and the Senate was seen by some as a potential challenge to the power and authority of the president. On August 17, 1991, Lt. General Asif Nawaz Janjua was appointed chief of the army staff replacing General Beg who had completed his term of office in this position and retired from the army. Lt. General Asif Nawaz was described as an ". . .old fashioned soldier preferring a distance from the media. . . ."[54] During the Gulf War, the prime minister had to deal with a bit of a flap that developed over a speech General Beg made in support of Iraq's position in the Gulf crisis. Until his untimely death on January 8, 1993,[55] the new chief of the army staff was less visible and more concerned with the issues internal to the military.

What May Be Concluded from Pakistan's Democratization Process So Far

The question may be asked, Has leadership in Pakistan pursued "government of the people, by the people and for the people" during this attempt at democratization? The answer is both yes and no. On the positive side, since 1979, there have been three rounds of local elections in 1979, 1983 and 1987 (albeit on a non-party basis), one set of national and provincial assembly elections (1985) on a non-party basis, and two sets of national and provincial assembly elections (1988 and 1990) on a party basis. There was a resurrection of political parties in 1986. The elections provided experience in contesting elections to new generations of Pakistanis and both sides (IJI and PPP) have spent time in office. Finally, there has not been a military coup since 1977.[56] On the negative side, the role exercised by the president which was facilitated by the Eighth Amendment is a concern for those who advocate that democracy in Pakistan should mean parliamentary supremacy. Furthermore, opposition to the government in power still tends to be equated with treason and the legal system is still being used to harass the opposition.[57] State institutions and public resources are still being used for personal gain.[58]

In summary, what do we know about Pakistan's current attempt at democracy? First, political parties are relatively free to contest elections and organization is critical for party success. Setting aside the charges of fraud leveled against the government in the 1990 elections which may have secured the success of the IJI, the PPP appears not to be a very well organized party. Benazir Bhutto has drawn heavily on her late father's charisma but she appears not to have learned the skills of effective election campaign management, nor, as her tenure as prime minister reveal, the skills of managing the government. On the other hand, IJI appears to be better organized and Nawaz Sharif's experience in contesting elections since 1979 has paid dividends.[59]

Second, political debate appears to be alive and well in Pakistan. The press censorship of the first several years of the Zia period has ended and there has been a literal blossoming of newspapers and journals. Furthermore, thanks to the Benazir Bhutto government, Pakistanis have electronic access to the outside world through Cable Network News (CNN) which is available to those who have television sets or access to one in Islamabad, Lahore and Karachi.

Third, although the military has been a threat to civilian government in times past, this institution has undergone a change in leadership and the new leadership appears to be more concerned with issues internal to itself than with presenting an alternative to civilian government.[60] The Pakistan Army has been described as a corporation in that its board of directors (the corps commanders) has followed its leadership (the chief of the army staff who is also a member of the board) in the three previous coups (1958, 1969 and 1977). The other non-elected source of power in the political system of Pakistan, the elite civil bureaucracy, in and of itself does not pose a threat.[61]

The only threats that may lead to an interruption of continued democratization could come from internal strife reaching a point whereby the military feels that the civilian government (a) does not have the "will" to deal with internal strife or (b) will not deal with internal strife. Nawaz Sharif publicly stated that the Twelfth Amendment was needed to deal with a deteriorating law and order situation in the country. The problem of dacoitry (banditry) in interior Sindh continues, however, and there is widespread concern over the major introduction of weapons into the country as a result of the Afghanistan civil war. The economy is a concern with fewer remittances from overseas workers flowing into the country, unemployment high in certain parts of the country and declines in foreign assistance when the United States assistance program finally runs dry in 1993.[62] In this respect, both the PPP and the IJI governments have pushed privatization and deregulation with the expectation that the private sector will play a greater role in job creation, the production of goods and the provision of services.

What if the government of Nawaz Sharif cannot control the violence that has engulfed the province of Sindh, fails to generate employment and economic growth with its economic liberalization plans or cannot stem the "political decay" that some observers maintain is the "greatest danger to democracy"[63] in Pakistan? The most rational solution appears to be to hold new elections and see if the voters want to replace those who currently hold power with another alternative. The option of a return to power of military leadership appears to be not viable at present.

In conclusion, it can be argued that democracy as defined in Pakistan is in place for the moment. The processes are there. The institutions have to be developed further. The government in power has to begin to work with the opposition if only for the reason that if the election process continues, those in power today may become those in opposition tomorrow.

Postscript

On April 18, 1993, President Ghulam Ishaq Khan "dismissed Prime Minister Nawaz Sharif, accusing him of corruption and mismanagement, and dissolved the Parliament."[64] These charges are similar to those Ghulam Ishaq Khan leveled against Benazir Bhutto when he dismissed her government in August 1990. The President appointed Balkh Sher Mazari, described by *The New York Times* report as a person "who heads a tribal clan of landowners,"[65] as caretaker Prime Minister, and announced that new elections would be held on July 14, 1993.

The dismissal of Nawaz Sharif brought to an end an unhappy partnership between President Ghulam Ishaq Khan and Prime Minister Nawaz Sharif -- a partnership which began to sour when Nawaz Sharif declared his intention to move a constitutional amendment that would limit the powers of the President.

This action by the President is constitutionally based. As was discussed earlier, the Eighth Amendment that was added to the constitution during the Zia period significantly enhanced the powers of the President. These powers enable a president to control the political process despite the presence of an elected Prime Minister. This is the third time that presidential power has been deployed to dismiss an elected government. In some ways, this action is a continuation of the struggle between the President and the Prime Minister with regard to who monopolizes power in the system -- a struggle that goes back to the early 1950s after the assassination of Liaquat Ali Khan in 1951. Resolution of this conflict is fundamental to the development of democratic institutions in Pakistan.

Post Postscript

On May 26, 1993, the BBC reported that the Supreme Court of Pakistan had ruled by a vote of 10-1 that President Ghulam Khan's dissolution of the National Assembly and dismissal of the Prime Minister were unconstitutional and that they should be returned to their previous positions. See also *The New York Times*, May 27, 1993.

On May 31, 1993, *The New York Times* reported that Nawaz Sharif and Benazir Bhutto "agreed. . .to hold their first meeting in five years to try to end Pakistan's political turmoil." Score one for democracy. Ed.

Notes

1. Jean Jacques Rousseau, *Du Contrat Social*, 1762.

2. This term was used by Harold D. Lasswell to describe the military and police. He employed the phrase "Garrison State" and defined it as a political entity where:

> . . .the dominant group is constituted by the specialists on violence, since force is the distinctive skill of soldiers and police. The specialist on violence rises in power as other skill groups subside, such as the

specialists on civil administration, party and pressure-group administration, and specialists on propaganda or persuasion.

See: "The Garrison State and Specialists on Violence," in *The Analysis of Political Behavior*, London: Routledge & Kegan Paul Ltd., 1948, pp. 146-57.

3. Second Edition. William Collins and World Publishing Co., Inc., 1975. Published in the USA.

4. Regarding democratic processes, it took the United States almost 130 years (from the ratification of the U.S. Constitution to the passage of the Article XIX -- 19th Amendment) to extend the right to vote to American women and 175 years (from the ratification of the U.S. Constitution in 1789 to the passage of the Voters Rights Act of 1965) to extend the right to vote to Afro-Americans.

5. A good example of this research is Gabriel A. Almond and G. Bingham Powell, Jr., *Comparative Politics: A Developmental Approach*, Boston: Little, Brown and Company, 1966.

6. For two works on this subject, see: Samuel P. Huntington, *The Third Wave: Democratization in the Late Twentieth Century* (Norman: University of Oklahoma Press, 1991); and Raymond D. Gastil, ed., *Freedom in the World: Political Rights and Civil Liberties 1987-1988* (New York: Freedom House, 1988).

7. For more analysis of this period, see: Keith Callard, *Pakistan: A Political Study*, London: George Allen & Unwin Ltd., 1957; and Khalid Bin Sayeed, *Pakistan: The Formative Phase*, London: Oxford University Press, 1968.

8. Keith Callard, *Pakistan*, p. 77.

9. *Ibid*.

10. Mirza was not known for his democratic sentiments. Callard cites a *Dawn* (October 31, 1954) news article in which Callard quoted Mirza as stating:

> The masses of this country are overwhelmingly illiterate. They are not interested in politics. They are bound to act foolishly sometimes . . . .People of this country need controlled democracy for some time to come.

11. Shahid Javed Burki, *Pakistan: A Nation in the Making*, Boulder, CO: Westview Press, 1986, p. 52.

12. For a more detailed examination of the Ayub period, see Herbert Feldman's two works, *Revolution in Pakistan: A Study of the Martial Law Administration*, London: Oxford University Press, 1967, and *From Crisis to Crisis: Pakistan in 1962-69*, London: Oxford University Press, 1970.

13. Iskandar Mirza is the source of another quotation regarding those from a government service background who occupied high political office during the 1950s (i.e., those not coming from a government service background):

> You cannot have the old British system of administration [and] at the same time allow politicians to meddle with the civil service. In the

> British system the District Magistrate was the kingpin of administration. His authority was unquestioned. We have to restore that. (*Dawn*, October 31, 1954, as cited in Keith Callard, *A Political Study*, p. 285).

14. See Edward A. Shils, *Political Development in the New States*, The Hague: Morton & Co., 1960, although Shils was describing Nigeria where he used this term.

15. Cited in Karl Von Vorys, *Political Development in Pakistan*, Princeton: Princeton University Press, 1965. Ayub also reproduced his famous memorandum in his book, *Friends Not Masters*, New York: Oxford University Press, 1967.

16. Joseph Lelyveld, "The End of Ayub -- And An Era," *The New York Times*, February 23, 1969.

17. See Robert LaPorte, Jr., *Power and Privilege: Influence and Decision-Making in Pakistan*, Berkeley: University of California Press, 1975, pp. 75-97 for a discussion of the Yahya period.

18. The postponement was due to the devastating cyclones and tidal waves which hit East Pakistan.

19. For an analysis of this period, see: Shahid Javed Burki, *Pakistan Under Bhutto, 1971-1977*, London: The Macmillan Press Ltd., 1980.

20. For those unfamiliar with military terms, in Pakistan GHQ stands for the General Headquarters of the Pakistan Army.

21. Shahid Javed Burki, *Pakistan: A Nation in the Making*, p. 71.

22. *Ibid.*

23. Bhutto also nationalized all domestically owned private educational institutions with the exception of those operated by foreign governments. It is interesting to note that during the past decade, domestically owned private English medium schools have become almost a "growth industry."

24. Shahid Javed Burki, *Pakistan: A Nation in the Making*, pp. 71-72.

25. The 90 days actually became 90 months.

26. In *Pakistan Under Bhutto, 1971-1977*, Shahid Javed Burki describes the events which led to Bhutto's execution in the following narrative:

> Bhutto's judgment that time would clear his name proved wrong. The Lahore Court announced its verdict on 19 March 1978, finding him an 'arch culprit' in an ambush in November 1974, the object of which had been to kill Ahmed Raza Kasuri, a one-time political protege turned opponent. The assassin missed his mark, but killed Kasuri's father. The Court ordered Bhutto's execution.
>
> The execution of the sentence was delayed for over a year while Bhutto's lawyers explored all possible legal avenues to save their client's life. The final legal pronouncement came on 31 March 1979 which the country's Supreme Court refused to review their earlier verdict. On 4

April 1979, Zulfikar Ali Bhutto was hanged at the Rawalpindi jail. (p. 202)

27. Shahid Javed Burki, "Pakistan Under Zia, 1977-1988," *Asian Survey*, Vol. XXVIII, No. 10 (October 1988), p. 1,086. Burki maintains that Zia ". . .also had the reputation of serving his superiors with unquestioning loyalty, an attribute that was reportedly confirmed to Bhutto by General Sahibzada Yaqub Ali Khan. Sahibzada was close to Bhutto and in 1976 was Pakistan's ambassador to the United States; he was consulted by the prime minister when the search was on to replace General Tikka Khan."

28. The Constitution (Eighth Amendment) Act, XVIII of 1985, 9th November 1985.

29. The term used in Pakistan for non-partisan. Since Zia banned political parties, candidates for office could only contest the elections if they disclaimed representing any political party and did not accept, openly, support from any political party. As a result, candidates drew support from their extended family networks, -- their *Biraderis*.

30. Newspaper reports of what the political parties were doing during the Zia period up to Junejo's resurrection of the Muslim League in 1986 involved using the term "defunct" in front of the political party name. This permitted the newspaper to report on party activities without being censored by the government.

31. For a thorough presentation of major events during the Zia period, see "Zia's Eleven Years: A Chronology of Important Events," in Shahid Javed Burki and Craig Baxter, *Pakistan Under the Military: Eleven Years of Zia ul-Haq*, Boulder, CO: Westview Press, 1991, pp. 155-182.

32. Local elections were held again in 1983 and 1987.

33. Shahid Javed Burki and Craig Baxter, *Pakistan Under the Military*, p. 172.

34. The United States had been encouraging Zia to fulfill his promise made shortly after the July 1977 coup to hold elections. This pressure increased after the new foreign assistance agreement was signed in the fall of 1981.

35. After the 1983 elections, a successful candidate remarked to me that once (not if) national and provincial assembly elections were held, people would lose interest in local government elections.

36. Landlord.

37. In a speech in Lahore in 1987, Junejo reminded his audience several times that he, Junejo, was responsible for the lifting of martial law.

38. This presented some awkward moments for the Junejo government. President Zia retained the position of Chief of the Army Staff and recommended promotions to Junejo as Minister of Defence. Junejo then would have to act on them in this capacity before they went to Junejo as Prime Minister. Rumors circulated that Junejo delayed rather than expedited certain promotions.

39. A measure to establish Islamic law throughout Pakistan -- a measure strongly opposed by women (Women's Action Forum and the All Pakistan Women's Association) as well as progressive groups in Pakistan.

40. Craig Baxter, "Restructuring the Pakistan Political System," in Shahid Javed Burki and Craig Baxter, *Pakistan Under the Military: Eleven Years of Zia ul-Haq*, Boulder, CO: Westview Press, 1991, p. 44. Baxter believes that none of these reasons were real:

> None of these seems to have been the real reason and none was put forward to me with emphasis in my last meeting with Zia in July 1988. Both Zia and his close associate, General Akhtar Abdur Rahman Khan [he was serving as Chairman of the Joint Chiefs of Staff Committee when he died in the same plane crash as President Zia], whom I met later the same evening, were more concerned with Junejo's assertion of his prime-ministerial role, especially with regard to the military.

Baxter also points out that Zia's dismissal of the federal and provincial cabinets and assemblies was later ". . .declared ultra vires of the constitution because neither Junejo or the provincial chief ministers had lost the confidence of the assemblies. . . ."

41. One assessment has already been published. See Shahid Javed Burki and Craig Baxter (with contributions by Robert LaPorte, Jr. and Kamal Azfar), *Pakistan Under the Military: Eleven Years of Zia ul-Haq*, Boulder, CO: Westview Press, 1991.

42. Shahid Javed Burki, "Pakistan Under Zia, 1977-1988," p. 1,087.

43. *Ibid.*

44. *Ibid.* Burki records a conversation he had with President Zia in which Zia stated:

> My instructions to Ishaq Sahib [Ghulam Ishaq Khan who served as Minister of Finance] are quite clear. I really don't care what he [Ishaq] does as long as the economy continues to function smoothly and the poor and the middle classes continue to see some hope for them.

45. On July 20, 1988, Zia had announced that national and provincial elections would be held on November 16, 1988. The next day, Zia announced that the scheduled elections would not be held on a party basis.

46. The President of Pakistan is elected "by members of an electoral college consisting of: (a) the members of both Houses [National Assembly and Senate]; and (b) the members of the Provincial Assemblies." Chapter 1, The President, Part III, The Federation of Pakistan, The Constitution of Pakistan, 1973. See Sahibzada Masud-ul-Hassan Khan Sabri, *The Constitution of Pakistan, 1973* (with all Amendments), Lahore: Publishers Emporium, no date, p. 52.

47. "Elections on Oct. 24," *The Nation*, August 7, 1990.

48. "Decision motivated by commitment to democracy -- Ishaq," *The Nation*, August 7, 1990.

49. S. Akbar Zaidi, "The Fall of the People's Empire," (Election '90 *Herald,* Special Issue), November/December 1990, p. 8. The statistics for the 1990 and 1988 elections comes from this source. It should also be mentioned that the PPP ran as the dominant partner in the People's Democratic Alliance (PDA). The other party was Asghar Khan's *Tehrik-e-Istiqlal* which has never won many seats in any election.

50. *Herald* (Election '90 Special Issue), November/December 1990, p. 3.

51. "Contest for Bhutto Successor Ends As a Top Party Picks Candidate," *The New York Times*, November 1, 1991.

52. Barnett R. Rubin, "Pakistan: No Stamp of Approval," *The New York Times*, November 1, 1990. Rubin indicated that although ". . .the National Democratic Institute for International Affairs issued a statement doubting that certain reported voting irregularities significantly altered the outcome of the elections. . .I would like to counter the widespread impression that by making this statement we intended to certify the election results."

53. Direct quotation from an interview conducted by the author in Islamabad, July 1991.

54. *The Nation*, July 5, 1991.

55. "Gen. Asif Nawaz of Pakistan, 56, A Champion of Democracy, Dies," *The New York Times*, January 9, 1993. The news report stated, "Shortly after being named to the post [as chief of the army staff], General Nawaz said the army had no role in politics other than to defend the civilian government and the country. . . .Former Prime Minister Benazir Bhutto. . .described General Nawaz as a true professional soldier. . . .He did what he said he would do -- he kept the army out of politics.'"

56. This is a bit of an exaggeration since Zia remained in power for eleven of those fourteen years in that as long as the military was in power there was no need for a coup.

57. The opposition would certainly claim that the government's allegations of extortion and corruption leveled at Asif Ali Zardari (the husband of Benazir Bhutto) is an example of harassment along with cases brought against PPP leaders who held office from 1988 to 1990.

58. According to Seyyed Vali Reza Nasr who cited *Herald* and *Newsline* articles which appeared in September 1991:

> In August 1991, IJI was accused of sanctioning illegal borrowing of some Rs. 1.2 billion from government-owned cooperatives in Punjab by the Ittifaq Industrial Group, which belongs to the [Nawaz] Sharif family.

See: Seyyed Vali Reza Nasr, "Democracy and the Crisis of Governability in Pakistan," *Asian Survey*, Vol. XXXII, No. 6 (June 1992), p. 536.

59. This appears to be the case despite the allegation that the IJI was a creation of the military's Inter-Services Intelligence unit. See: Seyyed Vali Reza Nasr, "Democracy and the Crisis of Governability in Pakistan," *Asian*

Survey, Vol. XXXII, No. 6 (June 1992), p. 523; and Mohammed Waseem, "Pakistan's Lingering Crisis of Dyarchy," *Asian Survey*, Vol. XXXII, No. 7 (July, 1992), p. 618. Nasr asserts that:

> It is an open secret in Pakistan that IJI was put together by the military's Inter-Services Intelligence (ISI), which brokered a deal between an array of right-of-center and Islamic parties to prevent a PPP sweep at the polls.

Waseem cites *Newsline*, April 1991, p. 39, as his source, saying:

> Brigadier Imtiaz, Internal Security Director in the Inter-Service Intelligence (ISI) reportedly helped organize the IJI in 1988 on behalf of the civil-military establishment.

60. The military has been called upon to restore law and order in the province of Sindh. "Operation Clean Up" was launched by the Pakistan army in July 1992. For analyses of the army's role in Sindh, see the articles which appeared in the October 1992 issue of *The Herald*, in particular: Ayaz Amir, "Strategic Withdrawal?;" Idrees Bakhtiar, "Partial Law;" and Mazhar Abbas, "State of Siege."

61. In a June 1992 article cited earlier ("Democracy and the Crisis of Governability in Pakistan"), Seyyed Vali Reza Nasr states:

> Democracy thus far has had an uncertain existence in Pakistan and an even more uncertain impact on the country's politics. The greatest threat to its viability has not come from its traditional foes in the bureaucracy or the military, at least not yet. . . .The greatest danger to democracy has rather stemmed from political decay and the subsequent crisis of governability that have emerged pursuant to the advent of the democratic process.

62. See Chapter 1, on the economy by Shahid Javed Burki in this volume.

63. See Seyyed Vali Reza Nasr, "Democracy and the Crisis of Governability in Pakistan."

64. Edward A. Gargan, "President of Pakistan Dismisses Premier and Dissolves Parliament," *The New York Times*, April 19, 1993.

65. *Ibid.*

About the Contributors

Lee L. Bean (Ph.D. Yale) taught at Yale and has been demographic advisor to the Pakistan Institute of Development Economics, research associate at the Population Council, and former chairman of the Sociology Department, University of Utah. Currently he is director of the Middle East Center, University of Utah. He has been president of the American Institute of Pakistan Studies and served as a consultant on population problems in Pakistan for the World Bank and the United Nations Fund for Population Activities. He has coauthored four monographs and numerous articles.

Shahid Javed Burki (M.Phil. Oxford University) was a Rhodes Scholar and Mason Fellow at Harvard. Former economic advisor to Pakistan's Minister of Commerce, he is director of the China and Mongolia Desk at the World Bank. He has written widely on both China and Pakistan. His most recent publications on Pakistan include *Pakistan Under the Military* (Westview, 1992); *Pakistan: A Nation in the Making* (Westview, 1986; 1991); *Pakistan: The Continuing Search for Nationhood* (Westview, 1991); *Pakistan's Development Priorities* (1986) coedited with Robert A. LaPorte, Jr.; *Pakistan Under Bhutto* (1980); and numerous articles on Pakistan.

Afak Haydar (Ph.D. Southern Illinois) is professor of political science and public administration and director of International Education, Arkansas State University. He is treasurer of the American Institute of Pakistan Studies. He is the author of *Basic Democracies in Pakistan* (1963) and articles on Pakistan and Islam.

Nasir Jalil (Ed.M. Harvard; M.A. Islamia University; M.Sc. Quaid-i-Azam University; doctoral student at Harvard) is on leave as Assistant Educational Advisor in the Ministry of Education in Pakistan. He is also on leave to the World Bank, where he is a consultant on a research project that reviews the World Bank Experience in the Education Sector during 1963-1992. He has coauthored with Noel F. McGinn a chapter on Pakistan in R. Murray Thomas (Ed.), *The Role of Education in National Development Plans* (1992).

J. Henry Korson (Ph.D. Yale) is professor of sociology, emeritus, University of Massachusetts at Amherst. He is a former officer and trustee of the American Institute of Pakistan Studies. He has held numerous fellowships, most recently at the East-West Center Population Institute, and served as a consultant at the National Institute of Population Studies in Islamabad. He has served as a consultant on research projects in Pakistan and as a lecturer at the Max Planck Institute and the Soviet Academy of Sciences. He is the editor of a precursor to this volume *Contemporary Problems of Pakistan* (1974) and is coauthor with M.S. Zand of *The Economic Value of Children in Pakistan* (1988). He is the author of numerous articles on modernization and social change in Pakistan.

Robert LaPorte, Jr. (Ph.D. Syracuse University) is professor of public administration, Pennsylvania State University. He has held several research fellowships in Pakistan and has been a visiting professor of public administration at Punjab University. He is the author of *Power and Privilege: Influence and Decision Making in Pakistan* (1975); *Pakistan's Development Priorities: Choices for the Future* (1986, 2nd printing coauthored with Shahid Javed Burki); *Public Enterprise in Pakistan: The Hidden Crisis in Economic Development* (Westview Press, 1989, coauthored with Muntazar Bashir Ahmed); and numerous articles on the political economy of Pakistan.

Anne T. Sweetser (Ph.D. Harvard) is assistant professor of anthropology, Connecticut College. Her dissertation is *The Power to Heal: Medicine and Society in the Pakistani Himalaya*. She is the author of several articles based on her work in Lahore and the Kaghan Valley, Pakistan.

Marvin G. Weinbaum (Ph.D. Columbia) is professor of political science and director, Program in South and West Asian Studies, University of Illinois. He is also the secretary and trustee of the American Institute of Pakistan Studies, and a trustee of the American Institute of Iranian Studies. He has written or coauthored, among other works, *Egypt and the Politics of U.S. Economic Aid*, (Westview Press, 1986); *Food, Development and Politics in the Middle East* (1982, with Louis Gold); *Presidential Elections: A Simulation with Readings*, (1974, with Louis Gold); plus numerous articles on Pakistan, Iran and the Middle East.

Anita M. Weiss (Ph.D. University of California, Berkeley) is associate professor in the International Studies Program, University of Oregon. She is the author of *The Application of Islamic Laws in a Modern State* (1986); *Culture, Class and Development: The Emergence of an Industrial Bourgeoisie in Punjab* (Westview Press, 1991); *Walls within Walls: Life Histories of Working Women* *in the Old City of Lahore* (Westview Press, 1992); and several articles on the status of women in Pakistan.

Lawrence Ziring (Ph.D. Columbia) is professor of political science and director of the Institute of Government and Politics at the University of Western Michigan. He is currently president of the American Institute of Pakistan Studies and has served as advisor to the Pakistan Administrative Staff College and lectured at several Pakistani universities. He has been a fellow of the American Council of Learned Societies, the Soviet Academy of Sciences and Oxford University. Among his latest publications are *The New Europe and the World* (1993); *The Middle East: A Political Dictionary* (1992); *Bangladesh: From Mujib to Ershad* (1992); *Pakistan: The Enigma of Political Development* (1980); *Pakistan's Foreign Policy* (1991); and numerous articles.

Acronyms

ACBAR -- Agency Coordinating Body for Afghan Relief
ACLU -- Afghan Construction and Logistic Unit
AIG -- Afghan Interim Government
APWA -- All Pakistan Women's Association
CBR -- Crude Birth Rate
CCAR -- Chief Commiseriate for Afghan Refugees
CD -- Chandrasekar and Deming
CDR -- Crude Death Rate
DHS -- Demographic Health Survey
EDI -- Educational Disparity Index
EEC -- European Economic Community
GDP -- Gross Domestic Product
GNP -- Gross National Product
ICC -- Islamic Coordination Council
IMR -- Infant Mortality Rate
IRC -- International Rescue Commission
MCH -- Maternal and Child Health
MMR -- Maternal Mortality Rate
MQM -- Mohajir Qaumi Movement
NIPS -- National Institute of Population Studies
NIS -- National Impact Survey
NMS -- National Migration Survey
NWFP -- North West Frontier Province
PFS -- Pakistan Fertility Survey
PGE -- Population Growth Estimate
PGS -- Population Growth Survey
PIDE -- Pakistan Institute of Development Economics
PLFMS -- Population Labour Force and Migration Survey
PPCO -- Pakistan Population Census Organization
PPP -- Pakistan People's Party
PWD -- Population Welfare Division
PVO -- Private Voluntary Organization
TFR -- Total Fertility Rate

UN -- United Nations
UNDP -- United Nations Development Program
UNHCR -- United Nations High Commission on Refugees
USAID -- United States Agency for International Development
WAF -- Women's Action Forum
WFS -- World Fertility Survey

Index

About the Book

Despite weeks of negotiation with the leaders of the Congress Party and the Muslim League, the British Cabinet Mission failed in its efforts to maintain a united India. As a result, in 1947 the Asian subcontinent was partitioned into a Muslim-majority but geographically divided West and East Pakistan and a Hindu-majority India.

Of the nations created after World War II, Pakistan is one of only two founded on a religious ideology: Islam. But religious cohesion did not mitigate the monumental problems that confronted Pakistan's leadership as it strove to establish the basic economic, political, and social institutions needed to govern a geographically divided nation.

After forty-six years of independence, Pakistan faces the twenty-first century with great potential, yet it must surmount tremendous barriers in order to attain its ambitious goals. This book considers the range of social, political, and economic problems facing Pakistan today. The contributors analyze the country's attempts to control explosive population growth, ease ethnic confrontations, and cope with a flood of Afghan refugees as well as to deal with the demands for education, women's rights, economic growth, and greater democracy.